Praise for *Tactical Transparency*

"Imagine the challenge of learning the tactics of communicating in a world where technology renders instantaneous, unscripted experiences, where the will of the people is spoken loudly across multiple immediate distribution points, and where the world has easy access to much more of the data and facts. Holtz and Havens deliver a book that starts a whole new conversation, one around the business impact of transparency and how corporate communications must change today to adapt, or risk much more down the road."

—**Chris Brogan,** social media strategist, chrisbrogan.com

"Does your organization host an online platform for open collaborative conversation? Even if your answer is no, understand that there are a number of web destinations where your employees and stakeholders are likely engaged in discussions already, forming networks of relationships and representing your brand. Communications professionals are no longer in control of the message, and your firewall is losing bricks.

Understanding how to communicate in these new and very popular social spaces—and understanding how to represent your brand and values through transparent and meaningful actions— have never been more important. In *Tactical Transparency,* John and Shel not only encourage but educate on how you, your employees, and all of your stakeholders can be true brand ambassadors in this new world."

—**George Faulkner,** author, *Blueprints: Social Computing at IBM*

"This is not a book about new technology but about new attitude. 'Tactical transparency' is about loosening up, lightening up, shutting up, and joining the conversation. Holtz and Havens make a convincing case for how to use social media to rethink and transform communications. Packed with case studies from successful companies, this book provides a road map to success in the new age of transparency."

—**Anders Gronstedt**, president, Gronstedt Group

"Nothing is more important to building and sustaining a community than transparency. People won't listen to you in the world of new media if you're fake. Authenticity is the currency of social networking, and John and Shel provide great case studies and insights on how to maintain your brand's integrity while still speaking your truth."

—**Alan Levy**, CEO, BlogTalkRadio.com

"Nothing is more vital in the world of business today than authentically communicating with clients. Monologue has given way to dialogue, and listening to the people who support your business builds the trust that will sustain an organization more than your stock price. Holtz and Havens clearly demonstrate the value of articulating a strategy for transparency that can effectively transform your organization to become aligned with the mindset of modern media."

—**Michael Port**, author, *Book Yourself Solid* and
Beyond Booked Solid

"Everyone knows that technology is changing the way we get and share information, what role the media and organizations play in our lives. What people don't understand is what their role is and what they need to know to be successful. Havens and Holtz know, and they are sharing their wisdom. You will be smarter having read this book."

—**Brian Reich,** author, *Media Rules! Mastering Today's Technology to Connect with and Keep Your Audience*

"Anyone can say anything about you in the freewheeling nooks and crannies online. That's scary for many companies, and they have a tendency to shut up or shout out (neither effective strategies). John and Shel dive deep into the nuances of transparency and provide you with everything you need to know. Companies no longer control the message (maybe we never really did). But following the advice in *Tactical Transparency*, we have something even better—the ability to successfully influence millions of people by showing what we really are."

—**David Meerman Scott,** author, *The New Rules of Marketing and PR*

"Honesty is the start of all success in a word-of-mouth world. This book will teach you how to openly embrace it, enjoy it, and expand your business."

—**Andy Sernovitz,** author, *Word of Mouth Marketing: How Smart Companies Get People Talking*

Tactical Transparency

How Leaders Can Leverage Social Media to Maximize Value and Build Their Brand

Shel Holtz

John C. Havens

Foreword by Lynne d Johnson

IABC INTERNATIONAL ASSOCIATION OF BUSINESS COMMUNICATORS

JOSSEY-BASS
A Wiley Imprint
www.josseybass.com

Published by Jossey-Bass
A Wiley Imprint
989 Market Street, San Francisco, CA 94103-1741—www.josseybass.com

Library of Congress Cataloging-in-Publication Data

Holtz, Shel.
  Tactical transparency : how leaders can leverage social media to maximize value and build their brand / Shel Holtz, John C. Havens ; foreword by Lynne d Johnson.
     p. cm.
  Includes bibliographical references and index.
  ISBN 978-0-470-29370-6 (cloth)
  1. Customer relations—Management. 2. Social media. 3. Interactive marketing.
  4. Business communication—Blogs. 5. Internet marketing—Management.
  I. Havens, John C. II. Title. III. Title: Leverage social media to maximize value.
  HF5415.5.H585 2009
  658.8'02—dc22   2008034930

Printed in the United States of America
FIRST EDITION
HB Printing   10 9 8 7 6 5 4 3 2 1

Contents

Part Three: Making It Real

To my brother, Craig, and his family,
and my sister, Cyndy, and her family.
I love you guys.
—S. H.

To my wife, Stacy, and children, Nathan
and Sophie Joan—the ones who keep me real.
—J.C.H.

Foreword

A few weeks ago, I moderated a panel titled "Data Geeks Unite! Building the New Tools for Getting Out the Vote, Getting Out the Corruption, and Going Hyper-Local" at Personal Democracy Forum 2008. There was much talk there about the information available to politicians about voters, as well as the opposite focus—what was available to voters about politicians—and how that information was being disseminated and used. At the end of the discussion, there was a strong consensus that there should be more open information available to both groups. A question directed to one of my technologist panelists was, why shouldn't Republicans have access to information about Democrats? The response was based in a business case example as opposed to a freedom of information one. The truth is, there's much work to be done in the governmental arena when it comes to questions of access to information. And exactly who does data belong to?

Well, just last week, Representative John Culberson of Texas told CNN, "The single-minded goal needs to be to shine sunlight in every dark corner of the Congress, to make the Congress and the government as transparent as humanly possible." As a user of microblogging service Twitter, his comment was a response to the upcoming governmental regulations to hit social media video sites like YouTube and Qik, particularly regarding how members of the House of Representatives use such services. Interestingly such social media services were the linchpin of Barack Obama's campaign. His campaign team even launched their own social media site and reshaped the face of politics by doing so, much like John F. Kennedy changed the nature of politics with TV as his media tool. But it's not only politics being impacted by the increasing technological changes; it's individuals, corporations, and entire industries as well.

This isn't news: technology has been the leading driver of business for a while now. Web 2.0 and its social media applications and web services—which include blogs, social networks, Wikis, microblogging services, location-based services, and the like—are all at the center of this change. And we haven't even begun to talk about the possibilities of the next generation of the Web—the semantic Web—when logic will bring human nature to the Web as an extension of how we currently use it to access data. Some even call this coming Web the ontological Web, where "information will be exchanged between applications, allowing computer programs to collect and process web content, and to exchange information freely with each other."[1]

But what does all of this talk about data, social media, and the future of the Web have to do with *Tactical Transparency?* Books like *Groundswell: Winning in a World Transformed by Social Technologies* by Charlene Li and Josh Bernoff, *Smart Mobs: The Next Social Revolution* by Howard Reheingold, *The Wisdom of Crowds* by James Surowiecki, and *The Power of the Many: How the Living Web Is Transforming Politics, Business and Everyday Life* by Christian Crumlish have all dealt with how communities and technologies have impacted the customer's relationship with brands, whether its about artists collaborating on the Web to mashup a company's logo, Digg readers revolting because a link to a "how-to" source was taken down, or even whether text messaging becomes the leading collaboration tool of the future. While a definitive case has been built regarding the customer's access to tools and information and how that access has changed relationships to companies (and government), a tactical transparency strategy is going to be essential to the future of business—and that's exactly what this book provides. How can leaders, individuals, and companies build brands, using today's technologies to create authentic communication processes with their shareholders? That is the main question that this book answers.

When I first met John Havens at BlogWorldExpo in the fall of 2007, I was on a panel called "Blogging Ethics: Making Tough Decisions," where we discussed the responsibilities of bloggers and commenters, issues of privacy and public behavior, as well as whether there should be a definitive difference between a journalist's code of ethics and one for bloggers. One blogger quoted me that day: "Blogging is free speech, journalism isn't always." What I meant that day was that most blogs work outside of the confines of a corporate structure, or are perhaps even less beholden to advertisers and other external agents, and therefore are more at liberty to speak freely about politicians, companies, and brands. What I meant was that bloggers outside of a larger entity had more freedom to have a *real* opinion than the news media. This is the first part of the open communication channel, the one on the side of the customer—the citizen journalist—who now has a platform for being open and sharing ideas.

Later that day, John and I talked on his BlogTalkRadio show about FastCompany.com's foray into social media, social networking, blogging ethics, and the Web. It was a long conversation, one that we never quite got to finish. We later met at SXSW Interactive in 2007, where we sat down for another radio interview, in which social media expert Chris Brogan took over as host in an interview with myself and Ronald Lewis of lijit to discuss building community and the new age of advertising. The theme always had been tactical transparency. Finally in March, John and I talked more directly about the themes pivotal to this book. On his and Shel's Tactical Transparency show we discussed the nature of transparency and how Company of Friends (FastCompany.com) and FC TV (FastCompany.TV) have helped increase communication/openness between the company I work for and its community. Throughout this relationship with

John and BlogTalkRadio, I've known him to be considerably concerned about what transparency means for both individuals and companies, and not only how it affects business but culture and relationships overall.

What I've learned in talking to John is that smart companies, those with tactical transparency strategies, are aware of how important social media is to their future. Those companies use social media to track the conversations being had about their products on the Web in community forums, on blogs, and on social networking sites like Facebook. The smart companies aren't just monitoring those conversations for some sort of research reasons, though the smart companies are having conversations with their customers. Because of this, Facebook, YouTube, and even Twitter are becoming de facto in marketing and public relations. Like Jet Blue on Twitter, responding to customer inquiries, or even the CEO of Zappos, who uses the service to have real authentic conversations with customers and who has encouraged all of his employees to have Twitter accounts. Being transparent is good. It's smart, but just how transparent should you be? Especially when transparency has been known to backfire for individuals, because Web data is forever and anything you've said or done can be found at any time by a simple search on Google.

That's why this book, *Tactical Transparency*, goes a step farther than other books covering social media's impact on the future of business. It outlines a course of action, providing a roadmap, not only through case studies but with guidelines as well. It's about how you or your company maneuver and manage transparency. Just how much information is enough? How much is too much? Why don't you read the book to find out.

August 2008

Lynne d Johnson
Director, Social Media
FastCompany.com

Tactical Transparency

INTRODUCTION

The Glass House of Business

You're in a restaurant with a great atmosphere, and you're eating your favorite dish. You've had a glass of wine, you're relaxed, and you're chatting with someone on your first date. You're doing some casual flirting, getting to know each other, when all of a sudden you find yourself opening up. You reveal a private truth or share an intimate story, and your date reaches over to hold your hand. Your vulnerability has allowed your date to trust you and share something of who he or she is in return.

Picture a first date of your own that went that way, and focus on that magical moment when you moved from small talk to real talk. There's nothing wrong with casual conversation, mind you. It's the usual approach to get to know someone. But when you are able to transcend those initial moments and catch glimpses of authenticity from another person revealing something about himself or herself, that's magical. Those moments of honesty in revelation are gifts, and they're instantly recognizable. Authenticity has a palpable feel to it, a stripping away of pretense that commands attention in any environment.

Transparency is a concept that has been thrust onto the business world as stakeholders increasingly expect authenticity from the businesses with which they have relationships. The context is different, of course (on-the-job dating is typically frowned on), but the desire to get a look inside is the same. For those facing adversity in the form of a workplace crisis or connecting on a deeper level with employees or customers, transparency is becoming a state of mind for tens of thousands of CEOs, managers, employees, and customers around the globe.

But let's be clear here because *transparency* is a term that's thrown around a lot in business today. And it's essential to note that whether an organization chooses to embrace any one tool or methodology that might lead to greater authenticity, it needs to be thinking about a transparency strategy because it will experience situations where transparent behavior will be the best strategy; an even better strategy is behaving transparently as a matter of course. In short, we are in an era and atmosphere that demand greater openness. You choose either to examine how your organization can work to embrace transparency or you appear opaque and behind the times to your employees and customers. Period.

Tactical transparency is the methodology elucidated in this book that will help your organization embrace and develop its unique plan toward bringing greater authenticity to your company and your brands. This empowering process will align your company with the philosophies articulated by media today, as Tia Carr Williams, CEO at EveryMedia and chief development officer at www.RNIA.org, explains:

> We're at the start of a transparency revolution, and information technology may well be the most powerful single force for transparency in our time. Whereas yesterday's dominant broadcast media were about one-way conversations, the multidirectional Internet is the opposite. No one controls its content—except for its users. Companies that are passively transparent are its victims. However, transparency is also a force that firms can actively embrace, using candor to build trust. Transparency is a new form of power and is becoming central to business success.

And here's good news: you can embrace transparency in stages. As Chris Anderson, senior editor for *Wired* magazine and author of *The Long Tail* and *Free*, pointed out in an interview when discussing his magazine's cover story about radical transparency:

> If you're currently saying nothing about your product line, try saying something. Radical transparency is the ultimate aim, but

each company is going to have to find their own path to that themselves that reflects their own corporate culture, their own competitive risk, and more important, who their participants are and could be. My point is: try being more transparent rather than less, and see what happens.

The majority of the interviews we conducted in order to include the contributions of these individuals in the book are a case study in transparency in their own right. They were conducted on BlogTalk Radio (where, in the interest of even more transparency, John is vice president of business development). By conducting the interviews on BlogTalk Radio, listeners could call in and ask questions. And the entire interview with each of these individuals is archived at www.blogtalkradio.com/transparency. The context in which the quotations we selected for use in the book were made is available. If we took anything out of context, you'll know.

Tactical Transparency provides dozens of case studies and interviews that address the implementation of transparency tools at the highest levels of the organization and the lowest. Transparency succeeds when it is embedded into the culture of a company, not implemented as a program designed to be exercised by only a few. Thus, this book can serve as a guide to transparency for senior leaders seeking to improve the reputations of their companies, communications professionals who will be tasked with managing the tools of transparency, and frontline managers and supervisors who will be responsible for running their parts of the business in a transparent, ethical manner. We see this book serving as a guide to help your organization create its own initiatives toward greater authenticity and accessibility.

The book has three parts.

The first three chapters, in Part One, explore the meaning of transparency and the requirements for a company seeking to become more transparent in a prudent, beneficial way. Defining what transparency means in the new media spectrum, Chapter One kicks off the book with several examples that illustrate the nature of transparency and why it is a critical business issue. This chapter explores the role of the Internet and social media in forcing the issue of transparency on organizations and the role the connected masses have played in exposing the dark side of opaque companies.

Chapter Two examines the characteristics of effective transparency. It explores this topic through a series of case studies, including Steve Jobs's letter to Apple fans about the iPhone, the HomeGoods Open House Blog, and the dark nature of astroturfing. Paull Young of Converseon defines astroturfing as "the deceptive and deceitful practice of creating fake entities that appear to be real grassroots organizations, when in fact they are the work of people or groups with hidden motives and identities."

In order to prepare to implement a transparent culture, it's important to have a checklist of the characteristics of a transparent organization, beginning with the company's core values and its approach to corporate social responsibility. Chapter Three provides just such a checklist with detail as to the underlying meaning of each attribute with accompanying examples of organizations already applying them. Chapter Three also features a step-by-step process for assessing the organization's readiness.

Tactical transparency gets practical in Part Two. These chapters explore different approaches and tools to employ when building transparency within different dimensions of the organization.

Chapter Four explores why opaque selling processes are problematic and how to be more open about them. Among the issues addressed are establishing conversation between customer and company. The chapter features interviews with Michael Port, popular speaker and author of *Book Yourself Solid,* and Matthew Knell and Morgan Johnston of JetBlue Airways, among others.

Investors, investment analysts, the financial press, and regulators all keep close tabs on companies that occupy the public space. Chapter Five examines the means by which transparency can increase confidence in your organization's ability to perform.

When things go wrong, companies are inclined to hunker down in a defensive posture. The case studies in Chapter Six look at how companies can serve business goals by becoming more transparent when problems emerge and during emergencies and crises.

Chapter Seven addresses the employee-employer relationship, since recent research suggests that most people interpret "corporate social responsibility" as a reflection of the way the company treats its employees. The chapter also looks at internal transparency pertaining to employee communications.

Although social media are at the heart of this book, there is no denying that traditional communication channels continue to play an important part. Chapter Eight turns to the role of traditional public relations and media relations, along with some recent developments, like the introduction of a social media press release.

Blogs by CEOs and other members of the senior leadership team afford companies an ideal opportunity to become more transparent. Chapter Nine offers case studies and extends advice on when a CEO or other senior leader should (or should not) blog. This chapter also explores the value (and risks) of a leader's engaging in conversations on other blogs.

Blogs and other forms of communications that address specific business issues are growing in popularity, and Chapter Ten treats this topic.

Whether employees write their own blogs or participate on behalf of the company in the conversation taking place elsewhere online, employees empowered to engage audiences often serve as the best, most effective spokespeople for an organization. (This is confirmed by the results of Edelman Public Relations' annual Trust Barometer study.) Chapter Eleven looks at how employee blogs and employee participation in other blogs can serve the organization.

Chapter Twelve examines podcasting and other multimedia. It examines how the nature of being heard or seen can change the spectrum of honesty and trust.

Chapter Thirteen discusses social networks like Facebook and MySpace, which continue to grow in popularity. The maintenance of individual profiles represents a relatively new channel for transparency, and a group dedicated to an organization or issue can also alter perceptions of a company's openness. This also addresses emerging social media channels like Twitter that afford new opportunities for transparency—and transparency done badly.

In spite of the new technologies, people remain hard-wired to communicate face-to-face. Chapter Fourteen examines opportunities for real-time, real-space interaction, notably participation in "unconferences" and other social networking events.

The chapters in Part Three provide you with the means to overcome the challenges you may hear from various sectors of the organization and put a planning process in place. The biggest concern most leaders have when exploring how transparent their organizations should be is the perception that they will lose control of their messages. The fact is, as Chapter Fifteen notes, they never really had control to begin with, and, in the age of social media, any control they might have had has evaporated.

Company legal eagles will no doubt want to stifle efforts to be transparent, and information technology departments will raise objections ranging from bandwidth and infection concerns to the cost of implementing new systems. In addition, people throughout the organization will object to the perceived loss of control associated with a transparent organizational culture. Chapter Sixteen weighs the benefits against risks and offers advice for overcoming objections.

Chapter Seventeen provides a template for managing a transparency plan. The template is also available as a download from the associated Web site (http://www.tacticaltransparency.com).

We conclude in Chapter Eighteen with a few observations about where transparency is headed. Anticipation of inevitable change can help organizations be prepared when the changes occur.

As you'll discover in the following pages, engaging your audience in authentic conversation and implementing steps to respond to that dialogue are the keys to tactical transparency. One of the seminal aspects of being transparent is simply to demonstrate that you're listening to the people central to your brand. This book shows you how to listen effectively and safely while providing lasting value for your organization.

Part One

STRATEGY

1

WHAT IS TRANSPARENCY?

A Working Definition

As Christmas approached in 2006, a blog appeared called "All I Want for Christmas Is a PSP." Charlie was trying to help his buddy Jeremy get the popular but expensive handheld entertainment system as a holiday gift. It took only a short time for dozens of people to check the publicly available domain registration and learn the site was registered to a marketing agency called Zipatoni.

The firestorm erupted. Some of the comments posted to the blog included these:

> "This site makes me want to get rid of my PSP."
>
> "Things must be going really bad for Sony if all they can afford to promote one of their flagship products are you monkeys."
>
> "If you want a PSP badly enough you should get together with an ad agency. Then try to sell the product through a lame Web site while attempting to speak down to what you consider your target audience."

Even after having been exposed as a fake blog, a deceptive marketing practice, the character Charlie continued trying to convince readers they were wrong. Writing in faux hip-hop style, Charlie said, "Yo where all u hatas com from . . . juz cuz you aint feelin the flow of PSP dun mean its sum mad faek Website or summ . . . you all be trippin." But the denials only sparked further commentary, which spilled over into message boards. Eventually Sony had to come clean, posting this message on the blog:

> Busted. Nailed. Snagged. As many of you have figured out (maybe our speech was a little too funky fresh???), Charlie isn't a real hip-hop maven and this site was actually developed by Sony. Guess we were trying to be just a little too clever. From this point forward, we will just stick to making cool products, and use this site to give you nothing but the facts on the PSP.—Sony Computer Entertainment America

The site is gone now. Recognizing it as the embarrassment it was, Zipatoni and Sony pulled it down. However, if you want to see what it looked like when it launched, halfway through its life, or just before it was deleted in mid-2007, all you have to do is visit the WayBack Machine at Archive.org, where Web sites live on forever.

• • •

In September 2005, media critic, blogger, and former *TV Guide* editor Jeff Jarvis wrote a post taking Dell, Inc. to task for its failures of customer service and technical support in his efforts to resolve computer problems. Jarvis's series of posts turned into a saga that was followed, reported on, analyzed, and spread by hundreds of thousands of people. One man's complaint dragged Dell's already fragile reputation through the mud and affected its share price.

It was a defining moment for Dell, which responded with an overhaul of its approach to customer service and technical support, including the launch of a blog. "Direct2Dell" which lays the company bare. Here company leaders, communicators, support personnel, and product managers engage in serious conversation with customers. Following the blog's success, Dell introduced the "Dell IdeaStorm," a site that allows any customer (or any employee, for that matter) to submit an idea. Other customers read the ideas, add their own comments, and vote to promote or demote them. Those that achieve broad support, gauged by the number of votes to promote, are turned into action items for management to consider. Several customer-introduced ideas have become reality, including the availability of Dell models running the Linux, not Windows, operating system. Dell also employs people to find and address customer problems reported on blogs like Jarvis's.

Dell's reputation has done a complete one-eighty. Even Jarvis is praising its efforts.

• • •

These two stories from real companies, Sony and Dell, portray the extremes of business transparency. Sony introduced a fake identity into an environment where reputation is based on authenticity. It was caught, as inevitably any attempt to deceive will be unveiled, and paid the price with a damaged reputation. Dell, however, began respecting the issues people raised and making their employees accessible to customers. Dell talked openly about problems and engaged customers in conversation about how to fix them. And Dell was rewarded with increased customer loyalty and a reinvigorated reputation.

The Transparency Debate

Raise the issue of transparency among businesspeople, and you are likely to spark instant and heartfelt disagreement. Transparency means different things to different people. Scholars tend to identify two categories:

- *Financial transparency.* Companies are required to disclose some financial information, such as earnings and profits, particularly if they are public companies. Other data, such as budgets and reports, may be disclosed if it serves the company's interests. Research has documented a relationship between the accuracy of analyst forecasts (for public companies) and financial transparency.

- *Governance transparency.* Exposure of the rules, processes, and behaviors that characterize how a company is run have been under a microscope since the business scandals that toppled companies like Enron and WorldCom.

There are books that address transparency from a holistic business standpoint, recommending the sharing of information among organizations and the exposure of data once carefully guarded by organizations. In their book, *The Naked Corporation,* for example, authors Dan Tapscott and David Ticoll recount the experience of a mining company that made its precious and proprietary geological data publicly available, along with a reward for anyone who could use the data to help the company find gold.[1]

These and others all are accurate and real definitions of *transparency.* In this book, however, we are most concerned with a company's reputation, the impact of forced transparency on a company's reputation, and the tools that companies can employ in order to bolster their reputation through transparency. It's a concept that encounters a lot of resistance, mostly because of a lack of clarity about what this kind of transparency means.

Before we get to a definition, though, let's tick off a few things transparency is not. First, it is not full disclosure. In other words, transparency does not mean you have to share absolutely everything about your organization. The idea that transparency could mean this is absurd. After all, most companies are prohibited by law from disclosing certain information. For example, companies agreeing to merge must maintain a mandated quiet period during which "no comment" is the only acceptable answer. Another example: a company that released its employees' health records would violate the Health Insurance Portability and Accountability Act. Companies can elect to keep all manner of information secret and not risk being viewed as opaque. "Being transparent doesn't mean I give you access to how much business

I booked yesterday or share with you what a customer in the intelligence community told me about how they want their systems designed," says Jonathan Schwartz, president and CEO of Sun Microsystems, an unabashed advocate of organizational transparency. "It means you're authentic with the marketplace."

Releasing information about products under development, for example, would give competitors an unfair advantage and could prove costly. Talks with governments about entering a new market could be very sensitive; public attention could derail them. Labor contract negotiations also belong behind closed doors. As General Motors' Christopher Barger noted on GM's "FYI" blog regarding a brief United Auto Workers strike, "These are sensitive times involving sensitive negotiations; a public blog is not the appropriate place for us to be commenting about them, nor do we think it's constructive to entertain a discussion of labor issues here."

In addition, being transparent does not require that you produce a never-ending sea of data and information, including copies of documentation the government requires be disclosed, in order to bolster the perception that you are keeping nothing hidden. Nor is it an endless series of meetings in which the same kind of information is offered face-to-face, accompanied by tedious PowerPoint presentations.

How Did We Get Here?

A definition of *transparency* to anchor this book must be based on the realities associated with doing business in today's business environment. Those realities have emerged as the result of the convergence of two separate and distinct trends: declining trust in business as usual and the increased public scrutiny under which companies find themselves thanks to the evolution of social media.

Declining Trust

In the days before the industrial revolution, a consumer (who wouldn't have a clue what you meant if you called her that) who needed a new pair of shoes would visit a cobbler. The cobbler would listen to what the customer wanted and then take the measurements he would use to cobble a pair of shoes that were just what the customer wanted. If while walking down the street, the heel separated from the sidewall, the customer could take it back to the cobbler who made it and have it fixed.

Today a consumer needing a pair of shoes goes to a department store that carries thirty brands. The clerk in the shoe department knows a bit about each one and helps the customer select the shoe that comes closest to what she had in mind, and then he gets the size that is closest to the size of the customer's feet. (She's probably somewhere between a 6 and a 6-1/2, but those are the only choices.) Should something go wrong with the shoe after the purchase, the shoemaker who made it—well, he's in the Philippines and doesn't speak English.

One of the consequences of the industrial revolution and its shift from individual craftspeople to manufacturing-oriented businesses was a widening chasm between customer and employee. In order to accommodate a global customer base and the command-and-control nature of the organization chart, companies began employing customer service representatives who responded to queries with canned, programmed responses. A company that had to communicate with the public did so through carefully crafted statements employing obfuscating corporatese and issued by designated corporate spokespeople.

The chasm between customer and employee thus widened. Companies grew more opaque, keeping their operations, leaders, and decision-making processes behind closed doors. Being opaque meant that it became unacceptable to reveal mistakes, problems, and failures; those were kept hidden in locked closets, which themselves were kept behind closed doors.

Most companies, even those embracing the behind-closed-doors approach to business, are run by decent people intending to run honest businesses in ethical ways. But there are always those who believe their opacity gives them license to engage in all kinds of deception in pursuit of personal power or financial gain. This belief that opacity shields a company from the glare of scrutiny led leaders from firms like Enron to engage in behaviors that shocked and enraged the population when they were exposed.

Those behaviors led to legislation forcing companies to be more open in their dealings, but the introduction of new regulations didn't quell consumer fury. Attitudes toward business began to change far beyond simple disgust. Customers began viewing their relationship with companies differently, as a partnership.

Coupled with these expectations about how they would be perceived by companies, customers began increasing the faith they put in buzz—the word of mouth being spread by people they know and trust.

The Evolution of Social Media

The original promise of the Internet when its existence became commonly known was clear. In the days before the Net, *New Yorker* media critic A. J. Leibling had it right: "Freedom of the press is guaranteed only to those who own one."[2] The Internet ensured the democratization of communication, that is, the ability for anyone to publish.

Unfortunately, publishing to the Net was not child's play. These were the days before HTML was a recognized initialism, before domain names could be obtained for $4.95 from GoDaddy.com, before hosting services that made server space available for pennies a day, before content management systems made creating an article as easy as filling in a form. Some intrepid souls nevertheless ventured into the Web creation space in order to stake their own claims to what was then referred to as "cyberspace."

They were joined only by programmers and coders working for Web development companies who feverishly slaved away creating sites for businesses, which dominated the Web. Everyone else sat back and lamented the geekiness required to participate on this so-called level playing field. In other words, creating Web content was expensive and technically challenging.

Neither is true any longer. Of course, you can still pay an interactive marketing agency plenty of money to create a dramatic, enticing Web site. But if all you want to do is tell your story, share your experiences, and talk with others who share the same desire, you can do it for free. A visit to Blogger.com or Wordpress.com, two minutes completing a registration form, and two minutes entering a headline and some text are all that's needed to become a publisher of online content.

The erosion of the technical and economic barriers to online publishing is not limited to Web pages. Consider video, which once was the sole province of professional video production shops. Sure, moms and dads shot video of their families, but the idea that a company could ever use a handheld camera and the editing software that comes with a computer to produce a video to convey a company message to thousands of people would have struck marketers or public relations practitioners as absurd. Today companies actually question whether they need a "YouTube strategy."

At the same time the barriers to online communication were coming down, the ease of publishing was inspiring greater collaboration online. Message boards (also known as bulletin boards, newsgroups, and forums) have always thrived online, but they were populated mostly by people who took the time and trouble to figure out how to use them. The new crop of tools was easy for anybody to use.

Motivated by the desire to provide and receive word of mouth, the result of the declining trust in corporate messaging, people flocked to these tools. Blogs were the first of the social media tools to erupt onto the business scene, making it easy for people to swap information with the members of communities of people who share the same interests. The concept that underlies blogging, for all the analysis and research to which blogging has been subjected, is simple:

- You can write about whatever you want. Your most recent article appears at the top of the blog's home page.
- Others can comment about what you've written.
- People can write about what you have written on their own blogs and link to your original article.

These fundamental concepts heralded a seismic shift in the way business is done. Before blogs, people unhappy with your business would tell ten friends (as the old marketing saying goes), who might tell ten friends, who might tell ten more friends. Today an unhappy Comcast customer videotapes a technician who fell asleep on his couch, and the video is viewed by millions on YouTube, becomes a source of discussion in both the blogosphere and the mainstream media, and morphs into a genuine reputational crisis for Comcast.

Consider just a few of the better-known instances when bloggers have pooled their collective expertise and resources to shine a light on blemishes that might never have been exposed in the days before social media:

- One document presented by the TV news magazine *60 Minutes II* as evidence of U.S. President George W. Bush's shirking of duty while a member of the Air National Guard was proven to be a forgery, ultimately leading to CBS anchor Dan Rather's departure from the network.
- A couple blogging about their journey across the United States in a motor home, spending their nights in Wal-Mart parking lots, were proven to be employed, and the motor home paid for, by a front organization created by Wal-Mart through its public relations agency.

- A Brooklyn-based camera retailer was driven out of business by its lost reputation after a blogger exposed its unethical business practices.

Yet these same bloggers—people sharing stories and experiences—have embraced organizations that open themselves to a closer look by the public at large. Here are some examples:

- Southwest Airlines' sole blog, "Nuts About Southwest," is a collaborative effort by a number of employees who represent the broad scope of workers, ranging from pilots and flight attendants to behind-the-scenes workers, mechanics, ticket agents, gate agents and baggage handlers. The CEO and the president chime in when appropriate. If there's a problem, it is addressed on the blog in the authentic voice of the person who's dealing with it.

- Another collaborative blog, "Fastlane," has provided auto enthusiasts, car buyers, and the auto press with a unique perspective inside the workings of one of the biggest companies in the world, General Motors. The blog is written primarily by vice chairman Bob Lutz, the company's top car guy, along with several of the members of the team who report to him.

- A newer entry into the collaborative blogging space, "Evolution of Security," is written by a handful of employees from the Transportation Security Administration (TSA), those uniformed people at airports who screen you and your baggage. Early reviews acknowledge that the TSA appears to be doing as much listening as talking; the blog is explicit in its solicitation of feedback.

- Microsoft, as we will see later in the book, initiated a complete reversal of its image by allowing its employees to blog. Instead of being viewed as a large, predatory, monolithic, and secretive organization, Microsoft is now seen as the aggregate of all those great individual employees who through their blogs talk candidly about everything from the scripting code being written for Internet Explorer 7 to how the company recruits employees.

But the social media space, with all its implications for the speed with which information about organizations moves, has evolved far beyond blogs and their audio cousins, podcasts. There are social networks of all stripes: democratized content networks where anybody can contribute to the information resources and add his or her two cents to how important any piece of content is; presence networks (also known as microblogging) that let people share information at the speed of light; content-sharing networks, where videos and images make the rounds; and virtual networking platforms like Second Life that transform the two-dimensional social networks of the Web into breathtaking three-dimensional worlds.

At one time, the need for transparency as an organization cultural imperative was far less vital than today. Getting a story into the *Wall Street Journal* could be enough to attract the attention of investors, and getting ink in the *New York Times* could motivate customers to part with their dollars in exchange for your products. Today the Internet provides organizations with their own means of distribution; reliance on traditional channels is dissipating.

"Is [*New York Times* technology writer John Markoff] valuable because he's at the *New York Times* or is he valuable because he's John Markoff?" asks Jonathan Schwartz. "Blogging suggests that it's because of the individual dialogue he has with the marketplace." There was a time, Schwartz says, that the importance assigned to a person or a product derived from the media outlet that chose to distribute it. "With free software, free content, blogging, all of that is being disruptive now," he says. "Facebook didn't need help from anybody to become Facebook. They are their own distribution, they are their own authentic engagement with the marketplace."

The lesson becomes increasingly clear as the social networking space evolves and matures. Be honest, authentic, and willing to engage in conversations—even conversations about things that are not exactly flattering—and your company will be respected. Goodwill accrues that can see you through difficult times. Reinforce the walls between you and your stakeholders, and they will turn against you using tools with far more serious repercussions than the old "tell ten friends" approach ever produced.

Our Definition

This book is about *tactical* transparency. Our concern is not philosophical but practical. What tools can you use, and how can you make them succeed in order to be sincerely but prudently transparent in the ways that matter to your stakeholders? We talk very little about regulatory compliance but a lot about what customers, consumers, investors, interest groups, and other publics can see when they try to look into your company.

To guide us in this exploration of the tactics of effective transparency, we have adopted the following definition:

Transparency is the degree to which an organization shares the following with its stakeholder publics:

- *Its leaders:* The leaders of transparent companies are accessible and are straightforward when talking with members of key audiences.

- *Its employees:* Employees of transparent companies are accessible to reinforce the public view of the company and to help people where appropriate.

- *Its values:* Ethical behavior, fair treatment, and other values are on full display in transparent companies.

- *Its culture:* How a company does things is more important today than what it does. The way things get done is not a secret in transparent companies.

- *The results of its business practices, both good and bad:* Successes, failures, problems, and victories all are communicated by transparent companies.

- *Its business strategy:* Of particular importance to the investment community but also of interest to several other audiences, a company's strategy is a key basis for investment decisions. Misalignment of a company's strategy and investors' expectations almost always result in disaster.

None of these dimensions of transparency is all or nothing. Leaders need to be accessible, but sensitive negotiations need to take place behind closed doors. Reporting problems that will affect the customer is a sound strategy; revealing every compound a scientist in R&D tried that failed to result in a viable product is the excessive flooding of people with unnecessary minutiae. The need to be transparent in this age of scrutiny always needs to be balanced with what is in the organization's best interests.

Conclusion

Transparency is not a choice. The business environment requires it. It is futile to try to hide bad news because somebody will expose it. It is equally futile to build walls in order to mask questionable business practices because they'll be revealed. It is in a company's own best interests to behave ethically and talk candidly.

"Nobody expects us to be perfect," Sun Microsystems' Schwartz says. "They do increasingly expect us to be genuine. Developers and customers want to do business with companies that are transparent. They know what's next for a product, how we are going to manage our relationship with them, how we are going to treat them."

Shining that kind of light on a company where people work hard, believe in what they do, and do it in a manner of which they can be proud will pay dividends to that organization. Yet transparency does not come easily, and it must be embraced across the entire company. At the same time, it's important to know what can't be shared. A defense contractor doesn't want the nature of its top-secret project broadcast to the world, nor does the government agency paying for this project.

To ensure transparency is practiced as a core company value but that it does not create undue problems, companies need transparency strategies. And they need to know how to use the same tools to practice transparency that are used to scrutinize them. They need to know how to become open members of the same networks their customers belong to. They need to know how to be transparent through conversation. These strategies and tactics occupy us for the rest of this book.

2

SOMEONE MAY BE LOOKING

Transparency Done Right and Wrong

Popular tech blog Valleywag.com told the story in November 2007 of how college student Kevin Colvin wanted to party on Halloween in Boston. But he was an intern at Anglos Irish Bank and was supposed to be at work on October 31 in New York City. He decided to blow off his job, telling his manager that "something came up at home," adorned the garb of a fairy princess (literally—with wings and a wand), and had his picture taken by a friend at the party. Enter Facebook, the massive social networking site where anyone's profile is instantly viewable by the Internet community at large. In the case of Kevin, this included his manager, Paul, whose return e-mail stated, "Thanks for letting us know [you wouldn't be at work]. Hope everything is ok in Boston. (cool wand)."

The picture and e-mail exchange exploded online with multiple reactions to Kevin's actions and Paul's response. Most felt Kevin might have grasped the fact that since his Facebook profile was available to the public (and that friends and colleagues at work would have already known about it), it may have been a more discreet choice to eschew the beer and tutu or simply avoid the phone camera altogether.

But the lines of privacy and professionalism are blurring. It is ironic that the speed with which personal media can be posted online lies in stark contrast to the permanency of our digital footprints. While social networking encourages a culture of authenticity, many of its most avid practitioners mistake the alarm of full disclosure for the ring of truth. While the freedom of press extends online, virtual voyeurism has encouraged a lack of universal standards that means one person's right of expression becomes another's cause for litigation.

Our public persona is murky online. Separating our private and professional lives used to be simple. Put on a suit and go to work; pop on some wings and go to a party. What were the odds your boss would be at the keg to bag you ditching work? But a friend "punchcasting" your photo online has become commonplace. (The term refers to services like www.kyte.tv that allow you to post media directly online without having to upload or save to your computer. Nokia and other carriers also produce phones that stream online video to a person's blog or site while they're shooting it live.) And a human resource recruiter is just as likely to find information you'd rather keep buried as your LinkedIn profile or online bio. As the author of Valleywag states in the post about Kevin, "Who says Facebook is the province of the young? Increasingly, the 30-something bosses of naive recent college grads are proving adept at turning the social network against its earliest adopters." H. L. Mencken was certainly prescient when he said, "Conscience is the inner voice which warns us that someone may be looking."

Companies like Enron brought the focus of corporate transparency to the forefront of the public eye. Through governance like the Sarbanes-Oxley Act, the call for financial and accounting disclosure has caused all organizations to open up their firms to specific public scrutiny. Another federal law, the Sunshine Act of 1976, "requires (1) most meetings of most Federal agencies shall be open to the public and (2) the fullest practical disclosure to the public of the government decision making process." Corporate social responsibility has become a self-imposed standard for many large brands like Starbucks and Ben & Jerry's, demonstrating a desire to promote trust with consumers coupled with the implied message that it's better to air one's dirty coffee than have someone else spill the beans.

While we can hope that the motivation for our current era of transparency stems from an inner desire to promote trust, the nature of modern communications ensures that hiding your head in the sand only increases the impact of your embarrassment when you get caught. At the very least, you likely won't have the support of your publics when you need it. As Paull Young, senior account executive at Converseon, states:

> Those of us who have even a rudimentary understanding of online communication and social media understand that it is not possible to hide anything online—everything will eventually become public. However, this knowledge is not widely shared among our colleagues, industry, or the public at large. In this way, you could say transparency is the process of ensuring someone is looking—thereby making your conscience publicly accountable.

This is unnerving. Who wants to cope with a higher level of accountability just because this new medium, the Internet, has come along, especially if you're concerned about your brand? Navigating the court of public opinion has always been perilous, but in the context of Internet culture, who can say what dictates authenticity versus full disclosure?

There's good news in all of this: you already have a context for transparency. You practice it in your daily life. Now you just have to translate your personal ethics into the framework of your organization. How we address the degree of openness we practice drives everything from our relationships with key audiences to how we handle trying times. Transparency is by nature challenging, confrontational, and risky because it is typically characterized by a candor and characteristics that are not often among an organization's priorities. It feels counterintuitive to admit mistakes or strive for authenticity in the dog-eat-dog, take-no-prisoners world of business. But it has to happen. The longer you veil your organization in preachy marketing rhetoric while trying to shield your operation from interested parties, the faster you lose credibility in the eyes of your social customers who demand authenticity and whose ranks swell daily. A company must determine where it will be transparent (internal policies) and how to encapsulate its core culture (communication channels) and reveal its message to the world.

The Four Characteristics of Transparency

The basics of situations requiring transparency fall into two primary camps:

- Something negative has happened, and you need to deal with it.
- You want to inoculate your organization against such problems by demonstrating your willingness to share information and disclose your business processes.

In either case you'll need to remain open by employing varying degrees of all of the following characteristics of transparency: objectivity, purpose, esteem, and navigation—or OPEN.

Objectivity

Knowing it's impossible to remain objective in the heat of conflagration or when dealing with something as vital as the integrity of your business, it is of preeminent importance that you demonstrate honesty and integrity in your actions that resonate with your audience. Employing multiple channels, from formal documents issued through traditional channels to informal videos of the CEO uploaded to YouTube, can earn you goodwill that will pay dividends when your reputation is under attack. Facts and figures help determine the plausibility of your case, but your heart is what sways potential ill will. Remember the four words people will ask when trying to determine if you're transparent or trite: *Are you for real?*

Purpose

Transparency needs to be accompanied by action. Although a sincere apology may turn an initial tide of disfavor, you need to implement a proactive campaign to galvanize your internal resources and face external pressures. A perfect example of this can be found in the response of JetBlue Airways' founder, chairman, and former CEO, David Neeleman, to his airline's canceling multiple flights over the course of Valentine's Day in 2007. Beyond his candid apology on YouTube, he worked with his management team to institute JetBlue Airways' Customer Bill of Rights as a way to manage customer expectations and empower them to participate with JetBlue Airways as valued customers. In this way, Neeleman and JetBlue Airways regained the trust of most of its customers and began rebuilding the brand in which it had built so much currency. When the airline encountered its crisis, the company innovated new practices that heightened customer confidence in how the airline would handle such events in the future. Such purpose and planning are key to any transparency effort. As Neeleman said in a later post, "Talk is cheap—action is the only thing that really builds your reputation, not just as a person, but as a company."

Esteem

The esteem in which your company is held is the result of a combination of several factors, including your record on corporate social responsibility, which itself is made up of a variety of behaviors, including your approach to the environment, your charitable activities, your role as a part of the communities in which you operate, and, most important, according to one study, the way you treat your employees. (A company with a solid track record will be given some slack over an uncharacteristic lapse, particularly if the company's leaders apologize and report on the measures taken to ensure no repeat.) Your values are another critical component of the esteem with which external publics hold your organization and, most important, how much you abide by those values when the going gets tough and it's easier or more instinctive to abandon them in favor of expediency. Regardless of all the communications your company issues trying to position itself, in reality it will be perceived based on what a customer finds when conducting a search of the company's name on Google.

Navigation

Companies must navigate their way through the complexities of marketplaces, regulations, competition, economics, and the dozens, even hundreds, of other variables that a company faces on a day-to-day basis. In particular, how you navigate a crisis can color your reputation for years to come. You need to have methods in place to respond quickly and candidly, without masking truths that will emerge anyway, that will allow an open dialogue with the people most precious to your brand.

Transparency Done Right: The Apple of My Ire

Apple fans are known for their zealous support of the latest technologies released by Jobs & Co. Dozens of fan sites, forums, and pod- and videocasts are dedicated to the discussion of what pioneering technologies will be released by the Apple innovators and when. It's the "when" part that became a heated controversy in early September 2007 when Apple lowered the price of the iPhone by $200 from its original price of $599 (from the previous summer) to spur holiday sales. After a fevered backlash online to what many early adopters called their "stupid tax" (buying early at a higher price), Jobs ended up apologizing in the open letter excerpted below and offered a $100 credit at Apple retail and online stores to iPhone owners:

> Even though we are making the right decision to lower the price of iPhone, and even though the technology road is bumpy, we

need to do a better job taking care of our early iPhone customers as we aggressively go after new ones with a lower price. Our early customers trusted us, and we must live up to that trust with our actions in moments like these.

It's important to note that Jobs's transparent tone is not overtly apologetic. He certainly doesn't grovel in his explanation for his actions and provides sound business reasons for the drop in iPhone price along with a mini-treatise on the nature of being a first adopter in the ever changing technology industry. However, as Forrester Research analyst Charles Golvin reported in an article for the Associated Press: "In the course of a day, he probably got an earful and a better sense of the extent of the discontent on the part of these very, very loyal customers. On second and third thought, he realized these were probably the customers you most want to make sure are satisfied and retain a very positive impression about Apple overall, not just the iPhone."[1]

In this way we can see how Jobs used tactical transparency and was OPEN (objectivity, purpose, esteem, and navigation):

- Objectivity. Jobs apologized for any inconvenience customers experienced but also explained his logic. Therein lies the key in regard to his tactical transparency: Jobs explained why Apple had taken the action it had, providing details about the decision-making process and the factors that influenced the decision. That was a big deal for Apple, generally regarded as a closed company. However you gauge his tone, sincere or smarmy, Jobs acknowledged that he listened to his customers and he responded to their concerns.

- Purpose. Jobs offered store credits along with his apology. His words were accompanied by action—savvy action, since shoppers returned to Apple stores to buy a hundred dollars worth of products that cost the company less than a hundred dollars to produce.

- Esteem. Love him or hate him, Jobs continuously creates the cutting-edge technology that drives the marketplace. Apple's reputation for quality of design and innovation stands it in good stead when it is challenged with conflict.

- Navigation. Some might have said that Jobs could have moved sooner to offer store credits, but the point is that he reacted quickly enough to stem a tide of rancor that could have seriously affected holiday sales or the faith of his core audience.

Transparency Done Right:
JetBlue Airways–Trick or Tweet?

The popular microblogging service Twitter.com (described elsewhere in this book) allows users to post short text messages via computer or phone that lets people know "what they are doing." It's an inherently personal medium, as people post the specifics of their daily activities, including everything from a meal they've just eaten to reactions to a political election. By following other people's Twitter messages, or "Tweets," users can also be alerted to what other members are doing and respond to their posts in real time, sometimes seconds after the initial Tweet goes live.

The ability to monitor this level of conversation has provided companies with a tool to insert themselves into discussions in a manner akin to walking up to group of people at a party. The behavior sometimes causes delight ("I can't believe this company is listening to me") and other times mild panic ("Big Brother is watching"). This mixed response proved to be the case when popular blogger Jonathan Fields heard from JetBlue Airways via their corporate communication manager and Twitter user Morgan Johnston. After Fields tweeted about seeing Star Trek icon William Shatner about to board a flight via JetBlue (the airline), he noticed that "JetBlue" (the person) was following him on Twitter:[2]

My mind starts spinning. I'm half freaked out, half awed. (My reaction is that) mega jet co has some dude dedicated to monitoring and responding to what's being said about JetBlue in the twittersphere (and) that's pretty damn cool. Cool because they care. And cool because have a clue that something called twitter not only exists, but might be a useful way for them to participate in the conversation.

In response to why he and JetBlue Airways are using Twitter and other social media tools to interact with customers, here's how Morgan Johnston responded to an interview for this book:

> With any of the microblogging tools available, people are able to broadcast what they're going through at the moment. If you can tap into and observe those types of activities while they're happening, you can help them much more immediately. Before they have a chance to go home and stew about it, you can help them while they're in the midst of the situation. Isn't that better than trying to recover a situation afterwards?

Johnston points out, however, that to avoid a Big Brother reaction from customers it's important for an organization to be (as he says in Fields's post) "less billboard and more information booth." But the point of his efforts is that JetBlue Airways is looking for better ways to *listen* to conversations around their brand so that they can react in ways to best help customers in an immediate and authentic way.

Transparency Done Wrong: Astroturfing

Astroturfing is a term referring to a formal public relations campaign designed to look like a grassroots or spontaneous outpouring of support (hence the analogy of real grass to fake). A recent example took place on a blog created by Edelman, the world's largest independent public relations agency, for Wal-Mart: walmartingacrossamerica.com. Following the adventures of a couple going cross-country in a recreational vehicle while stopping in Wal-Mart parking lots, the trip was funded by Working Families for Wal-Mart (WFWM) without proper disclosure of this fact. (CEO Richard Edelman eventually apologized for the campaign, citing the responsibility for the lack of transparency for the campaign was his firm's responsibility versus Wal-Mart's.)

This well-known case study is especially worth noting given Edelman's leadership role in applying ethical, authentic social media to client engagements. Richard Edelman was one of the first public relations practitioners to recognize the importance of social media and establish a practice around it. Yet the values emerging at the top of the organization had not yet filtered through the rest of the company, leading to damaging actions on the front line. If a transparency-savvy company like Edelman can make so egregious a mistake, so can anyone else. And what's important to note is that simply disclosing the fact the trip was paid for by the WFWM would have stymied the majority of online dissent. There's a vast different between questioning someone's judgment in creating a marketing campaign versus core integrity. The fact that someone got paid by Wal-Mart or its proponents doesn't inherently devalue the couple's journey, but if that fact isn't disclosed, the public assumes the company is trying to pull a fast one.

This example is a stark one. In fact, situations in which a company finds itself may be more subtle, enveloped in shades of gray. That won't stop a risk-averse public from noticing, though, and the questionable actions of one organization can reflect poorly on an industry at large. As Paull Young from Converseon states:

> Businesses are still working out how best to engage in the online space. Organizations see the opportunity to engage with customers in online communities and are trying to delicately balance the tightrope that is social media communications. Astroturfing by any organization harms the opportunities all businesses have to engage with their audiences online.

Transparency Done Wrong: Target's Dismissal of Bloggers

Amy Jussel, founder of the blog ShapingYouth.org, was unhappy with a Target campaign that depicted a woman in the process of making a snow angel with a bull's-eye positioned directly at her crotch. Noting in her blog that other campaigns she's highlighted could have a more negative influence on children than this one (her focus is on the impact of marketing toward youth), she nevertheless held Target to a higher standard because of its Disney-aged demographics. She called the retailer to express her concern over the image and reinforced the fact that she was a loyal customer for the brand. So it was a bit of a shock when Target's e-mail response came back to Jussel with a public relations person responding that "Target does not participate with nontraditional media outlets."

Suffice to say the blogosphere was not happy to hear Target's low opinion of citizen journalism after Jussel blogged about the incident. Multiple sites, including the Word of Mouth Marketing Association and the blog for Parents for Ethical Marketing, commented on Target's policy. The uproar eventually led to a *New York Times* article: "Target Tells a Blogger to Go Away."[3]

Although Target representatives noted in the *Times* article that its media focus is on the traditional outlets that cater to its core customer, Target's initial response was handled poorly. Jussel was a loyal customer expressing concerns over marketing that was inappropriate for children. Defending the campaign or noting its media focus should have taken a back seat to talking to Jussel on the issue. Although Target may have not pulled the ad in response to her complaint (it didn't), a smarter solution would have been to partner with Jussel for an interview on her blog or another initiative. Instead of alienating a loyal customer, Target could have reached her influential audience, however small.

One might wonder how any public relations person could allocate the time to connect with every person who complains about an issue like this one. Perhaps the better question, how-ever, is, How much more energy would it have taken to deal with the negative press from the *New York Times* article depict-ing your company dismissing an advocate for safer marketing toward children?

Be aware that your organization's policies toward blog-gers or anyone else do not determine how your business will be depicted in the blogosphere. The conversation rules your brand, so make sure your interactions with customers focus on dialogue versus dismissal.

Conclusion

If you're worried that someone may be looking, turn around. They are, or soon will be, and hiding is impossible. Begin the process of opening up communication channels between your employees and customers, and see how promoting trust will always be more profitable than spinning lies.

3

DO YOU HAVE WHAT IT TAKES?

Characteristics of Transparent Organizations

The president and CEO of a Fortune 500 company returned from a conference boiling over with enthusiasm for a presentation he had seen. First thing in the morning, he summoned his staff into his office and regaled them with tales of companies that had stayed ahead of the curve by adopting the philosophy, culture, and practices of "learning companies." Rubbing his hands together, he proclaimed, "We are now a learning company."

The executive's direct reports stole uneasy glances at one another. One of them, the vice president of human resources (HR), finally raised his hand a little timidly and asked, "What does that mean?"

The CEO seemed a little miffed. "It means that we're a *learning* company," he said, as though putting the emphasis on the adjective somehow would help people understand what it meant.

"Okay," said the HR vice president. "What do we have to do to become a learning company?"

The CEO was now getting visibly irritated. "We learn. We embrace *learning*."

"But how?" the executive continued to press. "What do we do differently?"

The CEO folded his arms across his chest and glared at his HR guy. "We learn," he said firmly, shutting off any further discussion.

It's easy to empathize with the HR manager's frustration. To embrace a new culture, the old culture has to change, and cultures don't change easily. Enough books, white papers, and reports have been written about organizational culture to fill a small library, but understanding the idea of culture doesn't require any study at all: *Culture is the way things are around here.*

People who don't fit into the culture—who cannot adapt to the way things are done around here—simply leave, a point reinforced by Sun Microsystems president and CEO Jonathan Schwartz. "Every organization *has* to have its own culture," he says. "Every employee either needs to bond with that culture and be a part of it, or find a place where they can feel at home. If you came to Sun and what you wanted was dictatorial hierarchy, sorry, wrong place," he says. "If, on the other hand, you love innovation but end up in an organization that didn't want to innovate, you'd end up bolting.

"The culture of an organization," Schwartz continues, "whether it's transparency or innovation or competitiveness, that has to be something everybody . . . feels a part of. If they don't, life's too short to just collect a paycheck."

New employees in an organization find themselves taking the culture immersion course. Every day they experience the culture, learning what works and what doesn't in their quest to get things done. The culture subsumes them; they become its adherents regardless of how much they may have resisted at first. To buck the culture is to reduce the opportunity for reward and recognition, two of the biggest drivers of employee commitment. But typically the more time we spend in a culture, the more we become part of it. Think of a benign, business-centric version of the Stockholm syndrome (which leads kidnap victims to sympathize and identify with their captors). Changing a culture is no easy task. There are consultants who charge large fees to help guide organizations on the path to culture change. (Some of them are even worth the fees they charge.) Most of them will tell you that you have to start by identifying the culture you want. Next, analyze the gap between the current culture and that desired state. The work of culture change then becomes taking the appropriate steps to close the gap by showing the workforce the advantages of embracing the vision and helping them figure out what they need to do differently in order to bring the change about.

To discover where the gaps in an organization are between opacity and transparency, let's explore some of the key characteristics of truly transparent companies.

Transparent Companies Do the Right Thing

There's a reason the executives running Enron concealed their efforts, from defrauding California residents by manipulating the demand for energy to cooking the books in order to hide red ink. They knew these things were illegal and they'd pay a price if they were caught. So arrogant and greedy were these executives, however, that they rolled the dice with the livelihoods of thousands of workers who went about their work diligently, proud of their company and completely unaware of what was going on behind the scenes. It's impossible to imagine Enron's management voluntarily inviting careful scrutiny of their business practices or openly detailing the processes by which its decisions were made.

Far too many companies breed cynicism among the public as well as their own employees by articulating values that its own leaders fail to embrace. "Words on the wall" is a phrase applied to carefully crafted values statements that are enshrined in frames in meeting rooms and common areas but bear little resemblance to the values that seem to govern the decision making executed at the highest levels of the company.

There is a story about a Fortune 500 organization in the mid-1980s that adopted a culture of quality, a dominant business fad from the late 1970s through the mid-1990s. This company, in the consumer goods business, spent millions on communication and training to steep the culture in the "Quality Improvement Process" (QIP). Several key concepts became mantras in the organization, including "zero defects," which was defined as "conformance to requirements" and enthroned as *the* criterion for the company's products. Under the precepts of QIP, no product would be shipped if it did not conform to requirements. The company's entire workforce of more than five thousand people went through weeks of training to learn the QIP way. Their performance metrics were adjusted to include quality measures. Quality, by God, would become a way of life at this company.

But a couple years into the process, management was faced with a decision. A large inventory of product that needed to be shipped in order to meet the company's sales goals did not meet the zero defects criterion; the product did not conform to requirements. For management to embrace the QIP culture in which it had invested so much time, effort, and money would require quarantining the product and identify the "root cause" (another bit of jargon the meaning of which everyone in the company knew), make adjustments to the manufacturing process to ensure it didn't happen again, and then correct the nonconforming goods so customers would get product that met the company's zero-defect promise.

You probably know what's coming: management opted to ship the product and not risk missing their numbers. Employees witnessed this decision and knew instantly where the bread was buttered. They could continue embracing the values of QIP, or they could emulate the behavior of their leaders. Few employees wondered which of these approaches was more likely to earn them reward and recognition. Within weeks, QIP became an afterthought; nobody took it seriously any longer, and employees reverted to old habits.

These days, it's growing increasingly obvious that customers want to do business with ethical companies. The evidence is clear:

- As the global warming message grows louder, companies that jump on the environmental bandwagon without making substantive change in the way they address the environment are accused of "greenwashing" and boycotted.

- Investment funds made up of green companies and companies that take social responsibility seriously attract increasingly large numbers of high-caliber investors.

- Students graduating from college and ready to join the workforce want first to work for companies they admire even more than companies that will pay the most. Consequently the companies that walk the values talk often get the best recruits, leaving the mediocre leftovers for their competitors.

It has become something of a hackneyed phrase that companies can "do well by doing good." We could debate whether this is true; in fact, an analysis of business performance shows that some companies have done extremely well without embracing a real culture of corporate social responsibility. To be sure, there are organizations that simply have such a great product or service, or are the only purveyors of those products and services, that people will continue patronizing the company and filling its coffers. But the reality of the business world today is that most companies have competition: their customers have alternatives. There are customers who will switch from one cheese spread to another if they learn that the company that makes their cheese spread of choice also produces cigarettes. Philip Morris changed its company name to Altria to conceal the fact that Kraft food products (acquired in an acquisition of Kraft) come from the same company that sells Benson & Hedges cigarettes.

Corporate social responsibility, when taken seriously as a core company value, is a symbol of ethical behavior.

If You're Not There Yet . . .

- Revisit your corporate values and determine if they need updating or revisiting.

- Implement reward and recognition programs to reinforce the values.

- Downplay success achieved through actions that contradict the company's values.

- Audit your corporate social responsibility programs. How are they perceived internally and externally? Do they focus on the right things (as opposed to, say, a pet project of the CEO's spouse)?

- Consider hiring a corporate ethics officer.

Transparent Companies Acknowledge Inescapable Facts

The skin care company Dove has scored big points through the use of both conventional and social media to promote its Campaign for Real Beauty. The campaign turns its nose up at the rail-thin beauties whose images grace the covers of fashion magazines and the ads inside, who star in television commercials for everything from perfume to breakfast cereal, who have become the ideal to which young girls aspire. Real beauty, the campaign argues, comes in all shapes and sizes.

The campaign's early marketing featured appealing, attractive women who were too tall, too short, full-bodied, or eerily pale. But Dove scored its biggest successes with videos uploaded to multimedia sharing services like YouTube. The first of these, called "Evolution," began with a very ordinary-looking model looking into the camera. Then, using stop-motion photography, viewers witnessed a remarkable metamorphosis: with the aid of a hairdresser and a makeup artist, the plain-Jane model was transformed into a stunning beauty. Wind from a fan whipped through her hair as her photo was taken and then imported into Photoshop, where her eyes were enlarged, her neck elongated, and other changes made that would create envy in an old-school practitioner of the airbrush arts. The final image was seen on a billboard hawking some beauty product as cars and pedestrians passed by. The visage of the stunning model was replaced by the words, "No wonder our perception of beauty is distorted." The video ends with information on a series of "real beauty" workshops.

The video, which lasts just seventy-five seconds, was a sensation, producing 150 percent of the return on investment that Dove's prior-year Super Bowl ad had generated. Inconceivably, the video, on which not a nickel of media buy was spent, won the Film Grand Prix at the Cannes Advertising Awards. Buzz over "Evolution" was huge.

Dove bucked conventional wisdom that suggests you can't repeat a viral marketing success by producing another video, this one titled "Onslaught." A rapid-fire assault on the senses, the video is a barrage of images of beautiful, thin models in advertisements extolling the virtues of face creams, diets, plastic surgery, and all manner of products designed to help women look like . . . well, like the models in the ads. The video begins, however, with an innocent, adolescent schoolgirl looking into the camera. The same girl appears at the end of the video, walking across the street with her schoolmates as the text superimposed over the images warns viewers to "talk to your daughter before the beauty industry does."

So far, all well and good. The Dove Campaign for Real Beauty has been widely praised for taking an alternative approach to marketing and for its attempt to redefine what it means to be beautiful (that is, not a rail-thin model).

The campaign, however, makes no mention of the fact that Dove is owned by Unilever, the Dutch conglomerate that also owns, among hundreds of other brands, Axe. The advertising campaign for the line of Axe personal grooming products for men is aimed squarely at the younger set and appeals directly to their desire for sexual conquest. In the commercials, which are wildly popular, to the point that members of the target audience have made their own versions and uploaded them to YouTube (much to the company's delight), young men use an Axe product and are instantly assaulted by every unbelievably beautiful young woman within sniffing distance.

It was inevitable that Unilever would come in for some heat because of the apparent contradiction between Dove ("you don't have to look like a fashion model to be beautiful") and Axe ("use our product and you'll score women who look like fashion models"). Anticorporate activists have been all over the inconsistency, creating protest videos and uploading them to the same channels Dove used to gets its socially conscious message across.

It would have been far better of Unilever to openly acknowledge the different approaches of its two brands. The explanation is simple. As a conglomerate, Unilever owns a number of companies that operate independently. Certain of the parent's core values are instilled in all of the companies it owns, but each company also has its own culture, its own markets, its own values. As another example of this concept, think of Rupert Murdoch's News Corporation, which owns some of the seamiest tabloid newspapers in England but also owns the *Wall Street Journal*. Nobody wonders why nude models don't appear in the *Journal*, but of course, Murdoch is completely open about the companies he owns.

Thus, the management team at Dove can certainly embrace a philosophy that recognizes the beauty in everyday women and be entirely sincere and passionate about that belief, while Axe can at the same time approach the marketing of its product through the most prurient (albeit entertaining) commercials on TV. Being open about the discrepancy, the exposure of which was as predictable as tomorrow morning's sunrise, could have headed off activists' use of creative media to dent Unilever's reputation.

Not all misalignments are as clear-cut as the Dove-versus-Axe issue. Consumer food companies like the Coca-Cola Company and Kraft have quietly been acquiring small companies that market organic food products. The appropriate documents are filed to comply with the laws that govern such acquisitions, but the ownership of these organic foods companies is kept quiet in the communications of the organic food companies. The parent companies fear the defection of loyal customers if they were to find out that that quaint little company that makes its organic stone-ground wheat crackers is owned by a company that sells millions of dollars worth of sugar-laden cookies rich in trans fats.

Did these food giants really think they could keep their ownership of organic food firms quiet? It was a forgone conclusion that someone like Phil Howard, an assistant professor of agriculture and recreation at Michigan State University, would draft a buying guide that made clear the connection between organic food brands and the companies that owned them, publishing the guide in *Good* magazine.

Once an organization recognizes that concealing such affiliations will result in unpleasant revelations later, they can begin thinking about how to leverage the relationship, which had to have positive attributes to lead to the relationship in the first place. Starbucks has built its green reputation through the marketing of its Fair Trade coffee, even though the sale of Fair Trade represents only a fraction of the coffee it sells. Of course, the sale of Fair Trade coffee is enhanced by the free distribution of coffee grounds for use as compost and other actions consistent with an environmentally conscious approach to business.

In a *PRWeek* article, Straus Communications president Michael Straus put it this way:

> If the parent company is willing to undertake a broader strategic sustainable initiative to contextualize the organic, then there is the possibility to use the acquisition to further their overall brand strategy. There is increasing pressure from consumers and their shareholders to address environmental issues, and they can't afford not to do anything and not be transparent.[1]

If You're Not There Yet . . .

- Inventory the relationships in your organization.
- Identify any potential conflicts between any of the entities on your list.
- Identify any relationships that could be fodder for protest or sources of criticism.
- Develop a strategy for addressing the relationships, not just in your annual report and regulatory filings, but in your marketing and communication efforts.
- If you need to alter any of the relationships or jettison any of the organizations that are incompatible with your values, develop a plan to do so publicly as a symbol of the actions you're taking to walk the talk.

Transparent Companies Trust Their Employees

Companies that discourage their employees from speaking openly about the company fear those employees will cause problems with inappropriate or incorrect information. In companies that do not treat their employees well, that fear extends to worries that employees will expose bad working conditions or, worse, become whistle-blowers revealing unethical behavior.

Given the volume of research that supports the value companies accrue from a bond of trust between leadership and employees, it's surprising that some companies continue to treat their employees like assets to be used up. Ultimately companies are made up of people, and people determine an organization's success or failure.

Lack of trust in employees manifests itself in many ways. A startling number of companies block access to non-work-related Web sites because a few employees have taken advantage of the privilege. This practice begins with the premise, "We can't trust *any* of you, so we're blocking access for *all* of you." That's a heck of a way to promote an actively engaged workforce! It's far better to trust that most of your employees will not abuse the privilege and will get their work done, and then to manage the few slackers (who would find other ways to waste time in the absence of Web access) by exception.

If You're Not There Yet . . .

- Revisit your employee communications and human resource strategies and implement changes that will support building greater levels of trust between management and employee.
- Take a few small chances. You'll probably be surprised when your employees reward your confidence in them.
- Develop clear and well-communicated policies that let employees know what the limits are, such as the unauthorized disclosure of company-confidential information.

Transparent Companies Have an Open-Book Mind-Set

Although there will always be financial information that it is unwise to disclose publicly, most of your financial dealings should be an open book, particularly if you are a public company. It was Enron's (our favorite example) closed-book mentality that led very smart leaders to believe, stupidly, that they could get away with unconscionable financial swindles.

If You're Not There Yet . . .

- Implement processes by which your employees will understand the company's finances, the role they play in the company's financial performance, and how they can adapt what they do to contribute more to the bottom line.
- Make employees accountable for the numbers they control.
- Share all the information you can with your employees and your publics.
- Give employees a financial stake in the organization's performance.

Leaders and Employees of Transparent Companies Are Accessible

A company that has laid itself bare and has nothing to hide needs to be prepared to talk about the company and address questions and concerns that arise from within various publics: the mainstream media, bloggers, financial analysts, individual small investors, or employees.

The days of senior management hiding in the executive suite and talking through slick corporate spokespeople are over. Studies like the Edelman Trust Barometer have made it clear that customers have shifted their trust away from traditional sources like corporate spokespeople to peers—people who are just like them, who talk in plain English without the obfuscation that accompanies corporatespeak.[2] Executives who are accessible and ready to answer questions and inquiries honestly and plainly will win loyalty from customers, investors, and other core constituents.

This does not mean executives must abandon all other duties and become full-time communicators (although communication with key audiences is one of the key tasks of any chief executive officer). There are countless tools and channels leaders can employ to be accessible, ranging from press conferences to a blog. There are even companies that accept questions throughout the year and answer them once each quarter. The answers are so candid and open that the leadership is viewed by the company's publics as accessible and open.

Unless it is enforced by a regulation, such as the quiet period that is required in any merger or acquisition in the United States, companies should drop the phrase "no comment" from their lexicon. "No comment" has a clear meaning to audiences: "We have something to hide." If your company is transparent, you may have matters you have decided to keep confidential, but that's different from having something to hide. There is always something you can say besides, "no comment."

In a transparent company, employees are accessible too. Companies that encourage their employees to blog on behalf of the company (like Microsoft, Iams, Sun Microsystems, IBM, Google, Honeywell, and Thomas Nelson publishing, to name just a few) know that employees will blog about their areas of interest and expertise, creating knowledge touch points between the experts the company hired and customers with information needs related to those areas of expertise. In transparent companies, every employee is a customer service representative.

If You're Not There Yet . . .

- Investigate the various means by which your company responds to inquiries and the results those methods are producing.
- Measure the number of times the company's senior leadership is available to answer questions from key publics.
- Review your policy that governs employee interaction with the public. Once you make the policy more liberal, ensure that your internal communication processes support the effort by providing employees with the background, information, and context they need to articulate the company's messages from the perspective of their own jobs and the work they do.

Transparent Companies Are Managed by Courageous Leaders

Most opaque companies are likely managed by timid leaders as they are unwilling to take risks. They figure that if the company's inner workings are not exposed to the light of day, they won't have to address any uncomfortable questions.

"Leadership, whatever else it takes, takes courage," says Michael Hyatt, president and CEO of Thomas Nelson publishing. "You've got to be willing, as a leader, to set the pace, to be the example, to model what you're asking others to do, and to be courageous in the face of people who might be fearful or are only looking at the downside. You have to focus also on what's the upside, and with very, very modest investments, the returns [on transparency] are huge."

Leadership sets the tone for an organization's culture. "When you have a CEO who blogs, it definitely sets the tone," says Jonathan Schwartz. "When you have a general counsel who blogs, it changes everybody's assumptions of what they ought to be doing on a daily basis. You're much more likely to get in front a problem, to make the problem known to people, and be much more aggressive and rapid in trying to solve the problem."

Culture change doesn't come easily. Often it takes pain to drive change; when a company is performing well, there is little motivation to do things differently. It could be a shock to the system that leads your organization to seek an alternative path. That was the case at Sun, which, according to Schwartz, had its mandate for change

> handed to us on a platter. We were in a very bad competitive position. So we were all of us interested in driving very aggressive change, in part because it was obviously needed. We had customer issues, we had technology issues, and hiding behind any of those wasn't going to help anything.

> The opportunity presented itself to speak directly to the marketplace and stop having our competition speak on our behalf or have a segment of the journalist community that only had old tapes to rehash . . . interpret [for us] what our strategy was.

Schwartz says the company's commitment to transparency altered the way it looks at getting its message out. "What is the purpose of PR?" Schwartz asks. "I've been relatively public in my view of some news distribution companies. I wonder what role they play in a transparent world. Sun is more interested in identifying conversations we can be a part of than saying, 'Here's a message. How can we push it out into the marketplace?'"

The biggest risk a company can take in these days of expectations of transparency and cutthroat competition is to take no risk at all. There are plenty of people out there who will tell you that there is risk to letting your employees interact directly with the public in a forum like the World Wide Web, to the CEO writing a blog, to giving customers insight into the design and development process, to pulling back the curtain to show what goes on behind the scenes. And they are right: there is risk. But in business, leaders engage in risk-benefit analyses as a matter of course. Courageous leaders reach for the benefit and minimize the risk, but do not give in to a lawyer who resists openness simply because some legal risk is involved.

It would be helpful to tell you how to get your leadership to be more courageous if you're not already there. But don't worry. In these uncertain times, leaders who don't take risks will probably not be in leadership positions for long. Their replacements may be more willing to face down resistance and undertake a transparency initiative employing the tools and processes that reflect tactical transparency.

Part Two

TACTICS

4

FROM PROSPECTS TO PEOPLE

Why Opaque Selling Doesn't Deliver Long-Term Return on Investment

> Transparency is just another way to be willing to
> engage with the marketplace. I don't just sell
> to my customers, I love my customers. I embrace
> my customers and ask them to embrace me. I ask
> them for their insights and input. As a result,
> the products we build become assets of those
> communities. Somebody who feels part of a
> community is going to be a much more aggressive
> evangelist for our products than someone who just
> paid $29.95 for it at a big-box retailer.
>
> —*Jonathan Schwartz,*
> *president and CEO, Sun Microsystems*

Raise your hand if you like getting spammed.

No takers?

How about junk mail? Flyers stuck to your windshield? Or best yet, calls during dinnertime where people pry into the financial specifics of your mortgage rate?

We've all heard the statistic that the average consumer is exposed to upward of five thousand advertising messages a day. Many of these impressions are unconscious (glancing at a billboard), and most are invasive. But the fact remains (and here's a simple definition) that as *consumers*, we *buy* things. And the majority of our purchases come after researching a product or service online, at a store, or as a result of the recommendation (or not) of friends or colleagues.

In other words, one way or another, we are always getting pitched—being told why buying something will bring us value. And although many of us won't admit it, we like being pitched. It means that someone thinks we're worth speaking to, even if it's largely because we apparently have disposable income burning a hole in our pocket.

And let's also admit an obvious but understated truth in business: everybody pitches. You may not have the formal title of salesperson, but we're always looking to influence someone to get what we need to get our work done. For example, which of these phrases have you heard or uttered in the workplace within the past three months?

- Can I get those sales figures by the end of the day?
- Are you getting coffee? I'd love a mocha-skim latte.
- Looking forward to your help on this project.

The words seem innocuous enough, but they do imply a desired response or action from the speaker. The phrases are a form of a sales pitch but veiled in the context of typical office-speak instead of the rhetoric of commerce.

If pitching is so commonplace, why do we dread phone calls from salespeople? Why do we cringe at a party when an aggressive sales rep spots us across the room and stalks us to the buffet? What changes the context of a commonplace request into an obnoxious sales tactic?

At the simplest level, we don't like being interrupted. And few of us likely schedule thirty minutes a day for uninvited sales pitches in our calendar. Context is king when it comes to hearing a sales presentation. If we're prepared to be pitched or have asked to be told about a product or service, we'll potentially be more open to buying than if we feel we've been blindsided.

The concept of permission marketing has taken root, popularized by marketing author and speaker Seth Godin. The notion arises from the barrage of interruptions we face in an era when time is at a premium. Permission marketing turns the traditional model on its head, getting an implicit "okay" from a prospective customer to talk about your products or services.

Most of us likely use terms stronger than "not enjoy" when it comes to the surplus of advertisements deluging our senses. And it's not just because of their volume. "This type of behavior is basically saying I don't care about you," Michael Port said in an interview. Port, the author of *Book Yourself Solid* and *The Contrarian Effect: Why It Pays to Take Typical Sales Advice and Do the Opposite*, continues:[1]

> The behavior says I don't really know anything about you, I just want to push my stuff onto you regardless of whether you need it or not and I'll send it to everybody I possibly can in hopes that I get a couple of people to respond because then maybe I'll make my quota. Salespeople like this figure if they spend $10,000 on a marketing campaign and they make $10,100 they've made a profit and don't care if they've irritated 6,000 people to do so. But the more evolved professional is going to take a very different tactic.

If you've ever worked in sales, you know how easy it is to lose focus on building relationships with customers and think only about immediate income. Whether you have to make your numbers or are relying on a commission to pay the majority of your salary, how to sell effectively becomes a pragmatic need versus just a philosophy or preference.

There's a horrifying scene in David Mamet's play *Glengarry Glen Ross* in which the character of Blake (played to the hilt by Alec Baldwin in the film) delivers an eviscerating speech to his lackluster sales staff. Anyone who's ever cold-called a prospective client hears these words every time they "dial for dollars" and play the numbers game in an effort to convert strangers into customers:

> You've got just one week to regain your jobs, starting tonight. Have I got your attention now? Good. 'Cause we're adding a little something to this month's sales contest. As you all know, first prize is a Cadillac Eldorado. Anyone want to see second prize? Second prize's a set of steak knives. Third prize is you're fired. . . . Only one thing counts in this life! Get them to sign on the line which is dotted! A-B-C. A-always, B-be, C-closing. Always be closing! Always be closing!![2]

The movie provides a chilling sense of the pressure experienced by salespeople living in the trenches of day-to-day pitching, relying on quick closes to keep their jobs and maintain some shred of dignity. The experiences of workers in cubicles are no different from those working in car dealerships. These frontline salespeople are often the lifeblood of a business, providing the revenue to keep a company afloat. How ironic then that they are often provided minimal resources to adequately develop positive relationships with customers and are pressured to focus on closing a sale versus providing value (and these do not automatically go hand in hand).

It is within this framework that one can see how opaque, or just less-than-transparent, sales processes have become the norm. The customer becomes dehumanized when a salesperson prioritizes an immediate purchase over a genuine relationship. Worse still is the assumption that following a uniform set of persuasive or even bullying techniques will transform a simple salesperson into the archetypal closer whose overwhelming confidence can convert the most stubborn prospect to sign on the dotted line.

It's not surprising that sales conventions often feature (literal) battle cries and multiple references to Sun Tzu's *The Art of War*. Rallying with colleagues for inspiration toward a desired outcome makes sense. What's unfortunate is that authentic relationships with customers take a back seat to the bottom line.

From Prospects to People

There is no denying that there is a sales cycle for any business, meaning the time it takes to introduce someone to your business up to the moment when this person buys. And you should organize your sales procedure to target the buyers who are most likely to buy what you sell. But due diligence regarding process should never usurp the currency of relationship when it comes to sales. When the sales process loses its transparency and dehumanizes a customer, it trades short-term gain for an overall loss of integrity. "David Ogilvy used to say, 'The consumer isn't a moron; she is your wife,'" points out Sean Bohan, an advertising and marketing executive at a New York–based international marketing agency:

> *When you take them for granted, tell them what they*
> *want to hear, and get aggressive, you may win the*
> *battle but you will definitely lose the war. The hard*
> *sell, the bum's rush, the used car salesman process*
> *is a waste of energy. It is not oriented to creating a*
> *relationship—it wants a sale at all costs. It makes the*
> *customer feel pressured, like they didn't get a fair deal.*

People often equate the sales process to dating. It's an apt analogy if you consider it can take the same raw courage to cold-call a complete stranger as it does to walk up to someone at a bar and ask to buy him or her a drink. But how often do cheesy pickup lines work versus a comment or joke that inspires genuine and authentic communication?

Here's the thing when approaching a sales situation: everybody knows what's going on. Potential clients know your end goal is to sell to them, and you know you want to sell to them. So why not reject the fabricated techniques in exchange for the chance to begin a relationship based on hearing your client's goals? Odds are you wouldn't be having the meeting if there weren't at least the chance you could work together, so stop trying to force a situation and focus on listening to how you best can fulfill the needs of your potential customer.

In this regard, transparency can remove the pall of urgency that often pervades a sales presentation. It's not unlike a dating situation when someone is trying too hard to impress; it's a turnoff. And in the same way, being passionate about your product in its ability to solve a client's problem or transform their business is attractive. In this regard, your influence provides clarity versus coercion.

The Tactics of Transparency

Transforming your mind-set to embrace the idea of relationship-oriented marketing can be a disconcerting paradigm shift if you're accustomed to traditional sales techniques. Swapping pre-determined tactics for authentic communication is scary. Like dating, the fear of rejection is huge in sales, especially if you feel that you've really worked to genuinely offer value versus simply closing a deal.

But being transparent doesn't imply a lack of preparation. Rather, it dictates the framework that motivates your actions and communications. For a variety of reasons, you cannot guarantee that a person will buy what you have to sell. But you can repeatedly demonstrate your desire to serve that person's needs as it relates to your business relationship. Here's how:

• • •

Get specific. Telling a potential client you know nothing about his business (unless you're just meeting him) displays a lack of professionalism versus transparency. It takes all of ten minutes to surf someone's site and get a basic understanding of what he does. Invest the time to read his "about us" page and latest blog posts. Visit Hoovers.com to learn more about the organization. Conduct a Lexis-Nexis search to see what the media have been saying about the company. Conduct a Technorati.com search to see what bloggers have been saying. More than ever before, Web sites reflect the culture of a company as much as its offerings. Investigate the things he deems important about himself to demonstrate in a meeting that you connect with his content in some way.

Make small talk big. There's a difference between exchanging banal niceties and highlighting authentic moments that connect you to another human being. Maybe she has a picture of her child prominently displayed and you can chat about parenting or bond about a sports team. The point is not to flatter and certainly not to pry. But people give a multitude of hints about who they are with their clothes, books, or even conversation with coworkers. Commenting on these things where appropriate demonstrates you have an attention to detail for things that matter to them.

Make your pitch interactive. After starting a meeting, there's always a moment when the potential client signals you to begin your presentation. So you give your succinct pitch tailored to the person who's listening. Make sure you're pausing to let him interject questions or comments. Demonstrate your awareness that although you're providing a service to help him solve a problem, you're interested in a partnership, not a dictatorship.

Give a call to action. Although this sounds like a technique, it's really more of a way to galvanize next steps or determine if a customer simply isn't interested in moving forward. Being specific and asking for what you want (in terms of clarity) is actually more transparent than hearing a client say she's not interested and replying, "Well, maybe I'll send you a brochure in case you change your mind." You should also be prepared to offer a next step that will provide value while advancing your relationship. Perhaps there's a free version of your software she can try or an event you can invite her to. Have these types of things ready so you have a time frame for a second point of contact.

Write down a connection point. Odds are there was a moment in the meeting where you connected on a deeper level with a potential client (with your big small talk, for instance) or you had an insight into a person you can follow up on that shows you were paying attention during the meeting. For example, perhaps the person you're meeting with mentions he loves taking videos of his kids but gets frustrated at the process of uploading them online. When you send an e-mail thanking him for the meeting, include a link to the Flip Video site (http://www.theflip.com/) and tell him it uploads directly online via a USB port. This isn't about bribing. It's about demonstrating that you listened to things he said and spent the time to try and help him out with something that's not directly related to a potential sale.

Practice good timing. Robert Scoble, the popular tech blogger, had a post called PR Done Badly (http://scobleizer.com/2006/05/14/pr-done-badly/) in response to the receipt of a number of pitches from PR folks during a week when his mother was ill, about which he had been blogging. When visitors commented that PR folks may not have known about his mother, Robert responded, "If a call doesn't start with, 'How you doing, I was reading your blog and my heart goes out to you,' I can tell that the PR person doesn't care about me. So why should I care about him and his pitch?" It's far too easy to read a current press release or someone's blog to know when a follow-up call would be inappropriate. Due diligence is an ongoing process, and one ill-timed communication can sour a relationship you've been working months to create.

Follow up. If someone tells you to call in a few weeks, do so. But be prepared with new ideas relating to your past meeting or do fresh research to keep up with what's going on at this person's company. You can connect in just a few minutes while also assessing what she really needs to continue your working relationship.

Partnering versus closing. Relationship building has touch points, and in a transparent sales cycle, you do have the right to know if and when you'll be able to count on a sale. If you've worked to achieve an authentic rapport with a client, you should be able to know the point where you've earned enough transparency equity to ask to send a proposal or contract as the logical culmination of your ongoing conversations. When seen in the framework of a partnership, however, sending a contract should be an exciting point of the process for both parties, with both eager to see the specific plans you've laid out. When the plan and the partnership are at the forefront of the proposal and contract, then the onus of the money takes a back seat to the return on investment the initiative will bring.

• • •

Here's how Michael Port describes his logic about closing:

Certainly that idea that you need to bring a conversation about a potential sale of a product or service to a close makes a lot of sense, but once somebody has told me why they want to achieve something and I believe that I can help them do that, I will often ask them if they want somebody to help them achieve their goal. If they say yes, then I say, "Would you like that person to be me?" I don't ever believe in making sales offers, what some people would call closing statements, unless you have the proportionate amount of trust earned to make that offer.

The literal steps of a sales cycle may be the same in an opaque or a transparent process. But as Michael points out, being transparent changes the dynamic of a working relationship: the salesperson loses the badgering reputation and aligns so deeply with a client's needs that he or she becomes an invaluable asset in achieving a client's larger goal. If this sounds heroic in stature, good. That's the mind-set you should have when serving someone else's needs.

This is a vital point in regard to transparency: the importance of serving. Nobody wants to admit they're in a position of vulnerability if they jump to attention when a client calls. But serving in this case isn't synonymous with adopting an imposed or obsequious attitude to get someone's business. That would be a tactic a client would see through, and nothing is a bigger turn-off (in dating and in business) than brown-nosing.

Think about this: people know when you're being real with them. It's okay to say, "I'd like to do business with you," when it's appropriate. But when your underlying motivation is always about pushing them to make a decision they're not ready for, they'll know it. In an ironic way, being transparent provides salespeople with the best tactic they could ever use: honesty. And in this regard, if you've worked to serve someone effectively, being forthright when you've earned the equity to do so will be more motivating to a client than any phrase or trick you could pull.

Being real is powerful. It is always fresh and unique in the work environment as in life.

Along the lines of the attitude to take when working with clients, Jason McClain, host of the podcast Evolutionary Sales and founder of the Institute for the Development of Evolutionary Awareness, defines transparency in business as

> being clear and direct about your desire to influence a client but that your grounding is from service and contribution to their outcomes. I have actually asked prospective clients, "How heavily do you want me to influence you here?" If I am coming from serving what we have determined and clarified they want, then I believe it is my duty to influence them beyond their limitations. And I tell them all of that.

Notice that Jason forms a partnership with clients, a relationship built around working towards mutually agreed-on goals. And he's bold in telling clients he'll influence them beyond their limitations and obviously is not inferring they'll pay him a larger fee than they originally intended. He's demonstrating his willingness to partner and build up a trust that would allow clients to let him influence them beyond a known comfort zone. It's this boldness and candor, coupled with his sense of duty, that shows transparent sales in action—and it's refreshing.

The Buck Stopped Already

Christopher Carfi, cofounder of Cerado, wrote the following Social Customer Manifesto on October 26, 2004:

> I want to have a say.
>
> I don't want to do business with idiots.
>
> I want to know when something is wrong, and what you're going to do to fix it.
>
> I want to help shape things that I'll find useful.
>
> I want to connect with others who are working on similar problems.
>
> I don't want to be called by another salesperson. Ever. (Unless they have something useful. Then I want it yesterday.)
>
> I want to buy things on my schedule, not yours. I don't care if it's the end of your quarter.
>
> I want to know your selling process.
>
> I want to tell you when you're screwing up. Conversely, I'm happy to tell you the things that you are doing well. I may even tell you what your competitors are doing.
>
> I want to do business with companies that act in a transparent and ethical manner.
>
> I want to know what's next. We're in partnership . . . where should we go?

Does Carfi sound as if he would respond to traditional sales tactics? His words reflect a core concern that consumers (and people in general) share: *you're not listening to me*. Notice that he desires a relationship with people he does business with versus simply being talked at. He wants a dialogue.

Carfi's manifesto is echoed in the Social Media Manifesto from Brian Solis, principal of FutureWorks:

> There has been a fundamental shift in our culture and it has created a new landscape of influencers and an entirely new ecosystem for supporting the socialization of information—thus facilitating new conversations that can start locally, but have a global impact. Monologue has given way to dialogue. Social media is not a game played from the sidelines. Those who participate will succeed—everyone else will either have to catch up or miss the game altogether.[3]

Solis's words are more than a challenge; they're a promise. Social media have given people the tools to retaliate when they feel they're not being listened to by large organizations. To demonstrate this, try typing the following phrase into Google: "US Airways Sucks." (There are sixty-seven thousand entries as of this writing.) Or enter the same phrase into YouTube, and you'll find multiple videos created by disgruntled customers, like the one uploaded to the video-sharing site by Joshua Lemon, who created the video while waiting for a US Airways flight. He shows numerous passengers talking about their ten-hour delays and ends the video by videotaping people on a flight (finally) and asking, "What's the US Airways motto?" In unison, everyone onboard choruses, "Fifteen more minutes!"

The point here is not to pick on US Airways (it offered Lemon a $250 voucher for his troubles) but to vividly demonstrate how customers can and are reacting to poor customer service or what they see as a lack of communication. While it may be argued that there have always been outspoken customers whose negative feedback hasn't drastically affected the bottom line of a large organization, it's vital for modern companies to accept the following facts:

- The majority of mobile phones let users shoot photos and videos.

- Services such as Qik and Pocketcaster allow mobile phone users to stream live video directly to a Web site or blog.

- Digital footprints, including photos and videos as well as text, live online for years, even decades.

- People can e-mail, publish, or link to someone else's video, picture, or blog in seconds, improving the likelihood that others will find that content, since Google and other search engines rank sites based on the number of inbound links. Thus, it's just as likely that someone searching for your brand will find content created by others about the brand as they are to find your official content.

- If a person feels he or she is not being listened to by a company, social media allow this person to quickly find someone who will.

Ignore or Explore: JetBlue Airways Case Study

Now witness how a large organization can use social media to open up the sales and communication process with customers by watching founder and former JetBlue Airways CEO David Neeleman's video at http://youtube.com/watch?v=-r_PIg7EAUw. Note that the video has had 309,235 views. And if you scroll through the 386 comments, you'll see that most of them are largely positive and express appreciation at Neeleman's/JetBlue Airways' attempts to remedy a difficult situation.

"Our corporate communications team recognized the YouTube video was a good idea right away," according to Matthew Knell, general manager of JetBlue Airways. Knell worked with Morgan Johnston and his communications team to shoot the video as soon as possible after the unprecedented flight delays in February 2007 took place:

> *Matthew*: A lot of people thought it was revolutionary. We felt it just had to be done. We used it as a first yardstick to see

what people would think who weren't directly involved in media. Its purpose was to communicate to a large group of customers in a viral way.

Morgan: We wanted to make sure that customer service contact information was always out there. We wanted to approach people directly and say we understand you were inconvenienced. We knew the video was going to generate a lot of comments on the YouTube site. But the decision was made—we knew that people were going to be angry. If we tried to censor that, we'd be violating a main tenet of our company, which is to respond directly to our customers.

Matthew: Along with the video we also sent out 8 million apology e-mails. We got a lot of responses back. Eighty-five percent were positive.

So the good news for brands is that they can use social media to connect to their customers and provide them a forum to voice their grievances where they know they'll be heard. Neeleman and JetBlue Airways also used their Web site to respond directly to their crisis. Here's an excerpt from February 22, 2007:

Dear JetBlue Customers,

We are sorry and deeply embarrassed. But most of all, we are deeply sorry. Last week was the worst operational week in JetBlue's seven year history. Following the severe winter ice storm in the Northeast, we subjected our customers to unacceptable delays, flight cancellations, lost baggage, and other major inconveniences.

When is the last time you heard a CEO say he or she was sorry and embarrassed? This kind of sincere regret alone would resonate with most inconvenienced customers who wanted to know they'd been heard and would be compensated for their money and time. This post, along with the YouTube video, demonstrated that Airways' top management wanted to communicate as quickly as possible and work to remedy the ill will fostered by customer delays.

Instead of ignoring the problem (which is fairly difficult when you're an airline and all your flights are down), they apologized quickly. It may feel remarkable in business today to see this happen, but it makes perfect sense when viewed from the standpoint of a relationship.

The Real Return on Investment for Transparency

Transparency in sales doesn't terminate with a purchase. Your relationship shouldn't end when you receive a check. Making a sale is actually the beginning of what should be a long-term relationship with a person or company you've aligned with to achieve their goals. And when something negative happens to your customer, whether or not it's in your full control, by responding immediately and providing tools for communication along with appropriate reparations, you make your transparency evident.

If you've partnered with someone to help fulfill the vision for her business, your return on investment will be measured in multiple sales versus a one-off purchase made by forcing someone's hand. And if you're not going to be transparent in your selling, what's your other option? The days of opaque selling are rapidly fading, and the Internet means you won't be able to count on the numbers game to make a sale based on algorithms and click-throughs. Pretty soon you'll find the Google searches with your name or business will reveal hits you won't want other customers to see.

Conclusion: Transparency Takeaways

To avoid impersonal sales tactics, follow these guidelines when implementing transparent tactics for your organization:

- We all pitch at one time or another.
- Nobody likes to be talked at. Focus on dialogue, not monologue.

- Explore the specific ways you can build a relationship versus make a sale.
- Align with clients to partner with their goals versus focusing on the close.
- Social media allow customers to complain and provide feedback. Make sure you let them know you're listening.
- Use blogs, podcasts, video, and interactive media (streaming audio and video) to provide a platform for direct, two-way communications between your customers and your business.

5

FOLLOW THE MONEY

Financial Communications

There are lots of folks who can monetize inefficiency. Transparency is much tougher to monetize unless you're on the side of creating value or delivering value. Being the intermediary for value is diminishing in social utility as well as financial value.

—*Jonathan Schwartz,*
president and CEO, Sun Microsystems

Both customer and investor confidence in business plunged during a compressed period of time during which bad behavior by those with fiduciary responsibility seemed to make headlines almost daily. Enron, WorldCom, Tyco, Halliburton, Adelphia, Peregrine Systems, and even Martha Stewart led publics to believe they could not trust the management teams who were, after all, employed to manage the investments made by the company's owners. Those owners included everyone from the mega-rich to frontline employees whose 401(k) plans (in the United States) often are heavily weighted with company stock.

The gap left by that eroded confidence was filled by regulations that forced companies to be more accountable and minimize the risk to investors in the future. The most onerous of these regulations, known as Sarbanes-Oxley after the two senators who introduced the legislation that created it, is also known, tellingly, as the Public Company Accounting Reform

and Investor Protection Act of 2002. Known colloquially as
SOX, Sarbanes-Oxley comprises eleven titles that dictate the
responsibilities of a company's board of directors and spell out
criminal penalties for dereliction of those responsibilities. In
effect, SOX makes lack of transparency a crime punishable by
fine and imprisonment. Fulfilling SOX's reporting requirements
is a costly investment of time and resources that could be allo-
cated to other business-critical activities. These efforts are now
mandatory, with criminal penalties for failure to comply, because
some companies opted for opacity over transparency as a means
of masking bad behavior.

While there is disagreement over SOX's effectiveness,
increased transparency into business seems to have raised the
confidence that was so shaken by the rash of malfeasance that
led to SOX's creation. In its most recent "Trust Barometer" study,
the public relations agency Edelman recorded tremendously
heightened levels of trust in business in general.[1]

We won't concern ourselves here with the details of SOX or
any other regulations that legally mandate company openness.
In fact, companies should view the legal requirements for transparency as a baseline from which to start. Transparency with
investors and the financial community is critical to a company's
survival, and ultimately to its success.

We have, and will continue to, explore the new tools of
social media as a central platform for achieving transparency.
Using social media, however, is not a requirement. A culture
of empathy for the investor is the central criterion for building investor trust, according to Dominic Jones, whose *IR Web
Report* is an acknowledged resource for information on how
well, or badly, various companies communicate with financial
audiences.

Expeditors International, for example, does not believe in
conference calls and limits its communications to its filings with
the Securities and Exchange Commission. "But they are extremely
well regarded by analysts," Jones says, "because of their quarterly

Q&A." During the quarter, investors submit questions to the company. At the end of the quarter, the company replies to them all in plain English, presented in a manner particularly empathetic to what investors are seeking from a company. "The technology," Jones says, "is not as important as the intent of management to understand investors' needs, fears, and hopes."

Jones hastens to add that many companies that do empathize with investors also want to use these newer channels to provide them with greater access to management. For a few organizations, honest, candid, sincere answers to questions through traditional channels may be adequate. Most organizations, though, can gain a considerable advantage by broadening its access.

DellShares

It was a desire to expand access to the company that led computer maker Dell to launch the first (and still the only) investor relations blog from a large company. "Financial information is static," explains Lynn Tyson, Dell's vice president of investor relations. "Companies talking about what's happening in their environment, in their sector, can be far more fluid. These conversations give people perspectives on the company that simply cannot be represented in a balance sheet or cash flow statement." Tyson's view of transparency is consistent with that offered throughout these pages. "Ubiquity of information is not the same as making all information available," she explains. "It's just that the information you *do* make available is available in as many places as it can be."

The need for that ubiquity was one of two overarching principles Tyson articulated in a proposal she called "Twenty-First Century Investor Relations" when she submitted it in response to a challenge from CEO Michael Dell to be more creative and take more risks with the company's communication. The second principle rests on the idea of the democratization of information: "A lot of people don't realize that investor relations departments are open to everyone. They are not the private domain of Wall Street."

Consequently Dell's investor relations department interacts with individual shareholders and even with people who are not yet shareholders as readily as they will someone who owns 5 percent of the company. They'll even take time to help a student with a research project.

Both principles are evident in "DellShares," a rare investor relations blog that was formally launched at the company's annual shareholder meeting in December 2007. "The main thrust of 'DellShares' is to be educational, to empower people, to help them better understand the company—and not just the company, but how the company operates and what their rights are as shareholders," Tyson asserts.

That focus is important, particularly for retail investors who don't necessarily have the same depth of knowledge as an investment analyst or fund manager who is able to spend time researching and understanding the company and the sector in which it operates. "Investing is essentially a bet on the future of the company. If investors' expectations are different from those of management, you have a problem," Jones explains. "Eventually you're going to disappoint investors and create a trust problem when they believe they've been misled or that management has not been transparent in its communications."

Before the Internet, disgruntled investors couldn't broadcast their disenchantment very far. There may be fifty thousand investor clubs in the United States alone, but they tend to be made up of individuals who live close to one another. Before the Net provided a tool for collaboration regardless of location, information didn't tend to spread from one group to another. Today trusted individuals who believe they have been burned by a company in which they invested can tell others in forums where their influence can have a considerable impact.

The increasing sophistication of social networks is making it easy to trust participants in these online communities. It was not always so, according to Gabriel Dalporto, chief marketing officer for Zecco Holdings, a company that has linked online trading to a vibrant network of members. In the days of investment forums on America Online and Usenet newsgroups, it was impossible to gauge the motivation that led an anonymous participant to make a claim about a company. "Buy!" someone might post to a newsgroup. "It's a hot stock and I'm snatching it up." In reality, though, that vote of support for a company could mask an individual who owns a lot of the stock and wants to see demand increase so he can unload his shares before the company collapses.

Zecco Holdings has introduced one approach to building trust within its communities: members can elect to have their holdings and their trades associated with their profiles. Thus, if someone says, "Buy, it's a great investment," it would be easy to see whether that individual has been buying the stock himself, holding it, or selling it. (The dollar value of investments is not disclosed, Dalporto notes, just the percentages of a total portfolio.)

Other solutions are increasingly being introduced that raise the confidence of those who engage in such communities. As a result, in a community of investors like those Zecco hosts, the opinion of a participant who has built credibility over time can generate considerable buzz. The resulting word of mouth could bolster a company's fortunes—or result in a reduction of its value.

It is recognition of the growing importance of the individual voice that underlies Dell's focus on retail investors. Fortunately, Dell as a company was already thoroughly sold on the value of blogs as a channel for building ties with a public based on the shining success of its customer-focused blog, "Direct2Dell." Tyson once counted Dell's corporate communications department, which developed "Direct2Dell," as her responsibility, allowing her to witness the process of implementing and developing the blog. "We found the dialogue and conversations on 'Direct2Dell' were phenomenal. We got real-time feedback and were able to respond to customers." It was clear, she says, that the same tenets could be applied to an investor relations blog.

Dell was undeterred by the fact virtually all other companies were shying away from the use of social media as a channel for engaging with shareholders. Tyson insists:

> The regulations don't apply to a blog any differently than they do to any other investor communications. It doesn't require a change in behavior or tone. We have learned the value of blogging. Our lawyers have learned it, our general managers have learned it. I can't overemphasize how powerful this last year [since the launch of "Direct2Dell"] has been. No [Dell] employee around the world doesn't know that it exists. People have learned that there is little downside to have conversations. They might have been concerned about it before, but they realize that none of their fears came to fruition.

Inevitable Change

Tyson does confess that her colleagues in the investor relations world (she is a member of the board of the National Investor Relations Institute) are watching ""DellShares"" carefully, since their organizations don't have the same degree of confidence in blogging and other social media. The investor relations community is extremely conservative by nature. Dominic Jones doesn't believe we will see too much adoption of social media in that community for some time by virtue of the glacial pace with which investor relations embraces new tools.

There are forces, however, paving the way for the adoption of social media as a compliant channel for satisfying Regulation Fair Disclosure, better known as Reg FD. This is the U.S. Securities and Exchange Commission's set of rules designed to ensure that public companies disclose material information concurrently to all investors so that no single segment of the investment community has an unfair trading advantage.

Jonathan Schwartz became the first Fortune 500 CEO blogger when he was promoted to the job; he was already blogging as chief technology officer of Sun Microsystems. On October 2, 2006, Schwartz posted an item that made a case for including blogs as a channel for complying with Reg FD:

> Reg FD doesn't recognize the internet, or a blog, as the exclusive vehicle through which the public can be fairly informed. In order to be deemed compliant, if we have material news to disclose, we have to hold an anachronistic telephonic conference call, or issue an equivalently anachronistic press release, so that the (not so anachronistic) *Wall Street Journal* can disseminate the news. I would argue that none of those routes are as accessible to the general public as this blog, or Sun's web site. Our blogs don't require a subscription, or even registration, and are available to anyone, across the globe, with an internet connection. Simultaneously.

Schwartz added the text of a letter he had sent formally to SEC chairman Christopher Cox making the case for allowing blogs and Web sites to serve as channels for disclosure. What ensued was a remarkable correspondence in full public view. On November 3, Schwartz wrote another post that concluded,

> As I've said before, transparency and efficiency are obligations as much as opportunities—a better informed investor can make better decisions, just like a better informed customer or developer.

The first comment left to that post was from SEC chairman Cox himself:

> I mailed the response to your letter yesterday, but since you're talking about transparency and efficiency in communications, I thought you might appreciate my taking advantage of the Internet's speed and potential for broad dissemination by posting here as well.

In the letter, Cox agreed with Schwartz about the power of the Internet and explained:

> Assuming that the Commission were to embrace your suggestion that the "widespread dissemination" requirement of Regulation FD can be satisfied through web disclosure, among the questions that would need to be addressed is whether there exist effective means to guarantee that a corporation uses its website in ways that assure broad non-exclusionary access, and the extent to which a determination that particular methods are effective in that regard depends on the particular facts.

Schwartz detailed his response to Cox's questions in another letter that he posted to his blog on March 8, 2007. The dialogue between Schwartz and Cox continues to this day.

"Chairman Cox made a point not to put a letter on the front of the SEC.gov Web site," Schwartz said later, "but instead to go inject into the corporate dialogue his point of view on how companies should be engaging with shareholders. There was change written all over everything he was doing. And that was because he, as a leader, wanted to go drive change."

Dominic Jones (who also wrote a comment on Schwartz's initial post) endorses the idea but does not expect to see it adopted soon: "There's a lot of resistance to this. It's quite a revolutionary concept."

Current practice relies on the distribution of news releases to satisfy Reg FD, where the information might be conveyed by media through a newspaper or TV news report or read on a Web site, such as Yahoo's financial site. Using a blog provides an opportunity for interaction. As Jones puts it, "You can't connect with a person reading a news release, unless they're reading a social media release, and that's another thing that's far out in the distance from an investor relations perspective."

Ultimately, though, Jones is certain the blogs, RSS feeds, and other social media tools will be folded into Reg FD. "It makes sense," he says. "Why are we using third-party newswires to distribute information when companies have the tools to distribute the information themselves?" All it will take is the ironing out of details. Wire services, for example, put material releases through a rigorous vetting process. When financial information is distributed by a service like PR Newswire or Business Wire, investors are confident that the content is authoritative. Building the same kind of credibility into a blog post will be necessary before the SEC is comfortable designating blogs as a means of compliance.

The Voices of a Company's People

Jones is also a fan of Schwartz's blog in general, which provides investors with something Dell's blog, "DellShares," does not. "'DellShares' is written exclusively by the investor relations department," he says. As a result, it is the voice of Lynn Tyson that articulates the company's strategies. "There's nothing from Michael Dell. Senior management is not active on this blog."

Sun Microsystems does not have an investor relations blog. The enterprise computing company does, however, have thousands of employees who use the blogs.sun.com platform to blog about their jobs, from employees on the front line up to the executive suite. Although these blogs are not focused on the world of investors, investors can gain tremendous insight into the company from what Schwartz and his employees post.

That insight, in fact, makes a compelling case for CEO blogging as well as employee blogging. Jones explains: "Investors need to know what they're buying. Investors are essentially hiring these people to manage their money; the money in the business belongs to the shareholders, and they need to know who's managing it. The more insight they have, the better."

Jonathan Schwartz agrees: "Shareholders love transparency because they can know more about what they're investing in. That makes us more appealing in the sense that investors are going to want to put their money into assets they understand well."

Because of corporate scandals that resulted in Sarbanes-Oxley, along with other concerns, retail investors are insisting on greater access to the management teams running the companies on which they have placed their bets. Sell-side investment analysts, typically employed by brokerage firms, used to focus their attention on the preparation of reports based on their unique access to the management teams of the companies they covered. Today, the clients of these analysts—mutual funds and hedge funds primarily—want more than just research reports. The principal work of sell-side analysts today is setting up meetings between investors and management. Jones identifies it as "the biggest growth business on Wall Street."

Blogs and other social media can serve as a way to provide that kind of access to everyone, including small investors with only a few shares of stock. "The idea that CEOs shouldn't blog comes out of a sense that a corporation is an entity," Jones says, "but that's misguided because investors aren't buying into a legal entity; they're buying into a business that is run by people. And they need to have confidence that the people managing it are competent, that they buy into management's strategy." A lot of investment decisions are made based on soft factors, not just the numbers, according to Jones. "Whatever the company can do to level access to management is a good thing."

Video can also play a role, although Jones sees more use of video as an investor relations tool in Europe than he does in North America. The idea that an investor can look a CEO in the eye can build trust. In conjunction with its annual report, athletic shoemaker Nike included a video interview with CEO Mark Parker, answering questions while wearing his trademark sunglasses. For a company leader to appear so unconventional may be unusual, but it nevertheless provides insight into the personality of the person making decisions that will affect the future of the company. "We're going to see more of that," says Jones.

Some companies worry that their executives won't come off well on video or would not make good bloggers. Jones dismisses these concerns: "If you provide the information investors are looking for, they won't care what you look like or how well you write. As long as he has empathy for whom he's communicating to, as long as his focus is on the needs of the audience, it just won't matter."

In fact, some companies employ a mix of such tools in order to provide greater access to management to a broader investor population. IBM's investor relations department recently relaunched its lauded podcast series, "IBM and the Future of . . .," which showcases the company's thought leaders in unscripted conversations about the upcoming role that technology will play in various dimensions of everyday life. Recent topics addressed include shopping, medical imaging, and mobile phones.

"It's a good strategy, a very clever idea," investor relations consultant Jones says of the podcast, which offers insight into the depth of the company's expertise. Ultimately the podcast raises the confidence investors need to have that the company is on top of new technologies and new trends. "Past performance is one thing, but investors are placing their bets on the future of the company," notes Jones.

Podcasts are also used to distribute recordings of conference calls between company leadership and key investment representatives. Conference calls continue to serve as the primary tool for engaging with management. As transparent as Jonathan Schwartz's blog may be, Schwartz does not engage in conversation with those who leave comments. Analysts and big-time fund managers know that they can get that dialogue during the conference call that accompanies earnings releases.

The motivation for making conference calls available as podcasts is largely financial. It's cheaper to host an MP3 file on a company server than to pay a company to make it available as a streaming media file. And while subscriptions to conference call podcasts aren't exactly surging, they do represent a convenience, particularly for people who are trying to keep track of several calls that often are held in a tightly compressed time frame during earnings seasons. For investors, analysts, and fund managers to be able to subscribe to conference call recordings and have them automatically show up on their computers, ready for listening or transfer to a digital media player, makes it easier to get caught up.

New-media tools may make it easier but are not required to engage in this kind of transparency. The desire to be informed in as close to real time as possible about the substance of conference calls has led to a cottage industry that produces transcripts available within minutes of a call's conclusion.

Several companies are finding other creative ways to use more traditional channels in pursuit of transparency. In March 2008, General Electric issued its annual report. In parallel to the distribution of the report, GE conducted a live Webcast, accessible exclusively on the World Wide Web. In the weeks leading up to the Webcast, shareholders were encouraged to submit questions that would be addressed during the session.

Ultimately six thousand questions were submitted, and 1 million people watched GE's leaders tackle as many as they could. The questions were selected and presented by objective journalists—one from CNBC, the other from the *Financial Times*. Since there was no way six thousand questions could be answered during a time-constrained Webcast, unanswered questions were aggregated into common topic categories and answered in a written Q&A posted to the company's Web site.

One reason for GE's push to improve accessibility and become more transparent is its multinational character. Companies viewed as secretive and unaccountable will find it increasingly difficult to execute their strategies, from introducing their products into new international markets to gaining community support for the construction of new facilities. Companies whose operations are particularly controversial are among those making the greatest strides toward transparency.

GE does not pretend to be perfect. Companies are managed by people, and people make mistakes. It's how a company addresses those mistakes that sets them apart in the eyes of investors. The German conglomerate Siemens, one of GE's key competitors, faced a major corruption scandal starting in 2006, when six of the company's employees were arrested on charges of bribery and embezzlement. Shaken investor confidence that was not addressed by the company's response to its woes could well account for the earnings warning the company issued in early 2008.

Other companies working in sensitive areas are also becoming more transparent because they have little choice. Monsanto, for example, faces tremendous challenges from nongovernmental organizations and activist groups opposed to the introduction of genetically modified seed into their agricultural ecosystems. "They have no choice but to be as open and accountable as possible," Jones says. "Without that, they are not going to be trusted."

ExxonMobil is working with more traditional tools to increase transparency and accessibility. Anybody, shareholder or not, can submit a question to be addressed at the annual meeting. Exxon posts a record of all questions and answers from the annual shareholders meeting, a practice not duplicated by many other companies. In addition, anybody can e-mail a question to any member of the company's board of directors and get an answer. "That's a nontechnical but very real demonstration of accountability that you don't see at other companies," Jones notes. "They don't crow about it, they don't make a big deal about it, they're just walking the walk."

Conclusion: The Risks of Opacity

A few very successful companies can get away with limited transparency, but most organizations need to provide access to management, which in turn needs to be candid and forthright in its conversations with investors and other stakeholders. A misalignment of expectations is the key risk to remaining opaque. Investors whose expectations for the company's direction and performance differ from management's will ultimately turn against the organization, finding it impossible to believe anything the company says.

Furthermore, organizations seen as opaque and taciturn increasingly will be denied the license to operate that is held by core publics, including local communities, legislators and regulators, customers, and the media. Whether a company's news is good or bad, the company should be the one communicating it, openly and as part of a dialogue. Companies need to be prepared to admit mistakes, Dominic Jones insists. "We are so overlawyered; we get told by lawyers never to admit we've made a mistake because it will make things worse, we'll get sued. But everyone makes mistakes; everyone is human. It's how you deal with these situations that sets you apart, that builds credibility, that builds goodwill."

6

WHEN THINGS GO BAD

Transparency During a Crisis

If ever there was a time for organizations to adopt a culture of transparency—and if ever there was a time when corporate leadership is most inclined to shutter the windows and hunker down—it is during an organizational crisis. The tendency to circle the wagons in a crisis is based on the very nature of a crisis: an unexpected and unanticipated event that threatens the organization's reputation, or even its very existence. From a communications standpoint, the crash of an airplane is not a crisis for the airline. It is certainly an emergency and definitely a tragedy. But it does not meet the criteria for crisis because an airline can anticipate and prepare for a crash, just as a railroad can establish procedures for a derailment and an oil company can expect that an accident could lead to spill from a tanker.

Crises are the reputation killers that catch a company unawares. Since there had never been a case of somebody poisoning over-the-shelf medications, the makers of Tylenol faced a crisis when tainted pills caused seven deaths in the Chicago area in 1982. It was the company's openness and leadership's adherence to its credo that put customers (not shareholders) first that led to the decisions that restored public confidence and deflected damage to the company's reputation.

Since the headline-grabbing Tylenol product-tampering tale, we have entered the era of the twenty-four-hour news cycle. Crisis communication expert Gerald Baron, author of the crisis handbook, *Now Is Too Late*, noted in an interview that we live in a global instant news world today, and most companies do not yet fully appreciate its implications:

> How you need to deal with rumors, with information going out, with people talking with each other, with how quickly something that is deep within the organization can be spread to various constituent groups, to stakeholder groups, has very much changed, and the primary driver of that change is the Internet. We communicate with each other regardless of distance much more quickly than we did before because we have the means of communication at the speed of light.

Public relations veterans are befuddled by the accelerated spread of information. For decades, they managed crises by calculating deadlines: How much time do we have before we need to make a statement for the nightly news at 7:00 P.M.? What's the deadline for an article going into the morning edition of the *Tribune* or the *Times* or the *Ledger?*

"There are no deadlines," says Baron. "There are no news cycles." Everyone in the news business, he says, even print newspapers, is in the broadcast business by virtue of their Web sites. Speed is the basis on which any news organization competes: "Not being prepared to deal with the speed of distribution of information is what leaves a lot of organizations flat-footed."

While it may be counterintuitive to prepare for unforeseeable events, transparency is an organization's most effective tool when it comes to a crisis. The honest explanation of what happened, a description of the steps being taken to address the issue, and plans to keep it from ever happening again can assuage a public experiencing a range of emotions, from fear to anger, sparked by the situation.

Before we discuss the role transparency plays in a crisis and how to achieve the kind of transparency that will serve your organization when things go south, we need to step back and cover some fundamentals.

What Kinds of Crises Are There?

Crisis communication literature has tackled the categories of crisis a number of ways. Here are three major categories to help determine what type of situation your organization may be facing:

• • •

Meteor crisis. Completely unexpected, a meteor crisis falls from the sky. It is usually characterized by randomness and senselessness and is viewed as a terrible thing. The organization affected is a victim in a meteor crisis, but nevertheless confidence in the organization is at risk. Consider the 2007 shooting in an Omaha, Nebraska, shopping mall. This was not the mall's fault, but people may opt to shop elsewhere after the shooting. How quickly and effectively an organization responds will determine whether it is perceived as complicit or innocent.

Predator crisis. In *The Insider*, Russell Crowe portrayed former tobacco executive Jeffrey Wigand, who delivered confidential company documents to *60 Minutes*. Some might argue that Wigand did the right thing (others will disagree), but from the company perspective, he was a predator: he was out to cause the company harm. In a predator crisis, the company is hardly a victim; it must have dirty laundry in order for a predator to air it. Other kinds of predator crises include behind-the-scenes disputes that go public, new regulations that expose safety or other shortcomings, and litigation that reveals unsavory business practices (for instance, an insurance company that drags its feet approving an organ transplant until after the patient has died).

Breakdown crisis. A breakdown crisis occurs when the company fails to perform. Organizations usually bring breakdown crises on themselves by taking shortcuts, deviating from ethical business practice, or showing disdain for the concerns of its constituents. Product liability lawsuits, recalls, environmental disasters, manufacturing accidents, and financial scandals (Enron leaps to mind) all fit in the breakdown crisis category.

• • •

When handling crisis communications, you should focus on achieving six main objectives:

- Maintain a positive image of the organization.
- Present timely, accurate, candid, up-to-date information.
- Remain accessible.
- Monitor communication channels to catch misinformation early.
- Maintain constituent support.
- Survive the crisis.

Crisis Principles

The need for openness and candor, no matter how painful it might be to admit a mistake, becomes clear when you explore some of the truths about crises.

The Public Is Risk Averse

In early spring 2008, Southwest Airlines found itself embroiled in a crisis when the Federal Aviation Administration fined the company more than $10 million for continuing to fly forty-six airplanes after it was revealed that these aircraft were not subjected to required inspections to determine if there were any cracks in the skin. While Southwest has been handling the crisis well (the situation was ongoing at the time of this writing), some of the comments left to the company's blog reveal the real fears such a disclosure produces. One customer wrote:

> I typically fly 75,000 to 125,000 miles per year for business. My safety is paramount; I have a family that depends on me for income and very much more. I trust every airline I fly to maintain the safety of its aircraft. You are lying. Everyone knows it. You know what the rules are, and you violated them. You

unnecessarily put your customers' safety at risk. Go to hell. I will
NEVER fly you again.

This comment reflects the reactions many are likely to have
to a crisis: they do not want to be put unduly at risk and resent
that they now have to face the hazards produced by the crisis.
Personal safety does not need to be an issue to inspire these kinds
of emotional reactions. Consider the case of Enron, whose
financial duplicity cost thousands of employees their jobs and
their retirement savings. As the bad news kept on flowing out of
Enron, employees at other companies worried about their own
security and wondered what their leaders might be doing behind
their backs.

These situations lead naturally to the next crisis truth:
emotion, not logic, prevails.

Emotion, Not Logic, Prevails

After the *Exxon Valdez* ran aground in Alaska's Prince William
Sound on March 24, 1989, Exxon's chairman, Lawrence Rawls,
added gasoline to the fire by failing to understand that he could
not win a logical debate with a public that perceived the disaster
in emotional terms.

Rawls personally was not comfortable in the glare of publicity
and was more at ease with the low profile his company had
historically maintained. Thus, when the *Exxon Valdez* spilled its
11 million gallons of crude, a U.S. record to this day, Rawls insisted
he could do more good coordinating the company's response
from his New York offices, where he could also avoid TV news
cameras and reporters' questions. In fact, Rawls *could* probably
accomplish more from his office, where he had access to his
staff, emergency officials, government representatives, and a
variety of other resources. But the perception he created by not
going to the scene of the ecological disaster was that of a cavalier
executive who didn't care that his company's tanker had caused

the deaths of half a million birds, forty-five hundred sea otters, fourteen killer whales, and a variety of other sea life. It was that perception of dismissal that led thousands of customers to cut up their Exxon credit cards and mail them to the company's corporate headquarters.

The *Valdez* case study raises another critical truth in crises: symbols characterize a crisis.

Symbols Characterize a Crisis

Ask most people to think about the *Exxon Valdez* crisis and tell you the first image that pops into their minds. Their answer, almost universally, will be the same: oil-soaked dead birds.

Every crisis has its symbol that is etched permanently in the minds of the public. Following are just a few symbols associated with crises that have been front-page news in the United States:

- *Enron.* Innocent workers leaving the company's Houston headquarters carrying their personal possessions in cardboard boxes, jobless, their retirement savings plundered.

- *Dow Corning.* The maker of silicon breast implants that allegedly leaked harmful substances into the bodies of patients who had received the implants did little to address the symbol of the crisis that nearly drove the company out of business: hospitalized women writhing in agonizing pain.

- *Rodney King.* The Los Angeles Police Department suffered massive reputational damage because of the videotaped beating of a defenseless crime suspect. The indelible image from that video of four police officers wielding their nightsticks against a victim curled helpless on the ground still haunts the LAPD and has led to suspicion of any police officer who might abuse his or her authority.

These crises occurred before social networks began populating the Net, enabling the spread of images—even videos that the mainstream media has ignored—before a company even has an opportunity to consider its response.

George Allen, a U.S. senator from Virginia, was a presumptive presidential candidate until cameras caught him uttering what many perceived to be a racial slur. During a campaign stop for reelection as senator, Allen noticed a representative of his opponent in the crowd videotaping his talk. Speaking directly to S. R. Sidarth, an American of Indian descent, Allen said, "This fellow here, over here with the yellow shirt, Macaca, or whatever his name is, he's with my opponent. He's following us around everywhere. And it's just great."

The mainstream media made no issue of Allen's comment. After all, *macaca* is not a recognized slur, and in fact the meaning of the word has been debated ever since the August 2006 incident. (Allen himself insisted that he made up the nickname on the spot and never meant it to be racially derogatory.) However, outraged individuals uploaded the video to YouTube and other online venues and blogged mercilessly about it. The blog posts and videos remain accessible today, and they will forever. The uproar forced the media to begin covering the story, ultimately leading Allen to lose an election that was supposed to be a sure thing for him and ending his presidential aspirations.

The exacerbation of a situation all but ignored by the traditional purveyors of news into a full-blown crisis occurred in a heartbeat—a matter of a day or so. According to Baron, the "postmedia world," in which news and information comes from sources other than the traditional news media, has become a driving force in the public information business.

There Are No Secrets

If a company's warts and foibles are subject to exposure on the best of days thanks to the microscope under which they are scrutinized by anyone with an interest or an axe to grind, that scrutiny is magnified during a crisis. The need to respond quickly can lead unprepared executives to equivocate or issue standard jargon-laden corporate statements even as new facts, not to mention rumors, are pouring into the public record via blogs, news reports, posts to message boards, Twitter tweets (messages of 140 or fewer characters transmitted to anybody who cares to follow you on their computers or mobile phones), YouTube videos, and a cavalcade of other channels.

The postmedia world, though, should not alter the appropriate approach a company should have taken to a crisis even before we found ourselves in this brave new world. Says Baron, "It doesn't change the basic fundamentals of what we need to deal with, and that is our ability to provide accurate, credible information out to various publics as directly as possible as quickly as possible." As for new media, Baron says, "Because people are blogging [means] that's another area we need to be watching and it's another medium, in effect, we need to be participating in."

Participation in the blogosphere might have saved Kryptonite from the damage its reputation suffered in the wake of the revelation that its Evolution bicycle lock could be picked with a Bic pen. Contrary to popular mythology, the company was aware that bloggers were actively covering the fast-breaking story. The initial revelation, posted to the online Bike Forums bulletin board, was visited over 340,000 times during the week after it was originally posted. A brief video showing the ease with which a lock could be picked was downloaded forty thousand times. Yet the company responded traditionally, issuing a succession of press releases written in typical corporatese. The first of these included the following statement:

> In light of recent demonstrations on the Internet that explain how to criminally defeat tubular cylinder lock technology, which has performed successfully for more than three decades, Kryptonite intends to expedite the introduction of its upgraded

Evolution and KryptoLok lines. These products will have the disc-style cylinder that has the same technology as the company's famous New York Lock.

Specifically, Kryptonite will provide the owners of Evolution and KryptoLok series products the ability to upgrade their cross bars to the new disc-style cylinder, where possible. This new cylinder provides greatly enhanced security and performance.

Kryptonite is finalizing the details of this upgrade process and will publicly communicate these details as soon as possible.

The replacement program, expressed in press release language and leaving many questions raised by bloggers and others online unanswered, led the situation to continue spiraling out of control. In an interview with blogger Dave Taylor, Kryptonite's public relations manager, Donna Tocci, said:

I've spent the time to research what is going on online and have created relationships with some of the more influential bloggers. I've treated this like I would do with any traditional media representative. I'm confident that, should something else come up like it did in September '04, I would be able to converse with a few of these folks and, should they choose, they could write about what is going on with us.

There is no way for a company to answer all of the individual blog posts or forum posts during a crisis. There isn't enough time in a day. Having your own blog or even a Web site on which it is easy to change content is a way to get some information out, but just like the traditional media, everyone wants their own quote that is unique to their own blog or news coverage. (Just like you!) Know who the influential bloggers are in your space, and start a conversation. Create a relationship or two, or ten.

Let's wrap up our discussion of crisis communication with a few additional case studies, one from each of the categories of crisis management.

Meteor Crisis: BigHa and the Jasper Green Laser Pointer

Odds are you've never heard of BigHa, a Corvallis, Oregon–based outdoor recreation company that manufactures and sells a select few items, including a unique recumbent bicycle and a handheld green laser pointer and other astronomy-related items. The green laser pointer, known as the Jasper, emits a laser that is visible for miles, making it ideal for pointing out stars and constellations; its primary use is, in fact, stargazing. That didn't stop a Jasper owner in New Jersey from shining his laser pointer at planes landing at John F. Kennedy International Airport in New York, prompting the media to suddenly label the device a weapon and a potential terrorist instrument of destruction. Copycat incidences began occurring at other airports across the country.

Fortunately for BigHa, sales vice president Noah Acres was already authoring a blog that had attracted customers who were fans of the company's products as readers and commenters. "The blog started as a way to discuss our products with our customers without having to go through the work of creating a whole new Web page," Acres said in a 2005 interview. In another interview, he added that the ability to speak with customers with an authentic human voice was another consideration in launching the blog.

The blog and the solid relationships it had helped the company build proved a significant factor when the airplane incident hit the company in January 2005. In a January 5 post, Acres wrote:

> Well, it's been an interesting week, to say the least. Monday (our New Year's holiday, as it turns out), the *New York Times* published an article saying we sold the laser involved in the New Jersey incident. That's where it started. Since then, we've done dozens of newspaper and radio interviews.
>
> I'm really shocked about the magnitude of this story. Here we are one day, a small company in Corvallis, OR (on a holiday!)

manufacturing and selling outdoor equipment, then the next day we're asked to be experts on everything from terrorism to the Patriot Act.

Most reporters have been really nice, and some have not. All have probably hyped this story to be more than it's worth (to be fair, I guess that's their job).

Comments were quick to poke fun at the controversy. One commenter sarcastically wrote, "Oh you horrible people, after watching the news I was horrified to learn you are selling demonic rays that blast out explosive light at over 186,000 miles per second [the speed of light]. How many will die, oh God? I hope Dan Rather makes up some documents and gets you convicted."[1]

Why the post to the blog in the first place? "I wanted to use the blog to confirm that, yes, this was the place [from which] the guy got the laser to hit the airplane, so I just posted a message on the blog that served as a warning to people. . . . I don't want any of our customers to get arrested for doing anything stupid."

Nevertheless, it got worse. Associated Press created a photo to simulate what the laser beam might look like hitting a plane. The photo made the front page of newspapers across the country, prompting an outcry against the company that made the pointer. Again, Acres turned to the BigHa blog to tell the company's story. (After all, what good would it do to rely on the traditional filter of the media, which was publishing the damning photo in the first place?) Acres wrote:

> If anyone gets a false impression of what a Jasper actually does, we can blame the AP and this stupidly absurd image they published.
>
> Seriously, who came up with that? Have they ever seen a green laser? That image gives the impression that a Jasper's beam is 6' wide and clearly visible during the day.
>
> Of course, they could have used one of the photos from our site, all of which are real. I guess they just weren't sensational enough and didn't give the impression that Jaspers actually have the capability of shooting down 747s.

A Jasper is 4" long and ¾" in diameter. It's powered by a 4 volt lithium battery. At < 5 milli-watts, it's 20,000 times weaker than your ordinary 100 watt light bulb, and this is at its absolute strongest. Don't you think if a $129 handheld Jasper could reliably be used as a weapon, some really evil people would have their hands on it by now?

A little perspective is in order. Pictures like this don't help at all.

The comments again mostly expressed support for the company and reinforced Acres' message that the Jasper is a harmless device; Acres also let stand the comments that took a contradictory position. Not doing so, Acres said, would have just prompted more comments. Besides, he adds, he was genuinely interested in what everybody had to say.

Acres pointed out that the company was confident it had done nothing wrong: no laws regulated the use of the laser and the company had warned people about the dangers of misusing the device. "Had we been at fault about any of this, perhaps I couldn't have been so open," he says. "But since we were so confident in our position, we were able to just put whatever we wanted to up there and have . . . a discussion."

Acres also used the blog to respond to a critical editorial in the *Toledo Blade:* "I was kind of upset that nobody called us for a comment or asked us for our side of the story, and I wanted to submit that letter to the editor to get my side in, and then I figured, I might as well post it to the blog."

Eventually the crisis subsided, in large part because of Acres' posts and customer comments.

Predator Crisis: GMnext and the Rainforest Action Network

As General Motors approached the hundredth anniversary of its founding in September 2008, the company rejected the traditional idea of producing a glossy coffee table book proudly regaling readers with the highlights of its first century. Instead it opted to focus on a conversation with customers and other publics about its future. GM identified five topics about which it wanted to engage through social media channels, including design, technology, and the environment.

GMnext.com is the hub of the initiative, although there are other venues; GM is actively encouraging its employees at all levels to engage in conversation on these topics wherever they may encounter them, from blogs they read to groups they belong to within social networks like Facebook. On the official site, visitors can find blogs, discussion groups, and a variety of other channels. One feature allows anybody to upload a photo, which is exactly what some environmental activists from the Rainforest Action Network (RAN) did, uploading a photo of a protest in front of the Detroit Auto Show accusing the company of "greenwashing," the practice of misleading consumers about a company's environmental practices or the environmental qualities of its products or services.

In the spirit of open conversation, and as a matter of policy, GM did not remove the photos and left open the utility visitors could use to comment on them. Christopher Barger, GM's director of global communications technology, explains what happened next:

> The first comments we started seeing come in were constructive introductions into the dialogue. You want to talk about green jobs, all right, that's a valid thing to be talking about in the future of transportation. We reached out to a few of the GM executives who had knowledge in that area and said, "All right, what's the answer for these guys? Would you please go in and respond?" A few of them did, so at first, this was working out exactly as we had hoped, a dialogue on subjects you wouldn't normally anticipate happening on one of our sites.
>
> The problem happened when a few of the more passionate members of RAN recognized, "Oh, wow, GM's not stopping this;

they're going to let everything go up." What we started seeing in very short order was a flood of the same comments, over and over again, or rather direct and not nice comments personally directed at the GM personnel who were out trying to participate in that conversation.

It became very clear when you get seventy-plus comments in the space of less than an hour that are pretty much [the same] word-for-word, that's not a conversation, that's just somebody trying to campaign you and take control of your site.

Reluctant to stop the two-way nature of the conversation that included candid participation from GM executives, Barger and the GMnext team made two decisions. First, they would freeze comments on the photos (while leaving the photos and all comments posted to date untouched). But second, they would move the conversation to another channel that would promote a genuine dialogue while preventing the more extreme advocates for the environment from flooding the channel and drowning out other voices. Here's Barger's masterful and candid final comment to the photos before closing them to further messages:

We appreciate the interest that's out there on this subject; obviously it's sparked a lot of thought. Frankly, engaging in a dialogue about subjects like these is why we created GMnext in the first place. Unfortunately, a handful of folks are obviously not interested in actual dialogue; they'd rather just use this platform as a soapbox to spew diatribes loaded with propaganda. And while we welcome other opinions and constructive conversation, we have no intention of letting a vocal set of activists hijack the conversation with invective and dogmatic misinformation. "Dialogue" doesn't mean "allowing ourselves to be campaigned by people with no interest in actual exchanges of information or even listening to anyone who disagrees with them." So for now, we're closing commentary on these posts—though we are absolutely keeping the posts and comments up on the site.

But if we just closed off the dialogue altogether, we'd be letting the dogmatics win—and that's not fair to the people who have viewpoints on this subject and who are interested in real conversation. (And by that, we don't mean "agreeing with GM"—we mean acting like adults, articulating actual arguments and listening to other viewpoints instead of shaking fists.) And we do want to hear from people who want us to do more in the areas of alternate propulsion, instead of just closing doors.

Given the obvious interest, we're planning a live chat very soon on GMnext.com with several of my colleagues who can take your questions on GM's progress regarding ethanol, plug-in hybrids, extended-range electric vehicles and fuel cells. We'll also try to line up some outside experts with no connection to GM, to provide their input on the state of technology today. So for those interested in actual conversation on this subject, please stay tuned for the chat—because this is something we want to do in short order.

General Motors was true to Barger's word and sponsored live chats, many of which addressed the issues raised by the situation, including whether the GMnext.com site was in fact an example of greenwashing. By switching to a discussion chat format, Barger was able to moderate questions before they were forwarded to the participating executives. "When we came back in with our live chats, we reached out specifically to the group and said okay, you're invited, come on in, and they have been participating," says Scot Keller, who was director of the GMnext initiative at the time the incident occurred. "We have been letting their questions come through, even to the extent where, as you might expect, they weren't very flattering. One was a very sharp comment about this being a corporate dog-and-pony show."

The first session produced 150 questions with only an hour in which the participants could address them. The most passionate among the audience submitted multiple questions on the same theme, leading Barger to select one to represent the bunch. At the same time, one individual was submitting multiple questions, which the team addressed by selecting one from that individual and then moving on in order to "spread the wealth around." In no way, he insists, did the comment moderation result in soft questions being fed to the GM executives; tough questions remained in the queue. "It has nothing to do with which ones are flattering or which ones do we want to answer, but the physical task of trying to manage that many questions coming in all at once," Barger says.

While some among the activists have accused GM of shutting down the conversation, the company has earned praise with those who were interested in the dialogue, which has continued unabated since the situation was addressed through openness and a desire to continue a true give-and-take between the company and its publics.

Breakdown Crisis: JetBlue Airways and the Valentine's Day Freeze

The Valentine's Day 2007 ice storm that hit New York City led many airlines with planes queued up for takeoff to return to the gate. Bad decisions, exacerbated by woeful understaffing and communications breakdowns, led low-cost carrier JetBlue Airways to keep its planes on the runway in hopes of getting its flights out of town. Instead, wheels froze to the runway, and passengers were trapped on the planes for as much as eleven hours. Food ran out. Tempers flared. Countless more passengers were stranded in terminals as flights were canceled. The situation turned into a runaway debacle for the company that had been a darling of the travel industry up until then.

It is easy to imagine how most companies would have addressed the situation. An official spokesperson would have read a carefully scripted statement with words to this effect: "We deeply regret any inconvenience the situation at New York's Kennedy airport caused for any of our passengers."

That's not what happened. JetBlue Airways CEO David Neeleman (who has since left the company and started a new airline in Brazil) produced a video in which he spoke, unscripted and off-the-cuff, about his mortification at what had happened, how it had happened, and what he planned to do about it. The video was not the only channel through which Neeleman issued a heartfelt apology.

There was no equivocation. On the JetBlue Airways' Web site, the statement was labeled, "An Apology from Dave Neeleman." It began, "We are sorry and embarrassed. But most of all, we are deeply sorry." Later in the missive, Neeleman wrote:

> Words cannot express how truly sorry we are for the anxiety, frustration and inconvenience that you, your family, friends and colleagues experienced. This is especially saddening because JetBlue was founded on the promise of bringing humanity back to air travel, and making the experience of flying happier and easier for everyone who chooses to fly with us. We know we failed to deliver on this promise last week.

There's an important point to be made here: in a crisis, a risk-averse public reacts emotionally. Yet people are often willing to forgive those who apologize for their actions. While legal counsel may object, claiming an apology can be construed as an admission of guilt, it's a sincere and genuine way to defuse the worst response to the situation. Several bloggers and industry observers echoed the sentiment of Jennifer Miner, who wrote on Suite101.com:

> Will David Neeleman win back the hearts, and loyalty, of former fans of JetBlue Airways? Only time will tell. The airline certainly shouldn't make such a huge error in judgment again any time soon. In the meantime, how many CEOs of Fortune 500 companies do you know, that would present as humble and contrite an apology as this one?"

Several other apologies have been forthcoming since then. For example, Mattel CEO Bob Eckert apologized in a scripted video, then explained actions the toymaker was taking to prevent a repeat of the 2007 crisis involving toys from China recalled because of lead paint. A study by Mediacurves.com, also available on YouTube, showed high levels of believability among test subjects viewing the video. Apologizing goes a long way—far enough that it may far outweigh risks that concern the legal eagles. (By way of disclosure, we need to point out that Shel worked in Mattel's communication department from 1984 to 1988.) The risk-averse public also wants to know what the company will do to redress the parties affected by the situation. In his video, still accessible on YouTube, Neeleman told viewers that the company would present vouchers to passengers affected by the delays.

Finally, the public wants to be assured that the company is taking steps to prevent a repeat of the situation. On his video, Neeleman's introduction was explicit:

> There are a couple things you can do; you can ignore it and pretend like it was an aberration, or you can do an examination and determine if there's something you can do internally to make sure that never happens again, and I wanted to assure you as the CEO of this company that the events that transpired last week and the way they transpired will never happen again.

Then Neeleman outlined the steps the company was taking, including training nonairport employees so they can be brought to the airport during similar weather situations, improving the reservation process to make changes to reservations, and beefing up the headquarters staff to ensure planes and flight crews can be paired quickly. He also introduced a customer "bill of rights," guaranteeing adequate compensation to passengers affected by delays in the future.

Nearly four hundred comments were posted to the YouTube video, which was also copied and embedded into other blogs and

Web sites (as well as JetBlue Airways' own site), many applauding Neeleman for his candor and the speed with which he took action to address the problems that allowed the crisis to occur. Neeleman posted another unscripted video on April 19, 2007, updating customers on another storm and JetBlue Airways' decision to cancel flights and admitting that there was still further to go in implementing the changes he had initially promised. He also listed some of the changes that had already been made. Indicative of most comments left to that video were these two:

> It's awesome that you, David, go in front of the camera so much and let us know what's happening. Most CEOs would just write an article online or something, but you make a great effort to update us, thanks!

• • •

> Honest communication is appreciated even when things haven't always been smooth, We always make the airline our choice for flying now. . . . Other airlines charge more and their expectations are easily met because you know the service will not be there. At least jetBlue rebounds and can commit to make a difference. Kudos to you David and your team.

JetBlue Airways has regained its customer loyalty and is flying packed planes. Not everything worked out perfectly, though. The company's board replaced Neeleman, the founder of the company, as CEO. The move was based on JetBlue Airways' growth and the need for someone more experienced to handle day-to-day operations, according to the company, which continues to praise Neeleman's communication skills.

But there was less skill involved than there was transparency. Neeleman, aided by his communication staff, did not equivocate, obfuscate, or hunker down behind a barrier of lawyers and spokespersons. He explained honestly what had happened, apologized, and outlined what the company would do to prevent a recurrence.

That's excellent crisis communication.

Conclusion

When faced with a crisis, most companies are inclined to shutter their windows and barricade the doors. Transparency is forsaken in lieu of a defensive posture in hopes that opacity will deflect attention and maybe, just maybe, the crisis will go away.

It's the wrong approach. During a crisis, more than any other time, transparency is a requirement in order to gain trust, reduce public fears, and begin the process of returning to normal.

7

EXPOSING THE COMPANY TO THE EMPLOYEES WHO MAKE IT WORK

Internal Transparency

If you ask most people working in corporations how to gauge their company's reputation, the answers come quickly, and with a bit of a derisive lift of the eyebrow, as in, "How can you not know this?" People typically respond that corporate reputation revolves around how the company treats the environment, how much money it donates to charitable causes, how good a neighbor it is in the communities where it maintains facilities.

If that's what you think most people consider corporate social responsibility (CSR), you'd be wrong. According to a study commissioned by the public relations agency Fleishman Hillard (a client of Shel), 27 percent of the respondents said they assessed CSR based on how well the organization demonstrated its commitment to the well-being of its employees.[1] This bears repeating: How well a company treats its employees is the number one factor that leads others to rate the company's corporate social responsibility. Only 3 percent said corporate donations were the key indicator.

Businesses frequently invest a considerable amount in promoting their charitable giving. The *Journal of Philanthropy*, according to a *New York Times* article, "highlights several companies that have made marketing alliances with nonprofit groups, dedicating a percentage of sales of certain products to a specific charity or agreeing to support a specific program or project."[2] The only problem is, with only 3 percent of respondents citing donations as the most important sign of CSR, you have to wonder how much good it's doing from a reputational standpoint—especially for companies that have a less-than-sterling reputation for how they treat their own workers.

This study should be important to human resource and employee communications professionals, who can now make a stronger case for more resources. It should also make some companies that have been dismissing employee concerns rethink their philosophies.

A company can approach the employer-employee relationship from a variety of angles. One is compensation and benefits, although study after study suggests that employees consider these to be entitlements. People get out of bed in the morning and show up because they get a paycheck in return. Building engagement among employees requires more. (*Engagement*, a word bandied around a lot these days since studies have shown that companies with large populations of engaged employees produce far higher profits, refers to the degree of discretionary effort an employee is willing to make on her employer's behalf.) For example, the belief that compensation and benefits are implemented fairly and consistently across the organization is a more important dimension than the actual amount of pay when it comes to the effect pay has on an employee's commitment to the organization and external perceptions of how the company treats its employees.

For employees to know that pay and benefits are distributed fairly, there has to be an overt effort to make sure they understand the philosophy surrounding compensation at the company and have insight into the practices that result in each employee's level of pay. In other words, the kind of transparency that throws open the windows for a look inside the company should apply to those already working within its walls.

Tales of inequity spread quickly and dampen enthusiasm for the organization. The leadership at one company, which we will refer to as Acme, thought it would receive kudos for its enlightened approach to a problem. A director-level employee who was an important asset to Acme had decided to quit and stay home with her soon-to-be-born baby. Acme instead offered to give her a larger office where she could keep a crib and promised her that she could take whatever time was needed to nurse and care for her child at work. This would have been an enlightened solution *if* the same accommodation was made for every working mother in the company. But lower-paid administrative assistants who spent sizable portions of their incomes to pay for child care didn't see it as enlightened at all. They were deeply resentful that one higher-level employee was given this treatment while they had to continue plodding along with the same child care burdens they had always carried.

Although the compensation these administrators received may have been good, maybe even higher than an industry standard, there was no perception that compensation and benefits were administered fairly. The administrators began to wonder what other inequities were hidden beneath the surface.

The lesson is clear: if your employment practices are beyond reproach, you need to make sure employees know what they are. And if they're not, you need to fix them. It is in a company's own self-interest in this new world of intense scrutiny and instant communication to treat its workers well, since the research suggests that treatment translates into positive views of the company's corporate social responsibility, not to mention increased levels of employee engagement.

Of course, there is more to internal transparency than an unfiltered view of compensation practices.

An Open-Book Approach

In 1983, the plant manager at a struggling engine rebuilding facility in Springfield, Massachusetts, bought the facility from its owner, International Harvester, rather than lay off employees. The plant was losing some $2 million every year, and the former plant manager turned owner, a devout Catholic originally from

Chicago named Jack Stack, needed to innovate in order to turn its fortunes around, especially considering that the country was mired in the effects of a recession.

After securing the financing to take the company independent, Stack and his partners, a dozen other managers from Springfield Remanufacturing, gave shares of the organization to all the employees in order to build commitment. Most of these were blue-collar workers on the factory floor who rebuilt vehicle engines. Just as the financing was completed, the company lost one of its most important customers. The debt-to-equity ratio in the company was a staggering eighty-nine-to-one, and the owners were paying 18 percent interest on the debt.

That's when Stack and his colleagues gathered the employees together, those physical laborers in their greasy overalls, and explained the situation in grim detail. That was the start of what Stack came to call "open-book management." It was important that every employee, no matter how low on the totem pole, could read the company's financial statements and understand them as well as any member of the board of directors of any corporation. Even more important, these workers had to understand how the work they did affected those numbers.

One employee, an hourly worker at the time who rose to a senior management position later, explained in an interview that employees not only appreciated the insight and the chance to learn the fine details, but they also reached a common epiphany: the company could run out of cash at any moment and they would all be out of jobs. The only way to avoid that fate was to pay attention to the numbers with the same kind of intensity a company controller and chief financial officer would give to the books. That employee, Ron Guinn, said, "If you bought a tool, you realized what the effect of that expense would be. It finally dawned on me that I didn't have to trust those thirteen guys in management. If I learned the numbers, I could figure out the business for myself and determine if it would do for me and my family what I thought it should do."[3]

Stack became the champion of the approach to management that involved sharing every wart, every scar, every problem, every issue with employees so that they could use their own ingenuity to overcome them. After 4:00 P.M. on weekdays, Stack was available to any employee with the most open-door policy available, at a bar on the edge of town where his employees hung out after work. That was just one sign of management's commitment to the company's success and the seriousness with which they took line of sight between the highest levels of the company and the front line.

When Stack and his colleagues took over the company, its share price was 10 cents. In 1988, the price fell from its high of $15.60 to $13.02. Employees responded by voting to defer bonuses in order to bolster the company's numbers. If ever there is a sign of commitment, it's when employees volunteer to give up income in order to help the organization. At Springfield Remanufacturing, the motivation underlying the vote was clear: employees believed that they controlled their own future and their own job security, and propping up the company would have a longer-term payoff than a one-time bonus. It was in their own self-interest to forgo the extra income, something they knew because of their understanding of the organization's finances. (It's worth noting that even at $13.02, the share price represented a 13,000 percent increase over the value of a share at the time Stack and his partners secured ownership of the company.)

People who visited the factory floor of Springfield Remanufacturing have expressed the same amazement at the degree of both business literacy and commitment on display among the workforce. An *Inc.* magazine article included this passage, recounting reporter Bo Burlingham's visit to the facility:

> I met fuel-injection-pump rebuilders who knew the gross margins of every nozzle and pump they produced. I met crankshaft grinders and engine assemblers who could discuss the ROI of their machine tools. I met a guy who worked on turbochargers and ran his area as if it were his own small business.[4]

Too often in business, leaders assume that frontline workers are not smart enough to understand the nuanced financial details of the business. A CEO once was overheard saying he had to remember to visit plant floors a couple times a month just to remind himself how smart these people are. They may work in a factory environment, but they also are Boy Scout scoutmasters, treasurers for the local Kiwanis club, and organizers of nonprofit fundraising events. They help their spouses with their businesses or run home-based businesses of their own. They build their own vacation homes. They are all adults, and for the most part they are capable, smart, and ready to contribute to something they believe in. It's too easy, this CEO said, while ensconced in the ivory tower of corporate headquarters, to forget this and begin viewing them all as children who can't possibly comprehend the details of the business and are incapable of hearing bad news without throwing a tantrum.

In fact, according to Jonathan Schwartz, president and CEO of Sun Microsystems, a company's transparent behavior can motivate employees:

> If you're a sales rep, it's wonderful to watch the customer relationship being talked about in public. If you work in operations, you love the fact that we brag about having extraordinary efficiency to bring products to customers that solve problems. If you're an engineer, you love the fact that we're in a global forum, that our technology is being talked about and is influencing the marketplace. There's a certain amount of honesty it drives as well. It causes us to be a lot more humble, pragmatic, and connected to the marketplace, and not so caught up on what's happening in the 650 area code.

Fast Company's Open Approach

Lynne d Johnson, senior editor of FastCompany.com, had never before worked in a company that received monthly reports from the CEO directed to all employees. John Koten, CEO of Mansueto

Ventures (which publishes both *Inc.* magazine and *Fast Company*), details financial information, lists those newly hired, and reports on content that has been published on company Web sites and magazines as part of his reports. Topics covered also include how employees in all operations can become more efficient and improvements that need to be made in various arenas. "I find the report very helpful within the organization," Johnson comments. "I've never had that anywhere before—usually only directors know this information. But within the company we don't just talk the talk, we walk the walk."

The report engenders trust among employees who feel a partnership with their organization that also leads to improved productivity. "If ad sales need to be made up, we know it," says Johnson. "It's no surprise to anyone." This allows Johnson and her colleagues to go directly to the sales team with ideas to help drive ad sales. In other words, the report inspires productivity along with a sense of engagement from employees for being included in the communication of vital information about their company. Even interns are allowed to attend staff meetings: "I've never seen that level of inclusion before," says Johnson. "In my experience, those meetings are typically only reserved for directors."

Mansueto Ventures/Fast Company's transparency is also reflected in the physical environment of its offices on the upper level of a high-rise in Lower Manhattan. Occupying an entire floor of the building, the rectangle-shaped space features modest offices facing expansive windows with a sea of open-faced cubicles interspersed throughout the space. It's a warm and inviting environment that reflects the working style and corporate culture within. As Johnson notes:

> The office we came from before in midtown was a typical office.
> You couldn't see over your desk to see who was next to you. Now
> I can just slide over to someone to talk to them. At our old office,
> you didn't know what was going on where, how. There was that

sort of hierarchy with offices. It's not that way now. The CEO, the VPs, anyone who has an office, they're the exact same size. No one's office is bigger than any other. That's a testament to what our company is about, that we made a move into an office like this and we have more collaborative spaces.

Johnson describes how employees have "scrums" (short for "scrimmage," a rugby term) where groups gather every morning during the course of a project literally to huddle at counter-sized desks to collaborate. The process allows everyone to know the status of a project from the viewpoints of all decision makers involved.

The CEO report and literal open environment of Mansueto's corporate culture provide two ways that tactical transparency can inspire and motivate employees to achieve great results for a company that respects their opinion.

"90 Days of Transparency" at BzzAgent

In February 2006, BzzAgent CEO Dave Balter decided to push corporate transparency by creating a blog to document over the course of ninety days the inner workings of his company. Employing writer John Butman to record his experiences at the "90 Days of BzzAgent Blog," the objective of the initiative, in Balter's words, was to

> talk about the business in real time with what was really happening and do it from an outsider's perspective to see how that would impact the perception of our clients and of our employees. In the end we found that this embracing of transparency, no matter whether it is from us to the market or from an outsider to the market, really changed how we behaved. Internally we'd have a concept, we would talk about what we were trying to do publicly and then our clients could have a really open dialogue with us about what was working and what wasn't. It has been a massive change in how we run the company.

Butman had parameters about procedure, documented in the "Transparency Guidelines" portion of the blog that contains points like, "employees must approve usage of their names." And although the experience was sometimes rocky (Balter took heat when he blogged that his employees were taking free products home rather than giving them to the BzzAgent volunteers who are the frontline brand zealots for clients), overall the initiative was a major success from an internal standpoint. Balter notes:

> The staff felt paid attention to—we would hear things like, "I finally know what another department is doing because John [Butman] wrote about some other department for a day." Clients would e-mail us or call and say "Hey, I saw this is happening [on the blog]. Let me give you my two cents." We created this sort of new association with clients. I'd have potential employees start interviews with, "I saw on there you are struggling to figure out this part of your process. Let me tell you what I think." It is just a whole different way of communicating with everybody who influenced us. We saw the blog as a positive influence because it really gave everybody around the business a role to play that was fun and engaged and that made them feel like they were part of the process.

Business Literacy

Jack Stack's open-book management approach at Springfield Remanufacturing focused almost entirely on the financial end of the business. There are other aspects of the business that can be exposed to employees—aspects about which employees in many organizations have long been kept in the dark. Ask yourself these questions:

- Can my employees list our most important customers, what they buy from us, why we're their provider of choice, what we can do to improve those relationships, and what we might do to damage them?

- Can my employees name our key competitors, how we compete with them, what their strengths and weaknesses are, and what our strengths and weaknesses are that might lead a customer to choose one of them instead of us?

- Do my employees know what we make and sell beyond the products or services for which they have direct responsibility? Do they know what our other business units do?

- Are my employees knowledgeable about the issues that could become obstacles to our ability to compete, such as legal challenges and regulatory threats?

Again, many executives view the faceless mass of employees as simple-minded worker bees, incapable of grasping the subtleties and details of these issues. That's decidedly not the case. When Aetna, the health care insurance company, was faced with election campaigns in Texas that increasingly focused negatively on health maintenance organizations (HMOs) like those Aetna offered, the CEO reached out to employees to explain the issue. The CEO's outreach was accompanied by a petition, which hundreds of Texas-based employees signed. These signatures accompanied the text of the petition in newspaper ads throughout Texas that said, in effect, "We work for Aetna, we're proud of what we do, we live in Texas, and we vote." Employee literacy on the issues effectively stopped the HMO bashing in the campaigns.

Executive Blogs

Jack Stack had a few things going for him that many organizational leaders don't have. His employees were all in one place. He could make his way to the Expressway Lounge at 4:00 P.M. every day and be available to all of his workers. For larger organizations, the senior leader simply cannot be in all places at the same time. Workers at the manufacturing facility in Bristol, Oklahoma, can't drive to the local watering hole for a beer with the CEO when his offices are in Manhattan's financial district. New media tools like blogs, however, make it easy for CEOs to have the same kinds of conversations and introduce the same kinds of transparency.

Of course, older tools work well too. Before Sears was acquired by K-Mart, the Sears intranet featured a section dedicated to CEO Alan Lacey. Among the various elements of this site was a blog-like page where Lacey could share his thoughts. Another section was titled "Alan's Listening Channel." Any employee could submit an idea or suggestion through this channel. Lacey read them all, keeping a few to deal with himself and parceling the rest to the appropriate member of the senior staff. Every idea submitted through Alan's Listening Channel was addressed and the employee given a reply. Many of the ideas were turned into action items.

Blogs, however, provide a variety of benefits that cannot be built into an online form. First, a blog affords the CEO an opportunity to speak in his own voice about issues that concern or interest him or her. The fact that the voice is authentic and genuine means employees get to know the CEO—the individual whose decisions determine how secure their jobs are and how much money there will be available for bonuses and profit sharing—as a human being. The comment feature means employees can engage directly with the CEO, something that formerly happened only at town hall meetings or chance encounters in hallways and elevators. A CEO who listens to what employees say has access to a wealth of knowledge that resides at the lower levels of the organization where the work is done.

That's the experience Paul Otellini had. Otellini, CEO of Intel, began an intranet blog in December 2004 after learning he would assume the leadership position the following May. His initial post to the blog explained his reasoning:

Why am I doing this? Well, it seemed like a good idea to be able to create an ongoing vehicle to share my thoughts and observations on Intel and our industry with our employees, and to allow you an opportunity to have a platform for your thoughts or responses. While this is intended as an internal blog, I recognize that it will become public—welcome to the Internet! As a result, please recognize that I may be a bit limited in my comments and responses to protect Intel, and that we may exercise some editorial privilege on your comments for the same reason. I want to be clear on this up front. This is the price of entry to this blog.

Otellini acknowledged the response from employees in a subsequent post:

First of all, let me say that I was blown away by the response to the Blog. We received over 350 comments in the first 24 hours, with more coming in every day. I did not read them all, but read many of them.

Other CEOs have reported the same kind of response from employees who are generally thrilled to have the leader's ear. Some, including Otellini, have made better decisions based on the knowledge and insights employees provide. Employees, for their part, feel more connected to the company and more in touch with the issues that matter to top management. Trust increases, and commitment and engagement grow.

The CEO is not the only executive who can blog. At eBay, the online auction company, former CEO Meg Whitman had a blog on the intranet (a practice continued by her successor, John Donahoe); so do division leaders like Rajiv Dutta, president of eBay subsidiary PayPal. Other companies whose leaders are blogging internally include Michael Roberts of McDonald's, and David Senay of Fleishman Hillard. One of the most interesting leaders blogging to employees is Bob Malone, who heads up U.S. operations for British Petroleum (BP).

BP's U.S. business was in serious trouble when Malone took over in 2006. Poor maintenance on the Alaska pipeline had led to corrosion and leaks, and similar oversights led to a refinery

explosion in Texas, costing employee lives. Employee dissatis-
faction was at an all-time low. Rather than notify the company
if they encountered a problem or an issue, employees were more
inclined to contact an outside source. Upon assuming his leadership role, Malone implemented a hot line that employees could
call and appointed former U.S. jurist Stanley Sporkin as an
ombudsman to whom employees could take issues and grievances.

Malone also launched a blog on the intranet. After introducing the ombudsman and the hot line, he received hundreds of
e-mails from employees expressing support for his actions and
offering additional recommendations. He determined that a blog
would be an appropriate and effective forum for reaching out
to and engaging in conversation with employees. In an e-mail
introducing the blog to employees, Malone wrote:

> To make it even easier to have a dialogue with all of you, I am
> going to try my hand at using what has become a very popular
> Web communications tool: a blog. Now, I didn't even know what
> a blog was until just a month ago, but evidently, in this cyber-
> world we live in, a blog enables two-way communications.

Malone planned to continue the blog only if employees used it
to engage in constructive conversation.

The notion that a blog provides a platform for the highest-
ranking leaders in a company to engage in a constructive dialogue
with employees at any level speaks to the need for executives to
do their own writing. In too many organizations, executive blogs,
both internal and outward facing, are ghost-written by members
of the communications team. Executives are accustomed to this:
someone else writes their speeches, the letters that appear at the
beginning of the annual report, and the columns that have
appeared in employee publications.

A blog is different. Introducing a blog, as Malone notes, is
inviting employees to participate in a conversation. To have
someone else write it is disingenuous; it's like saying, "I want to

have a meaningful dialogue with you. My assistant will represent me in this dialogue, so talk to him."[5]

There are other requirements for executive blogging:

- *Write short.* Employees don't have time to read long essays on the intranet, whether they're articles produced by employee communications or blog posts from the senior leadership.

- *Read comments that employees contribute.* She does not need to respond to every one, or even any of them. Response to comments can be handled through a subsequent blog post.

- *Write conversationally.* Employees are sick to death of hearing leaders spout comments about how a paradigm shift is driving a quest to become a world-class company through a realignment of core competencies and adoption of best practices.

Other Internal Blogs

The executive blog isn't the only type of blog that serves to create greater transparency within an organization. Consider, for example, a project blog.

Historically a project leader has submitted a memo to higher-ups, usually weekly, outlining progress made on the project during the intervening week. The information contained in the memo was limited to the handful of people to whom it was sent as an e-mail attachment, despite the fact that many other employees have a vested interest in the outcome of the project. Also, many employees who are not actively engaged in the project have knowledge they can bring to bear in order to solve problems or otherwise assist in the successful completion of the project.

Worse, years later when somebody else starts a similar project, there is no institutional memory the employee can access to find out about the previous project.

Now, imagine that instead of writing a memo, the project leader—and even members of his or her team—maintain a project blog. Posts to the blog can include the following information:

- Achievement of milestones
- Notification of setbacks
- Requests for information to help overcome an obstacle or reach a new milestone
- Reports of problems encountered
- Ideas introduced to enhance or alter the nature of the project

Imagine an employee who works in another department and has a work-related interest in the project (once the project is complete, it'll really help her department reach out to existing customers with a new benefit, for example). Upon reading about an obstacle the project team has encountered, the employee might think, "Hey, I know someone in the company who knows exactly how to deal with that," and then posts the solution to the blog. Problem solved. Three years later, anybody starting a similar project can review the earlier project blog, identifying resources that will help in the completion of the new project, as well as roadblocks to avoid.

A project blog opens the door into company processes that was previously closed to employees. Their only knowledge of project status came from the rumor mill and official updates, often delivered at quarterly town hall meetings or through articles distributed in the company's employee newsletter.

Further transparency could be created by an open discussion of the issues and challenges a company faces. A blog authored by the employee assigned to address the issue could not only keep employees up to date and informed, but facilitate a conversation about ways to handle the issue.

Think about some of the topics raised by management as critical to organizational success that we've read about for years:

- Customer satisfaction
- Quality
- Globalization
- Diversity
- Wellness
- Offshoring and outsourcing
- Creativity and innovation
- Teamwork

Here's how we normally communicate these initiatives. An article is printed in the company newsletter (or on the intranet) introducing the initiative. Senior leaders reinforce the messages from the article at town hall meetings and other face-to-face encounters. Employee communications occasionally publishes more articles about progress. Managers are asked to keep the issue alive by raising it in team or departmental meetings. There may even be specific goals managers must achieve that are built into performance measures.

With a blog, the executive tasked with the initiative can keep everyone up to date, post examples of employees and teams that have exemplified the theme, explore new approaches, report on what other companies (including the competition) are doing, relate customer experiences based on efforts to institutionalize the initiative, and express concern about lack of progress or backsliding whenever it occurs. And since it's a two-way conversation with employees, the blog generates new ideas, allows employees to raise concerns and share success stories, and brings what otherwise is a stilted campaign to life.

One additional type of blog that can create huge internal transparency is the blog authored by frontline employees themselves. Unlike the external employee blogs we cover in Chapter Thirteen, these blogs are maintained strictly behind the firewall and are for the eyes of other employees only.

The idea that any employee should be able to blog will strike a lot of traditional managers as an excuse to roll their eyes to the heavens. *Just what this company needs,* many of them will think. *A way for employees to avoid doing work so they can write about their cats.* In fact, employees who blog internally tend to blog about their jobs. They share knowledge they believe other employees will find useful. They provide updates about what they are working on. They offer their thoughts on what's going on in their departments and in their business units.

At one European company, Macaw, every new employee is given an intranet blog along with security card and office phone number. What do they use it for? Mainly to share knowledge and technological issues and solutions.

Blogging at Siemens USA was not implemented as a companywide effort by information technology (IT). In fact, one department that wanted to offer blogs to its employees simply installed a blogging package on its own local server, bypassing IT altogether. The department didn't get permission from human resources, legal, or any other traditional authority. In response to a question asking what management thought about this particular IT employee taking company time and using company resources to write a blog, a member of the employee communications department replied, "They think it's great. He's sharing his specialized knowledge with any employee anywhere in the company who can benefit from it. As for the time it takes, management doesn't care as long as his work gets done." Every few posts in the blog, though, dealt with a non-work-related subject: soccer. When asked about management response to this dimension of the employee's blog, the communicator responded, "Management doesn't care as long as his work gets done. Management also thinks it would be very cool if another soccer fan in another part of the company discovered this employee because of his blog and established a new knowledge connection that paid off when one of them was able to help the other accomplish something on the company's behalf, even if it took two or three years before that payoff occurred." Siemens USA has very enlightened management.

Many other categories of blogs could potentially be introduced in organizations. Teams can produce blogs for group input, for example, or departments can introduce blogs for publication of departmental news and information and feedback from other employees about those announcements. In fact, any employee, team, department, or business unit that needs to communicate with any other employee, team, department, or business unit in a two-way conversation could use a blog to achieve that level of engagement.

All of this internal communication among employees at all levels also helps prepare employees to engage with customers, whether it's face-to-face, over the phone, or online. It also helps prepare them to play the role of brand/company evangelist/advocate.

You may wonder what internal blogging of this nature has to do with engagement. The simple answer lies in the way provincial executives view employees talking to one another: they're against it. When employees can talk openly and freely about their work, they are usually more satisfied with their jobs. Of course, this open dialogue must take place within the boundaries of any constraints that may exist; employees working on top-secret projects for a defense contractor aren't supposed to be telling other employees what they're doing, and a culture of transparency doesn't change that.

Blogs May Be All That, But They're Not All There Is

Blogs, of course, are just one tool. Tools are the last consideration in a strategic plan; they must help achieve the objectives you have established, which are designed to meet measurable objectives on the way toward executing the strategy. Blogs are powerful tools; that's why so many companies are turning to them to help build a culture of transparency. But the culture that the blogs produce represents the end game, and there are other tools that will get you there as well.

This kind of approach to new media has been top-of-mind for Ludovic Fourrage, group program manager at Microsoft, who concerns himself these days with the employee population and, most important, the employees in the field who deal day-to-day with customers. Fourrage asked during an interview

> Enterprise 2.0 technologies, wikis, blogs, new ways to communicate . . . how do they really come together in the enterprise? I started to see a lot of changes not just in the technology, not just in [the] wiki or blog . . . but more profoundly in what it means in the enterprise to adopt those new innovations.

More than just complement to existing communication channels, these tools have

> to disrupt how enterprises operate today, how [companies] think about engaging with their employees, how they think about educating them, how they think about communicating to them. How do you empower (a) salesperson [in the field] to engage with the customer? If you're a marketer in the corporation, how do you leverage all these new ways of doing marketing and engage with the customer and the salesperson? I came to realize that utilizing these tools where anyone could be engaged represented a movement where we could democratize the enterprise."

Fourrage refers to this new approach as the "liberal enterprise." He explains that the term emerged as he was exploring the idea of the democratized workplace.

The liberal enterprise is at the heart of a Microsoft initiative called "Academy Mobile," which provides the tools and resources for any employee to create a podcast. While some may argue that this simply creates additional content overload for employees who now have so much more from which to choose, Microsoft believes that the answers to most questions employees in the field have are already in the field. By allowing employees to share their knowledge via podcasts, others can identify those that provide them with value and subscribe. Field personnel can play the audio podcasts in the car while they are driving to appointments. It's a far better approach to sharing knowledge than waiting for the next scheduled meeting or spending hours searching the company's intranet for e-mails, discussion threads, or documents. And it's transparent because it eschews the formal one-way, top-down channels of communication designed to control the information employees get in favor of a free exchange of knowledge among employees, exposing their work and their knowledge to anybody who finds value in it.

8

MEET THE PRESS

Traditional Public Relations and
Media Relations

While we have been focused on using the tools of new media to open the organization, the work of traditional public relations churns on. The increased participation in conversations through resources like blogs does not herald a simultaneous reduction in media relations efforts. According to multiple studies, Americans continue to put their trust in mainstream media, particularly when seeking information about news that affects them personally. The idea that social networks and the increasingly important public commons will replace public journalism is patently absurd, at least for now.

Yet the influence of social media on mainstream journalism can't be ignored. The public relations agency Brodeur & Partners conducted a study that asked journalists about the role blogs play in their reporting. More than 60 percent replied that what they read in the blogosphere affects the tone of their stories. Half believe that blogs influence their publications' editorial copy, and 75 percent admit to getting story ideas from blogs.

A book could be dedicated to examples of social media influencing media coverage, but the point is clear with just one example, offered by Todd Defren, a principal at midsized public relations agency SHIFT Communications. SHIFT, which represents NEAT Receipts, a company that makes a hardware-software solution for organizing receipts, had been trying for some time to get its client onto Gina Trapani's radar screen. Trapani is an A-list blogger who writes the LifeHacker blog, dedicated to various ways to get more organized. On his blog, PR Squared, Defren explains what happened next:

> The latest shut-out came in December of 2007, when Gina asked her readers, "How do you organize your tax receipts?" Since Gina wanted her readers' input, it's arguable that NEAT Receipts "deserved" a mention here, but keep in mind that this was just the latest in a string of defeats. . . .
>
> This time around, we decided to surrender: Gina clearly didn't want to hear from the PR crowd. But, we asked one of our client contacts to get involved in the Comments section of the December post. In the comment, our client identified her affiliation and briefly outlined how NEAT Receipts has helped its customers at tax time.
>
> As we monitored for any reaction to our client's comment, we soon noted a follow-up comment by Justin Martin, a writer for FORTUNE Small Business. Justin seemed intrigued by the many suggestions of LifeHacker's readers. When we called on him, Justin remembered our client's comment at the LifeHacker blog and readily set up an appointment with our NEAT Receipts contacts.
>
> Result? Big-time profile of a NEAT Receipts customer in the *cover story* of the March edition of FORTUNE Small Business.[1]

There can be no doubt that all that sharing of information among bloggers and the people who comment on their posts, as well as their commentary and analysis of what the mainstream media covers, is influencing what and how the media write. Everything is getting mashed together, leading some to suggest that the very nature of journalism is changing. Tom Foremski, a former *Financial Times* reporter who now covers Silicon Valley with the blog "Silicon Valley Watcher," noted that stories he writes get greater pickup on the weekend, when mainstream newsrooms are operating on a skeleton staff. Other observations about the impact of the Net on the business of news flow fast and furious, including observations like these:

- More and more readers go online for their news, even if the source is a mainstream outlet like the *New York Times* or CNN, which means they are reading individual stories instead of the package that once arrived on their doorsteps. Thus, the value of the package has been diminished, while the worth of the individual article has been raised.

- With multiple news outlets covering the same story, there are a lot of similar individual articles available. The stories to which most people link from their blogs and other online properties (like Facebook profiles) are the ones that will attract the highest level of readership. To what lengths are some journalists willing to go in order to write the most-read article?

- Journalism can now contain hyperlinks. Where these links take readers is as important as the article that contains them.

- Links are important not only within a story. Many news brands are now offering links to the most important coverage they have found on a breaking story. This evolving practice even has a name, *link journalism*, and how it is practiced is a subject of considerable debate.

While mainstream journalism continues to wrestle with its role in the era of the twenty-four-hour news cycle, the public commons, citizen journalism, consumer-generated content, and social media in general, reader habits also are going through a transition. Fewer than half of the households in the United States subscribe to a newspaper, a dramatic drop from thirty years ago when a sizable percentage of households subscribed to more than one newspaper. Newspaper subscriptions continue to plummet, which should come as no surprise to anyone with teenage children: How often do *they* turn to a newspaper for their news? The consequences of this downturn are worrisome. Between June 2000 and December 2006, seventy-two thousand editorial jobs were eliminated in the United States. In the meantime, the number of blogs that ranked in the top one hundred online news sources jumped from twelve to twenty-two in the six months between September and December 2006. Something is happening here (as Bob Dylan would say), but we don't know what it is.

It is in this environment that companies continue to try to tell their story through the filter of the media. How the media are addressing those attempts is worth some consideration here.

Transparency Channels

Transparency with the media begins with a simple pledge to keep the press informed about stories it's covering. Silence breeds suspicion, but regular updates quell distrust, assuming the information provided is accurate and honest.

UGOBE, a privately held company in the San Francisco Bay Area, sparked excitement at the 2006 DEMO conference when it unveiled Pleo, an interactive robot dinosaur. "The company was set to take the world by storm and make Pleo the number-one must-have product that holiday season," recalls SHIFT Communications' Todd Defren. "Unfortunately, the product did not hit the market in time for the 2006 holiday season."

In fact, the company estimated it could take as much as an additional six months before the product would reach store shelves. UGOBE didn't make that target either, extending it another few months, and then another few. Ultimately UGOBE wasn't ready to start taking online orders until summer 2007; as this book goes to press, the company anticipates availability in stores in summer 2008.

"The company was faced with the challenge of continuing the momentum from DEMO longer than anticipated and keeping existing fans talking, while expanding the fan base already lining up to buy a Pleo," Defren explains. "The other major challenge that UGOBE faced was addressing the media corps, who were not shy about expressing skepticism about UGOBE's ability to deliver on the Pleo hype."

UGOBE addressed all of these issues by remaining as transparent as possible through regular correspondence with both the media and the growing base of Pleo fans. "Several newsletters and e-mails were sent out leading up to the official launch," Defren says, "often directly from the company's founder." These missives detailed the challenges the company faced and how they were addressing them, keeping constituents updated on what was going on behind the scenes. These two notions, insight into decision-making processes and a look behind the scenes, are at the core of organizational transparency. The result, Defren notes, was "minimal uproar from either the press or consumers as each delay was announced. And all units sold out for the 2007 holiday season."

The UGOBE tale is one of traditional media relations carried to the extent necessary to provide a candid look at the situation and what the company was doing about it. The modern tools of transparency, though, can be employed by organizations, and against them, in a variety of ways never before conceivable.

Michael Hyatt, president and chief executive of Thomas Nelson publishing, was contacted by a trade publication about an interview. Hyatt knew the publication was not likely to report positively on the interview, so he put conditions on it: "I'll agree to the interview if you submit your questions in writing. Then I'll publish your questions and my full responses to my blog, and you can publish whatever you want, provided you give a link back to my blog from your article."

By exposing the full answers he provided before the interview was published, any quotes that were taken out of context by the publication would be available for anyone to see. Hyatt's credibility would rise while that of the publication would fall. It provided an impetus for the publication to treat Hyatt fairly in its final article.

Hyatt's approach trumps more traditional actions taken by company leaders who don't like the approach taken to coverage. Google CEO Eric Schmidt, for example, cut off online news company CNet after publication of a report to which he objected. Schmidt had responded to a query about some of the sensitive information that could be uncovered about people using Google by noting that Google archives only publicly available content. Proving the point, a CNet report revealed personal information about Schmidt himself, including his salary, the neighborhood where he lived, the charities to which he made contributions, and his hobbies, among other things—all obtained through Google searches. Schmidt forbade Google employees from talking to anybody from CNet for a year. That news spread quickly through the blogosphere, with Schmidt taking more heat than CNet. Schmidt, a smart and even-tempered executive if ever there was one, appeared petulant, hypocritical, and vindictive.

But such transparency can work two ways. In 2005, Ziff-Davis reporter David Berlind opened what he called a "media transparency channel." Berlind used a blog to provide readers with the raw, unedited research that he accumulated while developing a story. This would include original pitches he received by e-mail from media relations professionals, the entire transcript of interviews—everything. Transparency, Berlind noted in a post, "is the practice of unobscuring that which might otherwise be obscured for the benefit of those who deserve to see what's happening behind the scenes." The media transparency channel, he suggested, unobscures the raw material of reporting. If the *New York Times* had had such a channel, Jayson Blair's fabrication of news stories might never have happened and the two editors who resigned in the wake of that scandal might still have their jobs. (Blair resigned from the *New York Times* following accusations of flagrant plagiarism. An internal report determined that thirty-six of the seventy-three national news stories penned by Blair included fabrications and content copied directly from other sources.)

Berlind didn't stick with the effort long. He noted that it required a significant amount of "heavy lifting," as he put it, that an interface that made it easy to expose the raw material of journalism simply didn't exist. Given existing technologies, it took too much time. But other efforts by traditional journalism outlets are following in Berlind's footsteps, creating greater transparency about their processes and, at the same time, the companies journalists work with in the production of news content.

At *Wired* magazine, for example, some stories are being written in public. Instead of waiting for the finished, polished copy, writers are posting their research to blogs and inviting public comment in the hopes of unearthing additional information and correcting misinformation. "The corrections that our readers make and their comments make a new form of journalism that is interesting and useful even though it's not all sort of perfect and polished and sealed with a bow and published with a 'publish' button," says Chris Anderson, *Wired*'s executive editor. "It's sort of an open-sourcing of research."

Wired may be the first publication to adopt this technique to its reporting, but it isn't the first time such an approach has been undertaken. Bloggers Robert Scoble and Shel Israel published chapters of their book on business blogging, *Naked Conversations*, to a blog for reader comment, and used the feedback they got to improve what they had written.[2]

From a writer's perspective, there is huge value to getting that kind of crowd-sourced input and feedback. From the publisher's perspective, it attracts attention and builds interest in the finished product. From the reader's perspective, it's an opportunity to get a preview of the content to come, as well as a behind-the-scenes look at the evolution of an article or a book. From the perspective of the company whose efforts are the subject of the article, however, the prospect can be horrifying.

Even the polished articles of traditional journalism are subject to new twists that can keep media relations experts awake at night. For example, a growing trend among the Web sites of news outlets like CNN allows readers to comment on some articles. Google News, a prime source of news for many people, has a policy that allows comment in a story reported on the news aggregation site by individuals and representatives of organizations cited in the story. "We're hoping that by adding this feature, we can help enhance the news experience for readers, testing the hypothesis that—whether they're penguin researchers or presidential candidates—a personal view can sometimes add a whole new dimension to the story," Google News team engineers Dan Meredith and Andy Golding wrote on the official Google News blog. While this feature, accessed by a link titled, "Comments by People in the News," may lead some to believe inaccuracies can be corrected, it also provides opportunities for other parties cited in a story, including competitors and activist groups, to foster inaccuracies. The slim hint of control companies believed they maintained by employing professional media relations appears to be slipping away even in the arena of mainstream journalism.

How can companies cope?

Brian Solis, principal of FutureWorks, a high-tech public relations agency, believes these issues can be addressed through companies' behaving transparently in their dealings with all audiences:

> Whether it's media relations, influencer relations, or blogger relations—and even analyst relations—let's just remember that at the end of the day, this is all about people. For some reason, especially in the traditional communications world, we tend to forget about the "relations" in public relations. We're so consumed with buzzwords, industry jargon, and hyperbole that we expect those who receive our news and pitches to have the same level of excitement that we have. In fact, it's pretty easy to get caught up in what we write and wind up most of the time speaking at people, confusing messages with conversations.

Transparency, to Solis, refers to the practice of talking to people as people and truly understanding their ecosystem as a way of inspiring and directing how you engage with them. "Remove the

BS from PR. Learn about what you represent and why it matters to the people you're trying to reach," he says.

Traditional means of burying bad news won't work in today's media environment, according to journalist Tom Foremski. In the days before the blogosphere, companies required to report bad news would distribute their press releases on Friday evenings or just before a holiday, knowing the news would be seen or heard by fewer people and might even escape the attention of some news outlets. Today, news that doesn't make the morning edition of the paper can still make the online edition, and news that doesn't make the mainstream press at all can still spread like wildfire on the Internet.

Companies that obfuscated their numbers in an effort to hide the real story might have once gotten away with it, but not today, with tens of thousands of interested parties picking through the numbers and reporting their findings online.

Social Media Relations

Some tools have evolved that move old-school media relations into the world of social media and, as a consequence, provide new opportunities for transparency. The "Social Media Release," an evolution of the old workhorse, the press release, was inspired by a Foremski-penned blog post titled, "Die, Press Release, Die, Die, Die." In the post, Foremski complained about the narrative format of the traditional release, which could hide information while making it difficult to take advantage of the interactive, multimedia World Wide Web that served as the platform for his reporting. Foremski called for changes to the press release to reflect the online world to which journalism has been moving.

In addition to clearly articulating the core news facts of a release, Foremski wanted to see the incorporation of multimedia elements, the addition of social media tools, and the development of tags that make it easy to find and use the information contained in a release. This rethinking of the traditional press release into the Social Media Release is designed to take advantage of emerging technologies while also making it easier for people to share the company's news with others through their blogs, Web sites, or traditional media outlets.

Social media releases have been issued by a variety of organizations, such as Ford Motor Company, Gatorade, Coca-Cola, Intel, Cisco Systems, and Novell. Social media releases have these elements:

- Elements of the release, such as news, quotes, boilerplates, and contact information, are separated into sections, with core news facts presented in concise paragraphs or listed in bullet format, making it easy to identify the news and copy-and-paste pieces of the release into an online article or blog post.

- Multimedia, including audio, video, screencasts, animation, and images, are available for incorporation into online articles and blog posts.

- Social media tools are included, such as Technorati tags that writers can use to see what others have written on the same topic, social bookmark accounts that make it easy to offer archives of relevant pages, and RSS feeds that enable writers to subscribe to updates.

- The means to share the release are built in, such as links to Digg, del.icio.us, and other content-sharing resources.

Transparency accrues from a variety of elements of the release. For example, by separating executive and customer quotes from the narrative of a traditional release into their own sections, it becomes difficult and unwise for those writing the release to fabricate the quotes. Outside the context of the narrative, quotes that don't sound the way a person talks will be even more obvious. The addition of video brings the speaker's facial expressions and tone of voice to the fore while also offering glimpses behind the scenes. Adding comments to a press release transforms it into a conversation starter rather than a deliverable. Including tags that launch a search of blog search engine Technorati to discover anything that anybody else is writing about that topic further exposes the company to remarks outside their control, but obviously remarks that don't concern them, since they freely offer the tags as a research tool for journalists.

Hiding a negative message in circuitous narrative text will be harder in the social media version, which can be used as fodder for conversation by journalists, bloggers, and even company representatives (including the CEO) themselves.

The adoption of the social media release has also spurred the creation of a cousin, the social media newsroom, which employs the same sensibilities to the online repository of resources journalists use to cover a company. In addition to the official company biography of the CEO, for example, a social media newsroom would include a link to the CEO's LinkedIn profile (assuming she has one), providing additional insights into the CEO's background and any other information she has elected to share with other members of the network. Social media newsrooms, like the one developed for General Motors Europe, also include links to blogs that cover the company, another research aid beyond the company's control.

Conclusion

The question of how journalism and social media will mesh, and how they will stay separate, continues to vex journalists and the people and institutions they cover. The mandate for companies and the public relations professionals that serve them, both in-house and in the agency world, is clearer-cut: be honest, be open, be accessible, and provide journalists (including citizen journalists) with the tools that make it easier to report accurately.

9

THE VIEW FROM THE TOP

The Role of Leadership

Over at "The New PR," a wiki that serves as a community-built resource for communicators seeking information on new media, a page listing CEO bloggers has grown to impressive proportions. Nearly thirty countries are represented. Some, like Austria, Hungary, and Israel, feature only a couple of names. But there are fifteen in the listing for the United Kingdom, forty-one in France, and close to two hundred in the United States. True, not every one of these names is a CEO. Constantin Basturea, who set up the wiki, uses the term generically to designate people in leadership positions in their organizations. And while some of the companies represented are very small, others are well-known organizations like Macmillan Publishing, Boeing, Lenovo, Pitney Bowes, NBC, General Motors, Marriott International, Sun Microsystems and McDonald's. The list is by no means comprehensive. Only those who have discovered "The New PR" and elect to contribute to it have added to the list.

Why are these senior executives blogging? According to Dave Taylor, who writes about leadership and online strategies through his "Intuitive Systems" blog, CEOs shouldn't touch blogging with a barge pole. Blogging, he writes, "often [puts CEOs] at odds with legal and financial constraints that limit the public actions of executives, particularly those of publicly traded companies." He continues:

> [CEOs'] primary role is to *raise money for the company*. They are
> the lead on strategic planning (along with the Board of Directors)

and are somewhat involved in corporate tactics (though that's really the purview of the President of the company), but notice that I didn't say anything about "communicating the company message" or even "inspiring the employees" or "engaging customers." For companies of any size, CEOs have more important tasks than writing articles for the company weblog.

In this chapter, we examine the role of leadership in general and the CEO in particular in illuminating the organization.

Despite Taylor's assertion that a CEO's primary role is to raise money, most would agree that the CEO's primary responsibilities are articulating a vision and leading the organization toward that vision. An enlightened CEO recently said that CEO should stand for "Customers, Employees, and Owners." These are the three publics with which CEOs must concern themselves, this particular CEO insisted, since without their support, the company cannot succeed.

CEOs have employed a variety of tools in their efforts to reach these audiences: press releases and official corporate statements, speeches, conference calls with investors and analysts (a routine practice when quarterly earnings are announced), press conferences, and road shows. In its early days, the Internet did little to alter the landscape through which executives could communicate beyond introducing a new distribution channel. Slowly, though, some executives recognized the power of engaging directly with audiences, fans and critics alike, in the forums where conversations about their companies were taking place. Participation in these forums predates social media. Several years ago, tax preparer H&R Block's former CEO, Mark Ernst, personally responded to questions about the treatment of seasonal tax workers in an old-fashioned bulletin board on Yahoo's finance site.

What could have devolved into a frenzied bashing of the company turned instead into a respectful discussion with many participants praising Ernst for his willingness to engage directly.

His conversational approach to correction misperceptions, as well as his openness to continuing improving the company's handling of communication to seasonal employees, defused the situation.

Today social media make it even easier for CEOs to have these kinds of conversations. "Today, more than ever, people want authenticity in the people that they do business with," says Michael Hyatt, president and CEO of Thomas Nelson, the sixth largest trade publisher in the United States and the largest publisher of Christian materials worldwide. "We're seeing that [demand for authenticity] ourselves in the whole environmental movement. I don't think you can create trust and build brand equity without transparency. You can try to do it, and some have been successful in doing it, but if you put people's faces, names, a personality on the company, it's that much easier to love and trust."

Hyatt began blogging with an independent blog—not a part of the Thomas Nelson Web site, although he did write candidly about his job and his company. "From Where I Sit" gained attention throughout a number of sectors, including the publishing world and the audience for Thomas Nelson's products, and it gained widespread attention when he published a proposed set of blogging guidelines for his employees and asked for public input. In that post, he cited three reasons for encouraging his employees to blog. Key among them was opening a window into the publishing business. That is, he wanted to increase Thomas Nelson's transparency.

Thomas Nelson's employee blogs are covered in Chapter Eleven, which looks at the role of employee blogs. Hyatt uses his own to achieve the same purpose. In fact, he found so much value in blogging that he started a second blog that *was* an official part of Thomas Nelson's Web presence, "As I See It." Eventually he folded his personal blog into the official one.

"At least a third of my job needs to be spent on communication," Hyatt says. "There are a lot of ways to do that, [such as] e-mails, phone calls, and speaking publicly. A blog is just another tool to do what a good CEO does: communicate." Furthermore, Hyatt says, blogging helps him crystallize his own thinking around issues his company is facing "and put it in a format that makes it transferable and accessible to other people on demand, when they want it."

Even boards of directors can support a CEO's blogging efforts. Hyatt says his board endorses his efforts. So does the board of directors at Beth Israel Deaconess Hospital in Boston, whose CEO, Paul Levy, maintains an independent blog, "Running a Hospital." "The board likes this thing," says Levy, who formerly ran Harvard Medical School's hospital. "They like the openness. I have a wonderful board that agrees with me that an institution is strengthened in the public eye [when the public can see] what's good and what's bad about how it does its business."

What Openness Means

Organizations steeped in an opaque culture resist discussion about anything sensitive and disclosure of anything they are not required to disclose. Transparent organizations don't have problems with these topics. Levy, for example, wrote a post about his salary titled, "Do I Make Too Much?" The post attracted a lot of attention in large part because the candid discussion of his income startled so many people. Levy's salary was a matter of public record, but Levy went beyond that Massachusetts-required disclosure to expose the process Beth Israel Deaconess's board employed to settle on his pay, something most leaders wouldn't want to discuss unless they were forced to. But Levy asks, Why not? "These are nonprofits, they're public institutions, they get public subsidies in the form of tax exemptions, they are publicly funded in terms of research and clinical care from the state and federal government. They're every much as public a body as the government is in many respects, so why not tell people how decisions are being made?"

That kind of candor has earned Levy praise from public advocacy groups like Healthcare for All. "Reaction from legislators, when I talk to them, has also been very, very positive," he says. It has become easier to recruit because the staff is proud of the hospital's reputation as an open organization. Even patients have told him that they like the idea that he's tackling these issues with a blog.

The fact that a CEO blog reaches employees as well as other audiences is important to Sun Microsystems president and CEO Jonathan Schwartz:

> I like to think of ourselves as a very simple business. We want to recruit all the developers in the world and then we want to help them develop applications that require innovative infrastructure that we like to sell to the world. But there are a lot of moving parts inside Sun, and to put in a blog why we're doing all the things we're doing allows me to communicate not only to the marketplace, but to all employees.

Paul Levy agrees:

> Part of the job of a CEO is to explain your mission and actions to the public. Why wouldn't you use one of the greatest communication tools that exists to do that?

Hyatt adds that transparency means addressing issues the company is not required to address, particularly given that it's a privately held organization. "There are things we don't have to talk about but will, and there are things we don't have to talk about and won't." He'll be happy to share Thomas Nelson's revenues, he says, but not its profitability. "That's something I don't want in the hands of my competitors. But [what I talk about and what I don't are] subjective on my part. At the end of the day, [I have to be concerned with] what serves my company, what will serve my shareholders. Transparency about most things generally does that."

Bad News, Controversy, and Misperceptions

Part of being transparent is addressing the bad news any organization faces from time to time. When Beth Israel Deaconess Hospital faces bad news, Levy just posts it, he says. He also addresses criticism head-on. Once, he recalls, he met someone in a grocery store who told him about a new medical device he found intriguing, leading him to write about it on his blog. The advocacy group Center for Science in the Public Interest took issue, writing a scathing post condemning Levy for writing about the device because a member of his faculty had a business interest in the product. "So I put in an addendum that said the Center for Science in the Public Interest was kind enough to point out a connection with a faculty member here; sorry, I didn't know about it." Thus ended the controversy.

Thomas Nelson's Hyatt faced a similar attack following Hurricane Katrina. Hyatt had seen a TV news report in which victims of the devastation lamented the loss of their Bibles. "Like every other American, we wanted to help," Hyatt recalls. Since the company publishes Bibles, Hyatt figured they could do something about this and shipped 100,000 Bibles to Louisiana.

"We got huge backlash from some people who felt [the hurricane victims] need groceries, clothing; the last thing they need is a Bible. There were scores of comments, some vitriolic and hateful." Hyatt left the comments alone because, he said, "that's part of what it means to be transparent." He was delighted when his employees began commenting as well, defending the company's action. "It was a pretty lively conversation."

Hyatt also used his blog to address a media inaccuracy. "We changed our editorial standards a year ago," he recalls, changes that were inaccurately reported by the publishing industry's principal trade publication, *Publishers Weekly*. The incorrect reporting caused a firestorm of controversy aimed at Hyatt's company.

Hyatt considered writing a letter to the editor but decided against it, knowing any correction would be brief and would appear toward the back of the publication where nobody would see it. He opted instead to take *Publishers Weekly* to task on his blog, where thousands of people who mattered to Hyatt saw it. The controversy was quelled within twenty-four hours.

In fact, both CEOs agree that their blogs have altered their organization's relationship with the mainstream press. Levy finds passages from his blog posts appearing in news coverage; what he writes is actually influencing reporting on his hospital. "I try not to scoop our own press office or a reporter," he says. "That would be bad form." But, he explains, there has been more than one instance in which he wrote a post on a topic a reporter was covering without knowing an article was in the works. "A reporter will call our press office about a particular story and say, 'Don't tell Paul I'm working on this, I don't want him to blog it.' My poor press person gets in the middle because she didn't know [I was going to write about it]; she has to tell the reporter I did it on my own."

These days, Levy says, his press officers keep him apprised about stories reporters are covering so he won't inadvertently beat them to the punch on his blog. Hyatt also agrees that his blog has changed his relationship with the media. "The leading publication in the publishing industry has ten thousand readers," Hyatt says. "My blog has six thousand readers a week. Through my blog, I have direct access to a similar audience that matters to me."

In addition to reacting to controversy and problematic media coverage, CEO blogs enable leaders to address dicey issues. Levy, for example, has no problem taking on labor unions over the tactics they employ in their efforts to unionize his and other Boston-area hospitals. In a handful of posts, Levy has criticized the Service Employees International Union. "Once or twice," he says, "someone from the union has commented on the blog." The conversation that ensues can run the range from "jokingly familiar to a hot and heavy dispute," Levy notes. That conversation, including Levy's measured and thoughtful responses, remains part of the public record, a view into the organization, its views and positions, and its approach to issues that affect it.

Hyatt, too, encounters people both in the comments section of his posts and in person who take issue with what he has written. These include fellow publishers and even customers he meets at trade events. "But that's conversation," he says, "not push-back against my blogging."

Do CEOs Need a Blog?

While Schwartz, Hyatt, and Levy, along with other CEOs from companies large (like Marriott International) and small (like the UK's Butler Sheet Metal), are blogging, there is no rule that CEOs must, or even should, blog. As Dave Taylor points out in his anti-CEO-blogging screed, the ranks of the highest-ranking bloggers at companies like General Motors do not include the chief executive officers.

Whether a CEO blogs should depend on a number of factors:

• • •

Will the blog produce better communication between the organization and a key stakeholder audience? Michael Hyatt and Paul Levy argue that the blog serves as a more effective vehicle than some others. Mark Elbertse, chief executive officer of Netherlands-based Tulip Computers, also views blogs as an alternative channel for organizational communication. In an interview, Elbertse explained that his board of directors questioned him on the time commitment blogging required. His answer was that he spends no more time on communication now than he did before. He has simply reallocated some of the time he used to invest on less effective vehicles to blogs. And it cannot be reiterated enough that communication is one of a CEO's primary responsibilities.

Is the CEO in the best position to handle these conversations? At General Motors, most of the conversation revolves around cars. CEO Rick Wagoner deals with the business side of GM, while vice chairman Bob Lutz is the senior executive responsible for vehicles. It makes more sense for Lutz to handle those conversations. Wagoner has, however, occasionally authored an article appearing on one of the company's group blogs.

Will the CEO make the commitment to keep the blog current? A CEO inclined to shut down in the face of a crisis would make a terrible blogger. Blogging about the company's good times, only to go dark when things go south, will do a company more harm than good. The appropriate frequency of posts on a CEO blog is a question that arises frequently. Most experts recommend two or three posts a week at a minimum. When Richard Edelman, president and CEO of the world's largest independent public relations agency, began his blog, "6 A.M." in September 2004, he committed to posting weekly. An uproar ensued, with bloggers insisting that one post per week was woefully inadequate. But Edelman has been consistent and steady in posting, and nobody today questions his commitment to his blog (which is one of several by Edelman staff appearing under the "Speak Up" label on the company's Web site).

Will the CEO commit to writing the blog himself? Blogs are all about conversation. A CEO who blogs is stating clearly to readers, "I want to have a conversation with you." To have a surrogate write the blog is a cynical approach to such participation. A lot of consultants insist that ghost-writing for the CEO is an accepted practice and that blogs shouldn't be any different from speeches or other channels for the boss to reach his audiences. Blogs are different, though; they have surged onto the landscape precisely because of their authenticity. There's nothing wrong with someone editing a post the CEO has written, particularly if the CEO blogger discloses this approach. And Marriott International CEO Bill Marriott doesn't actually write a word. Instead, he dictates his post into a digital recorder, leaving it to his staff to transcribe. Visitors to Marriott's blog, "Marriott on the Move," can choose either to read or listen to posts. Either way, they're hearing Marriott's authentic voice.

Is the CEO genuinely interested in a conversation with representatives of the company's publics who choose to comment on his posts? The best blogs are not one-way communication channels; companies have enough of those. A CEO who is interested in a one-way communication should choose from among the many existing channels that accommodate that model. Blogs specifically enable a two-way dialogue. If the CEO isn't as interested in listening as she is to speaking, then a blog is the wrong vehicle for her.

· · ·

Even if a CEO opts not to blog, that doesn't mean that CEOs cannot blog. While this may seem like a blatant contradiction, Rick Wagoner from GM has had his say on a GM blog. The blogs are group efforts. Even the highly regarded "Fastlane" blog, dedicated to a discussion of cars, is penned not only by vice chairman Bob Lutz (who gets most of the credit), but also by various members of Lutz's team. "FastLane" served as a platform for Wagoner in 2006 when he opted to discuss GM's turnaround efforts in the context of conversation. "While 'FastLane' is typically dedicated to discussion about GM products and services, Chairman and CEO Rick Wagoner has chosen to use this forum to update you on GM's turnaround progress," an editor's note on the blog read. Wagoner's post generated a flood of comments, most complimentary, others critical, and still others offering advice.

Southwest Airlines' Gary Kelly took the same approach, offering his first contribution to the "Nuts About Southwest" blog—a group blog authored by a representative sampling of Southwest employees—to address an issue that had grown to critical proportions among the discount airline's customers. At a May 2006 shareholders' event, Kelly announced that the company was experimenting with changes to its seating policy. (Southwest passengers are not assigned seats, instead taking any open seat they find once they have boarded.) In the post, Kelly addressed ("straight from the horse's mouth," as he put it) the rationale for the experiment. He concluded his post:

> We are currently conducting extensive research and if our research and testing (which some of you may be involved with) proves that we can bring in more Customers (without alienating our existing Customers) and increase overall Customer satisfaction, but at the same time not increase our boarding times or our costs, then I don't see a reason not to do it. I haven't given any time frame—just that it won't happen next year.
>
> I know that several of you have commented that you don't want the current seating policy to go away because you see it as a part of what makes Southwest "Southwest," but I'll remind you that many people felt the same way when we transitioned from plastic boarding cards to electronic boarding cards. Things change and we can't ignore that fact. One thing that will never change, however, is our dedication to you—our Customer—and we will always make decisions with your best interests in mind.
>
> So, stay tuned . . . we promise to keep you informed of this and all of the changes at Southwest. And keep telling us what you want, we LUV hearing from you and we appreciate your business!

Customers left 648 comments to the post, the vast majority voicing support for the open-seating policy. It was that direct feedback following his explanation for the company's experiment—a look inside the process by which the company makes its decisions—that led to Kelly's decision to scrap any plans for assigned seating and opt for some revisions to the open-seating system. In a follow-up post, Kelly wrote:

As many of you know, the question about whether to keep our open seating or to assign seats has been *the* Southwest question for the past couple of years. Proponents of each process have been very vocal and heartfelt in support of their positions, and my post of last summer generated more than 700 comments (including those on a followup post). To those who weighed in on this issue, thank you, and I assure you that your voices were heard.

Even if the CEO doesn't maintain his own blog, he can still speak with a critical audience through a blog, assuming the company has had the foresight to establish one, as GM and Southwest have.

Finally, there's no reason a CEO cannot turn to another medium, social or traditional, to be accessible and transparent. As Bill Marriott records his blog posts into a digital recorder, there's nothing to stop a CEO from recording a podcast instead of writing a blog post. The CEO of Pepsi Cola's former Quaker-Tropicana-Gatorade operation in Chicago, John Compton, took questions from employees, delivered via the company's employee communications manager, and responded to them without reading them in advance. His answers were candid and thoughtful, providing employees insight into both his thinking and his personality.

Other Executives

The CEO isn't the only executive with senior-level credibility who can take up the keyboard in order to communicate with audiences. Here are a handful of senior executives who write about topics related directly to their areas of responsibility or expertise:

- Randy Tinseth, vice president of marketing for Boeing Commercial Aircraft, authors "Randy's Journal" on the Boeing Web site. When Boeing lost a bid to develop a new breed of aircraft to refuel military planes in flight, Tinseth used the blog to articulate Boeing's position, which resulted in a dynamic conversation with readers. Again, the conversation provides insights into Boeing's response and the actions the company planned to take.[1]

- David Churbuck, senior vice president of Web marketing for computer maker Lenovo, maintains a personal blog at Churbuck.com, where he addresses business issues alongside personal observations.

- Eric Kintz, vice president of global marketing strategy and excellence at Hewlett Packard, blogs about "marketing, web 2.0 trends, software, digital photography, digital entertainment and anything else that is on my mind" at his "Digital Mindset" blog.

Each of these executives, and the thousands of others from across the spectrum of business and industry, provide behind-the-scenes views of the organizations they represent. They discuss processes, procedures, problems, and solutions in a candid and sincere conversation through which they learn as much as they share. GM's Lutz has noted that the comments to his blog provide the best intelligence he has seen in his forty-plus years in the automotive industry. Why? Because they are the thoughtful contributions of people who care most about cars, generated from ongoing discussion and offered because Lutz has made it clear that he wants to hear what they have to say.

"It's a great investment of my time," says Michael Hyatt. "For our employees, for our industry, for our position in the industry, I don't know of a better return."

Conclusion: Blogs Are Tools

Blogs, like any other communication channel, are, at their core, just tools. A CEO or other organizational leader is equally capable of carrying on a conversation that flings open the windows into a company through a podcast, a message board, or even a profile on a social network like Facebook.

Blogs get the attention and have attracted most CEOs and leaders because they have become widely accepted, are as easy to access as any other Web page, and are simple to maintain. The key to leader transparency is to find the right leaders and identify the channels that will work best for them and their audiences. That may be a blog. But whatever tool ultimately is selected, it's the sincerity and authenticity of the conversation that matters most.

10

EN-GAUGE THE CONVERSATION

How Issues Blogs Show People You're Listening

> The point is that we're McDonald's and everyone knows us. We're a big brand, we have size, we have influence. We're already part of the discussion anyway. People already talk about us, so the idea is [that] we want to be engaged in that conversation and post the good and the negative.
>
> —Bob Langert, *vice president,*
> *corporate social responsibility, McDonald's*

Whatever the size of your brand or the nature of your business, you have a unique angle on it. If you aren't communicating this value proposition online, you're conspicuous by your absence. More important, if you haven't created a conduit for customers to interact with your brand, you're sending the message that you don't care about their opinion. Whether that's true is irrelevant: if people think you're not listening, they'll eventually start talking about you (in ways you won't like) and buying from someone else.

Blogs that focus on a specific business issue provide two distinct advantages for any organization:

- They provide an opportunity to demonstrate an area of expertise.
- They provide a forum for people to talk about your ideas and brand.

Customers feel overwhelmed at the thought of trying to reach out to a large organization. Blogs and other forms of communication that focus on a specific topic within an organization demystify a company. Readers get to know the author of a blog through his or her authentic and candid writing style (or their voice in a podcast) and relish the thought of joining a conversation about topics they care about; it beats simply being talked at.

Issues blogs do more than just prove you're listening: they allow you to gauge customer sentiment. What will people say about the issue if you let them? How are you proving you know what you're talking about? Should the criticism you're hearing drive you to make any changes?

In this chapter, we focus on four organizations employing issues blogs as case studies for how opening up to an audience on specific topics can provide a transparent platform that establishes trust and other benefits for your brand:

- McDonald's
- Verizon
- Boston's Beth Israel Deaconess Hospital
- Ben & Jerry's

How McDonald's Proves It's "Open for Discussion"

Bob Langert, vice president of corporate social responsibility (CSR) at McDonald's, admits he didn't fully grasp how to blog when he first started "Open for Discussion" (http:// csr.blogs.mcdonalds.com/). "People said I spoke too much from a corporate voice," he admits. "So I've learned to make my posts shorter, more relevant, and I respond quickly to comments, typically within twenty four hours or less." But his passion for his subject matter and his desire to connect with readers outweighed any initial hiccups he may have had with online etiquette, "I really like blogging," he says. "When I started doing this about two and a half years ago, I didn't know what I'd get into, but it's really exceeded my expectations."

But here's the main point about Bob and his fellow contributors to "Open for Discussion": it's not about them. "Our number one criterion for the blog is that the people engaging with us are having a meaningful exchange."

The content of the blog focuses on five components of CSR:

- Balanced lifestyles
- Responsible purchasing
- People
- Environment
- Community

The tone of the blog is transparent and candid, as demonstrated by a post from January 14, 2008:

> McDonald's just received a food services sector report from the Roberts Environmental Center at Claremont McKenna College. We graded an A+ on their sustainability scorecard. Of course, we are pleased with that. When looking at the raw scores, I noticed we had a 44 out of 100. This is humbling, and tells us there is much more to do.

The candor of the final sentence is not only refreshing but surprising. McDonald's is saying it needs to improve on something? In public? Online, where it will live forever? But after the initial shock of that revelation, the typical response to such humility is appreciation and empathy. Customers appreciate that such a large, powerful company like McDonald's is candidly expressing its desire to improve. That expression naturally inspires trust since there's no apparent motivation for such transparency except to connect with the reader. In a post, Langert explained why he has taken this approach with the blog:

> We'll be the first ones to say we have a lot to learn. We don't view it as a weakness but as a strength to recognize that there are issues [we have to deal with at McDonald's]. Any organization that thinks they have it all figured out is probably not going in the right direction. And until you start facing where those challenges and tensions are you're not going to have a continuous improvement process.

As with so many other blogs, readers are passionate about the subjects Langert tackles. A great specific example along these lines from McDonald's is a series of comments left to a 2006 post responding to criticism about toy Hummer trucks McDonald's put in Happy Meals, a promotion that raised the ire of environmentalists opposed to the SUV's carbon emissions and gasoline consumption. Reading the post ("Toys and Environmental Protection") and the comments that follow provide an excellent case study for the type of conversation that takes place when a forum is opened for people to discuss specific issues. Bob begins the conversation/post by recognizing there's an issue to discuss: "I see we've received some comments about the use of Hummer toys as Happy Meal promotions in our U.S. restaurants," he wrote. "I can see why the question is being raised." He goes on to cite specific upcoming CSR reports and an "unscientific poll" he conducted among staff members with children to get their take on the placement of Hummers in Happy Meals.

The comments Langert's post inspired run the gamut from, "It is offensive to say you are a company that is moving forward and going in the right direction and then to promote something like a Hummer," to "You people are idiots—ask a kid what he'd rather play with, a Hummer or a Prius, and unless some granola-crunching parent sticks her nose in, the kids will choose the Hummer every time."

It's important to note these conversations also serve as a powerful source of feedback for organizations that initiate them. Conversations like the Hummer discussion represent a form of free research for a company to assess how consumers received a campaign, product, or service. A more central measure is in the authentic relationship established with readers. As Langert states, "We measure ROI in trust. We want people to say the blog is transparent and that it's open and that it's real dialogue." The degree to which Langert is achieving such transparency is evident in statements like this one, produced as part of McDonald's communication effort during a difficult situation:

> We hosted a panel for a conference with sustainability expert Julia Hailes. She had some tough criticism for us in terms of how she viewed McDonald's and our history. She wrote a blogpost on her experience and I blogged back. I found it to be rewarding. Part of my vision is that we all get a better understanding of each other over time. Sometimes you agree, sometimes you don't. But minimally, you're advancing an understanding.

Advancing an understanding is a powerful way to create authenticity when people discuss important issues surrounding a brand. Providing a forum for such open dialogue also certainly extends beyond the mandated obligations to comply with regulations.

Can You Hear Them Now? Verizon's Policy Blog

Verizon's Policy Blog (http://policyblog.verizon.com) provides an excellent example of an organization reaching out to audiences on issues directly related to its field of expertise. Whereas CSR issues affect every organization on some level, it's only folks like those working at Verizon who can write about broadband and telephony subjects with authority and aplomb.

John "CZ" Czwartacki is the executive director of external communications for Verizon and a frequent blogger on the site. Noting that conversations happen online among knowledgeable and influential people, Czwartacki points out that maintaining Verizon's policy blog provides "some table stakes to add and learn from those existing conversations. Those discussions in the policy space in technology and telecom and other issues that come across our doorstep are ones we want to be a part of."

This point demonstrates an important distinction for issues blogs not shared by a typical journal-oriented or general issues blog: they let you throw your hat in the ring with other leaders in your industry to demonstrate what you know. As you display your acumen over time, you can become a trusted voice in your field and encourage customers to trust you and your brand.

Czwartacki also notes that the larger conversation on a topic takes on a life of its own that your blog/brand should be a part of, even if the talk is sometimes negative:

> Blogs didn't invent the disgruntled customer. They didn't invent someone who is a brand advocate, either, but those folks are having conversations somewhere, whether it is over the back fence or at a message board. That's why it's important to note that we don't own our brand—the conversation is the owner of our brand and it is affected by the wisdom of the crowd.

It's terrifying to concede that the conversation is the owner of your brand until you remember that you can be part of that discussion. And if your business can provide unique insights, people will welcome your thoughts even if they sometimes disagree with you. You can also discuss general issues without divulging proprietary secrets and have an established platform when you want to make new announcements. But if you're silent eventually people will assume you don't know what you're not talking about or, worse, have something to hide.

Physician, Reveal Thyself: CEO Paul Levy's Blog

"Part of your job as CEO is to explain the mission and the actions of your organization to the public" says Paul Levy, CEO of Beth Israel Deaconess Hospital in Boston, in reference to his blog, "Running a Hospital" (http://runningahospital.blogspot.com/). "So why wouldn't you use one of the greatest communication tools that exists to do that?"

Levy's blog, although not formally linked to Beth Israel Deaconess's Web site, has become a focal point for news about the hospital for the local and national press. He's gained notoriety for the transparency of his thoughts, as evidenced by his January 28, 2007, post, "Do I get paid too much?" In it he discusses and divulges his salary with a candor and specificity rarely heard of in regard to the sensitive subject of executive pay. In an interview for this book, he noted:

> The *Boston Globe* does an annual story on all of our salaries [CEOs of Boston area hospitals] because [that information is] filed with the state. . . . So it's not as though it's a secret to the world what these salaries are. I actually thought it would be an interesting topic for people to think about in terms of governance of nonprofits. How does the board of directors or board of trustees make a decision as to the appropriate level of compensation of the CEO? So I put it out there, and it has by far been the most popular post. Why should it be taboo if it is already public?

There's a first-strike mentality to Levy's actions that demonstrates an excellent aspect of tactical transparency: if there's public information about you or your organization, stake a claim in the conversation around an issue before someone else does first. Having a blog about the issues surrounding your organization helps you center a conversation and frame the issues before others might question your motives or intent.

When questioned on whether the hospital's board of directors takes issue with subjects raised on his blog, Levy points out that "they like the openness. I happen to have a wonderful board who agrees with me that an institution is actually strengthened in the public eye by being honest about what is good and what is bad and how it does its business." Levy's inclination toward transparency has also led to other benefits from his posts. The Beth Israel staff, for example, knows it is accountable to the public for its performance because Levy openly shares clinical data in his blog, placing staff performance in the public spotlight:

> The blog has helped create accountability for the organization because the doctors and the nurses here know that their progress in terms of reducing infections and eliminating harm in the hospital is public. It gives them just a little extra incentive to do even a bit better than they'd be inclined to do anyway. That kind of public accountability goes a long way. The reaction by public interest groups like Healthcare For All (http://www.hcfama.org/) has likewise been very positive, and the reaction from legislatures has also been very positive.

Here's an intriguing point for managers: your blog reflects directly on your employees. Even if your personal blog is not officially linked to your organization, if readers know where you work, your words can affect employees' actions. This doesn't suggest that you should use your posts to manipulate behavior. Instead, you can help inspire higher levels of accountability when providing a public sounding board. If your focus, like Levy's, is to explain your mission in an effort to improve, the accountability will engender trust from the customers who follow your efforts through your blog or other communications outlets.

Ben & Jerry's Social and Environmental Assessment

Ben & Jerry's, the iconic makers of ice cream flavors like Phish Food and Cherry Garcia, has published reports on its social and environmental performance for more than eighteen years, long before most other companies had considered the notion of transparency or corporate social responsibility as it's defined today. Reading their reports provides an excellent framework for any organization to prepare its own CSR missives. The tone of their reports is affable and positive while not pulling any punches, as demonstrated by thoughts from the 2006 report written by "chief euphoria officer" Walt Freese. Noting that the company does "inevitably make mistakes," he goes on to state that "we want to be a company that is led by our values, not by circumstances." Humility and passion provide a solid background for authenticity, and Freese's words lend credibility to Ben & Jerry's efforts to stand by their core vision.

An intriguing part of the 2006 report comes in the reaction to Ben & Jerry's release of a Black and Tan ice cream flavor. Not realizing the cultural implications of the name chosen (the term refers to British paramilitary troops sent to defeat the Irish Republican army in the early 1920s), they apologized for the "international flap" and stated, "As a global brand now, it's clear that we need to be more aware of potential cross-cultural misunderstandings when we plan for product launches."

When it comes to issues blogs, the black-and-tan scenario serves to reinforce the notion that online conversations are international in scope. Cultural implications can greatly affect a conversation around your brand.

Eschewing the Issue

Consumers are demanding authenticity from the companies that create the products and services they buy. Whether it's the name of an ice cream or a toy truck in a Happy Meal, separating your brand from a consumer's experience is not up to you any longer. The conversation is your brand, and avoiding the central issues surrounding it will only alienate you from the people who most want to hear your expert thoughts on a subject. Employing tactical transparency to create an issues blog of your own means you get to talk about subjects close to your business—and close to your heart—before others beat you to the punch. And it's not going to go away, as Mike Prosceno, director of new media at SAP, wrote:

> The topic of transparency and what that means from a corporate or social responsibility perspective is not going away. It's going to become more and more important for how a corporation acts, not only in the marketplace, but in the communities that the corporation is vested in around the globe. Whether you're an oil and gas company or a software company like SAP, it doesn't really matter. These issues affect all of us.

What to Do Next

Get to know some popular policy blogs to see how you can focus on a central issue over a prolonged period of time and create dialogue for better understanding. These three examples are outstanding:

- Google's public policy blog: http://googlepublicpolicy .blogspot.com
- Cisco's "High Tech Policy" blog: http://blogs.cisco.com/gov/
- The "Know HR" blog: http://www.knowhr.com/blog/

11

FROM THE INSIDE LOOKING OUT

Employee Involvement

In Chapter Seven, which addressed transparency in the financial and investment community, investor relations expert Dominic Jones made an important point. The voices of employees, articulated through employee blogs to which the public has access, provide investors with insight into the depth of talent and subject matter expertise available in the company. Depending on the level of the employee, these blogs can also spotlight the quality of the company's management. And these, Jones said, are critical considerations that influence investment decisions.

Making those voices available requires a company to be willing to allow, even encourage, its employees to blog—or take advantage of other social media channels—on its behalf. Not many companies have placed enough trust in their employees even to entertain the notion. Yet the companies that have encouraged their employees to blog, like Thomas Nelson publishing, IBM, Microsoft, and Sun Microsystems, have experienced none of the consequences so many companies fear, and they can readily point to the benefits.

The Blurring Line

There was once a clear line separating communications with external publics from communications with employees. In fact, in many companies, it wasn't unusual for employees to hear news about the company from external media, since internal communications focused more on human resource and workplace topics.

Most organizations have moved beyond that, adopting a more strategic approach designed to foster understanding of the company's plans and the role employees are expected to play in achieving the company's goals. Of these companies, a smaller subset engages employees more actively. But even in companies with the most enlightened communication and engagement models, the internal and external communications functions often report to completely different parts of the organization chart.

This is a curious division given that most leaders hope their employees will be model ambassadors for the organization. A lot of organizations go so far as to implore their employees to be company or brand ambassadors. When at a PTA meeting, a church picnic, a family barbecue, or the kids' soccer game, workers are encouraged to be enthusiastic about the company and its products.

Social media have changed that dynamic. A Facebook group can be the new meeting place, supplementing (and sometimes even standing in for) a PTA meeting or a night class. Some employees have their own blogs. Others read blogs and post comments. Others are sending message bursts in Twitter. Some are doing all three, and even more.

If you work for a company of any size at all, search Facebook (you'll need an account) for your company name. Odds are you'll find groups of employees already congregating there, most often in public view and talking about work. They have set these groups up because it's becoming the common means of networking, particularly among people who aren't geographically able to get together face-to-face. These groups exist for people who went to the same high school, for people who like the same band, for people who have the same hobby. There are groups for gamers, for people who share common social and political causes, for farmers, for fans of this or that podcast, and for people who love the same car models. Why wouldn't companies expect people to set them up to talk to other people who work for the same company they do?

It is not reasonable to address this by forbidding employees to talk online about work. The Internet has become the watering hole, the smoker's circle, the coffee bar. It's where people talk. Part of management's role in the era of social computing is ensuring that employees are equipped to represent the company well in these conversations.

The first step to earning positive employee involvement online is what you might call the inoculation approach: treat your employees well, and don't behave in a way that gives them a genuine reason to trash the company to members of their networks. There has been a general improvement since we saw that footage of dazed Enron employees walking out of their workplace for the final time, carrying cardboard boxes filled with their possessions. In fact, a combination of the transparency mandated by Sarbanes-Oxley and the voluntary additional steps many companies are taking in their own self-interest means that poor treatment of employees will be exposed more quickly and condemned, leading to a reputational hit that could affect everything from sales to recruiting. Consider the case of video game company Electronic Arts, which was targeted in a blog post by the anonymous fiancée of an employee. The blogger, later identified as Erin Hoffman, was distressed that her betrothed, Leander Hasty, spent so little time with her as a result of his mandated eighty-five-hour work week. The post attracted widespread attention, leading to fifteen job offers for Hasty (he accepted one) and the distribution of a memo to employees by human resource executive vice president Rusty Rueff acknowledging the problem and promising to fix it.

It would have gone much better for Electronic Arts if the problem had been addressed before a frustrated bride-to-be took her grievance public. More companies seem to understand that now, which could be one reason the annual Edelman Trust Barometer's most recent findings indicate a boost in confidence and trust of business.[1]

The real opportunity, though, goes beyond preventing problems caused by disgruntled employees. It rests with committed, engaged employees who will represent the company proudly online and serve as a first-line public relations team.

Communication to employees needs to support employee online engagement. That engagement can take a number of forms, including participation in social networks like Facebook groups, blogging, participating on someone else's blog, file sharing (such as uploading workplace photos to photo sharing sites like Flickr), and others. Two of these categories, blogs and participation in social networks, warrant special attention.

Employee Blogs

Most leaders are inclined to laugh when hearing the idea that employees should blog on behalf of the company. Yet the companies that have taken that step report an overwhelming positive outcome compared to few, if any, minor problems. Michael Hyatt, CEO of Thomas Nelson, sees three key benefits deriving from employees who blog for his company. As he put it on his own blog:

1. To raise the visibility of our company and our products

2. To make a contribution to the publishing community

3. To give people a look at what goes on inside a real publishing company

Hyatt believes the twelve employees who have taken him up on the challenge have done precisely what he hoped they would, and he plans to encourage more employees to start similar blogs. "One of the things we've said to our people, and one of the ways I've tried to encourage blogging, is to say, 'You have a voice in this conversation, and it needs to be your voice.' My employees are free to disagree with me." They need to be respectful in the conversation, Hyatt says, something he has addressed in the guidelines to which employees are required to abide. "But we don't need to have a monolithic, uniform corporate response. We can have a dialogue about this, and it just happens to be in the public square."

IBM probably better fits the mold of companies that might expect to encourage its employees to blog. "What we're doing this for is to learn," Mike Wing, vice president of strategic communications at IBM, said in a November 2005 interview as the company's employee blogging initiative was launching:

> We think blogging is a big deal, and we don't know yet what the real full nature of that big deal is. It goes way beyond diaries or opinion or even marketing or PR. It's an unprecedented empowerment of individual human expression, a fulfillment of the original promise of the web in which everyone can become a publisher.
>
> Our hope is to engage. IBM is a company based on expertise and collaborative innovation; those are basically the company's business model. It's no longer product manufacturing that's the center of gravity for this company. This is an emerging space where the prime value is expression of and access to expertise. As important as it is for IBM to express its expertise, to make it visible by exposing to the world a lot of really smart people with a wide range of experiences and knowledge, more important in the long run is what we're going to learn in the process, the relationships we'll hopefully be able to build that wouldn't have been open to us or others otherwise.

IBM's employee blogs have become an integral part of the conversations about innovation, technology, and collaboration. (The English-language blogs are available at http://www.ibm.com/blogs/zz/en/.)

Other examples of employee blogging efforts include the following:

- The technology consulting firm EDS has its "fellows"— technologists who have achieved special distinction—writing for "The Next Big Thing," a blog where they discuss the future of technology.
- Southwest Airlines recruited twenty or so employees representing a cross-section of the workforce to provide insight

into not only what the company does but the quality of the employees who do the work. "Nuts About Southwest" is widely read and commented on.

- The U.S. Transportation Security Administration is using "Evolution of Security," a blog specifically to host a dialogue. The bloggers—an airport worker, an analyst, a former air marshal, and a communicator, among others—often pose questions to readers in their quest for conversation. The conversation led the agency to put a halt to practices implemented locally at some airports but not authorized by the TSA itself. The practice was revealed by readers of the blog, and the post acknowledging them for identifying the problem was titled, "Hooray Bloggers."

Even journalists find value in what employees write. Chris Anderson, editor-in-chief of *Wired,* the flagship publication of the computer generation, admires how Microsoft has turned its brand image around by turning the marketing model on its head:

Microsoft had taken a losing proposition in terms of its brand perception—its PR efforts, messaging, the trust that consumers felt in it. It was having a hard time getting traction [using] conventional means. And by simply going to this kind of bottom-up, blog-led, individual-voices-versus-corporate-voices, it kind of reversed paths, and was now seen in a new way. It was trusted and respected by people who weren't going to be impressed by press releases and advertising and corporate speeches. If Microsoft can do it—a company that is somewhat controlling and secretive—and they can embrace the risks and uncertainties associated in letting people blog without filtering, then maybe everybody can.

One more point about employee blogging harkens back to a study released in 2005 by the public relations agency Edelman and Intelliseek.[2] "We have clear evidence that consumers and other important stakeholders make decisions about products and brands based largely on what a company's employees say about them," Christopher Hannegan, senior vice president and director of Edelman's employee engagement practice, said when the report was issued. "And now blogs provide these same employees with access to a mass audience as never before. So companies need to understand that two powerful forces are beginning to converge in a way that will have a direct and growing impact on their business."

Employee Participation in Social Networks

It's not unusual, when searching Facebook groups, to find a multitude of employees who make no effort to hide their disdain for the company. On one such group, populated by workers at Hallmark card stores, a torrent of comments criticizing the company is tempered by an employee who argues that she likes working for Hallmark. That single comment can offset the perception created among those who peruse the group, including those who might be checking the company out before applying for or accepting a job.

But again, while balancing negative commentary is great, the more important role for employees is representing the organization to other publics in a positive manner that reinforces the brand the company wants to build.

Consider General Motors' GMnext campaign. GM leadership has identified five topic areas about which it wants to have conversations with consumers: design, technology, the environment, reach, and "ideas." The initiative was launched against the backdrop of the company's hundredth anniversary. In addition to hosting conversations on the GMnext.com Web site, where employees are encouraged to participate, the company is asking employees to have conversations on behalf of GM wherever they encounter them: on blogs, in social networks, on message boards, as well as in face-to-face situations.

Says Christopher Barger, director of global communications technology:

> We recognize that the issues we're going to be talking about are of interest to many different communities out there in the social media. It's not just going to be us saying, "Come on in and talk to us at our house." We're going out and trying to take active roles or active parts in other conversations, not the dominant role, not helicopter in and take over the things but to be part of these conversations, to learn from what's being said elsewhere and incorporate that into the GMnext efforts, as well.

It's not just executives from the automaker engaging in these conversations. Any employee is able to weigh in on any such conversation they may encounter without first seeking approval. "[Those employees will] be joining in the conversation as individuals with an interest in those particular [topic] areas," according to former GMnext director Scot Keller. "We see that as nothing but a positive."

Keller makes another important point: employees will participate only in conversations that interest them and focus on subjects where they have subject matter expertise or a strong interest. It's the same idea that drove employee participation in a special GMnext wiki before it was unveiled to the public. The wiki was designed to let retirees, employees, customers, and other publics build the company's history. An employee who was involved in a plant opening is far more likely to contribute an article about that plant opening than about, say, a stock split.

Employees also are contributing to an internal-only blog about the initiative, weighing in with numerous comments to posts authored by twenty or so employees to engage the global community of employees in a conversation about GMnext. The level of participation, according to Barger, reflects the genuine interest, even passion, that employees have for the company and the GMnext effort.

Customer Service and Technical Support

There is little that annoys an expert blogger more than a frustrating encounter with customer service or technical support. Search Technorati, and you'll find a treasure trove of posts by influential bloggers complaining about customer service and technical support. Every time someone reads a blog post about a technical support nightmare, he has a brand experience. Every time a prospective customer hears someone tell a customer service horror story, she has a brand experience.

The simple fact is that customer service and technical support are reporting to the wrong box on the organization chart. These functions are, along with socially active employees, the front line of public relations—the place where most people in the public will intersect with the company—and should report there, or to corporate communications or even marketing. These departments are sure to treat the functions as more than cost centers and afterthoughts. We are not alone in this belief. McKinsey & Company and Forrester Research have both made similar suggestions.

If you've ever worked with customer service or technical support within your own company, you know that it is not the primary goal of these departments to serve customers. It is, sadly, to keep costs cut to the bone. Rather than gauge success by the number of happy customers whose problems have been solved, these departments record the length of time devoted to each call. The less time spent with a customer, the more effective the department is seen to be. That's exactly opposite of how customer service and technical support should be. Companies should be eager for the opportunity to serve a customer to interact with her and seek to maximize every precious moment a customer gives to us. It's highly probable that the money your company saves by getting customers off the phone as fast as possible is less than the value of the hit your brand is taking as the social network buzzes about your inadequate, unfriendly customer service.

There are three ways to ensure a positive brand experience when customers (not to mention other critical audiences) contact your company through technical support or customer service:

- Get the company to invest what is needed to adequately staff and train the department.
- The people who staff the customer service and technical support departments shouldn't wait for calls to come to them. Social networks make it easy to find people who are having trouble and offer to help.
- Every employee in the company is a potential customer service or technical support representative.

That last point is a radical concept, but an important one. Rather than blocking access to social networks, blogs, and other social media sites, employees should be actively engaged in these spaces, representing the organization by being available to answer questions and solve problems.

Shel has had several direct encounters with employees of companies about which he blogged, underscoring the importance of building a corps of employees empowered to address customer issues wherever they encounter them. In one instance, Shel posted a negative experience about the off-airport parking company, Park 'N' Fly to his travel-related blog. He received the following reply from an administrative assistant named Caryn Healey:

> I can see that your experience was less than satisfactory and less than our desired level of service. While I can't change what has already happened, I would like to ask if you might let me make it up to you. Park 'N' Fly is a good company, and we are really trying to get our Customer Service levels to the highest standards. Info like this helps us. I do apologize for the service you received, and would LOVE to have that driver's name, or any other driver's name that has treated you less than satisfactorily. I would like to

send you some free parking too, can I do that? There is absolutely no reason for this kind of thing to be allowed. And we thank you for sticking with us this long.

Here is an employee who is not a customer service representative who found a dissatisfied customer and knew she could take action to solve the problem, not report the problem to the appropriate department.

Still, customers calling for service or support are clear targets for excellent experiences. Thus, treating customer service and technical support representatives as communicators can strengthen the brand experience by creating positive buzz through social channels. An employee who can reach out to solve a customer's problem makes buzz even better and the brand even stronger.

Conclusion

Being transparent internally with the employee audience is important not only to build employee engagement but to prepare employees to participate more effectively in social networks, representing the company well, solving customer problems, aiding in the recruiting effort, inspiring and reassuring investors, and bolstering the company's corporate and product and service brands.

Rather than block employee access to these networks, companies should make social networking sites readily available to employees and provide them with the tools and resources to provide accurate information and take appropriate action to address unhappy customers, inaccurate rumors, and opportunities to bolster the company's reputation and tell the company's story.

12

TRANSPARENCY BEYOND TEXT

How Audio, Video, and Interactive Media Build Trust

How much do you read in one day? If you add up the number of e-mails, text messages, magazine and newspaper articles, and other content you digest in one day, it's no wonder we escape to music or video after work to decompress. Media that move beyond text, however, engage our minds in different ways and capture our attention in a more visceral manner. Think, for instance, of a music review. As powerful a wordsmith as a critic might be, would you rather read about Eric Clapton's amazing solo during "Layla" at Madison Square Garden or listen to or watch an audio or video clip? Other media don't demean the importance or ubiquity of text, but offer a compelling way to build trust and community with your consumers or employees.

"Backstage with Barack"

Barack Obama understands the power and reach of social media. He and his campaign staff actively utilize multiple platforms such as Facebook, Digg, and Twitter (you can see all of the communities he's involved with here: http://my.barackobama.com/page/content/hqblog). However, many would argue it's his eloquence in presenting a speech that has captivated audiences since his introduction to the political arena with his keynote message to the Democratic Convention in 2004. While the sound of his voice and carefully crafted words are compelling, his physical demeanor and posture lend even more credibility to his presentation. By witnessing how he chooses to emphasize a word or phrase with a gesture, or noticing the softening of his features when speaking of his family, a viewer is able to build a level of trust with his message that the written medium can't match.

Barack and his staff have also proven to be artful in how they leverage the trust they've established with tactical steps toward gaining the upper hand in the presidential race. A prime example of this is a video Barack appears in for his "Backstage with Barack" campaign, which you can watch on YouTube: http://www.youtube.com/watch?v=eGysjOixVNs.

As a way to "open up the political process," Barack offers the chance for anyone who will make a donation to his campaign to potentially be selected as one of ten people (plus their guests) to go to Denver to attend the Democratic convention as he formally accepts his nomination. He states in the video that "there are no strings attached. You don't have to be well connected, you don't have to know someone powerful, you just have to be a part of this campaign" and "you'll be supporting our movement to bring change to America."

Here's why this video is an excellent example of how video can build trust while still being tactical—essentially, Barack is offering a chance for his constituents (aka fans) to see him in person, not unlike *Good Morning America* offering a chance for viewers to see a popular band live in New York City. But if you like Obama, sending five dollars for the chance to go to Denver is a small price to pay to both support your candidate and get the chance for a free trip. In other words, good PR can be transparent while still achieving a purpose. And if you prove you're listening as well as speaking (as Obama and his campaign do via their multiple social media platforms), you provide even greater opportunity to build trust since you demonstrate a community versus one-way focus.

And the more you listen and capture various conversations via video and other multimedia formats, the more you'll be in the right place at the right time to hear the ways consumers are already genuinely connecting to your brand (or campaign, in this example). Your job is not to manipulate what they say or how they say it, but to give them the vehicles to communicate what's important to them.

Not all people are writers, but most are storytellers in one fashion or another. After people grow accustomed to being on camera or using interactive media, they begin to feel an intimacy with these other mediums to express themselves; it's as if they were talking to a friend. The context of the situation where they're being recorded is important, but the medium's power is not just about the watcher but about the creator and subject. The prevalence of webcams and audio/video chat communities like BlogTalkRadio and Paltalk demonstrates the fact that we like to be heard and seen by our family, friends, and peers. Using video and interactive media for business echoes that innate desire and provides a powerful tool to enhance a connection with consumers.

Mike Donnelly's Video Diary: How Coca-Cola Is Listening

Coca-Cola recently designed an interactive campaign around the virtual world Second Life that asked entrants to create an "experience machine" that would vend the Coca-Cola brand experience instead of a bottle or can of Coke. (Shel was part of the marketing communications project team for this effort.) Given that the laws of physics don't apply to Second Life, residents could put their imaginations to the test. The winning entry would be transformed into a digital asset that Coca-Cola would give away for free to any Second Life resident who wanted one.

The contest, known as "Virtual Thirst," received a lot of press and attention from bloggers. Not all of the notice was positive, however; many potential entrants complained that the prize, a visit to California to help bring their winning idea to life, was too puny for an organization the size of Coke. Others worried about taxes they'd have to pay on a prize, that they couldn't submit entries using blogs versus the other channels Coke had created, and that they would be required to assign intellectual property rights for their ideas to Coca-Cola.

Mike Donnelly, marketing director at Coca-Cola and the project lead for the Virtual Thirst program, had been participating through the comment section of several blogs. He didn't simply set people straight, but participated in a conversation as an active and equal participant. To address the ongoing discussion of the four major areas of criticism, Donnelly recorded a video blog to respond to concerns and complaints. Here's a quote from the video, which was recorded without a script and posted to multiple locations, including YouTube: "We want to learn how to become better marketers. I'm doing this video blog specifically to share with you some of the most common comments that have come up so far and to address them as best I can."

A specific reaction to the concern over the prize for the contest was for Coke to reward half a million Linden dollars (the currency used within Second Life that has a real-world monetary value). "We hear you," Donnelly says in the video, "we're adding to it [the prize] and don't blow it all in one place."

The video went a long way to inspire trust in Donnelly and Coke inasmuch as his posting his thoughts and responses demonstrated he was listening to what people were saying about the initiative. Donnelly's video was personal and real, far different from a trite corporate statement distributed over the news wires. In the video, Donnelly explained that he tried to get around the tax issue by having a long conversation with his legal department but eventually lost: "You'll have to take that one up with the IRS," he said on the video. And Donnelly's delivery of the news was less apologetic than it was matter-of-fact, which shows that being transparent doesn't mean being weak or overly vulnerable. A lot of being transparent simply involves letting people know you're listening and are trying to address their needs, virtual or otherwise, and explaining why your organization made the decisions that it did.

One of the most vocal critics of the campaign, writing on the "Business and Games" blog, wound up embedding the video in his own post, adding, "All I can say is—WELL DONE! A very informal and concrete reply, showing they listened and understood what they were hearing. Where they went wrong in their response to the Coke/Mentos hype, by going corporate on our asses, this time they show their human face."

When the Nuts Saved *Jericho:* How CBS Showed It's Listening

When CBS announced it was canceling its drama *Jericho*, there was a huge outcry from passionate fans in forums and blogs to keep the show on the air. But it wasn't until Shaun Daily, a host with social broadcasting service BlogTalkRadio, urged his listeners to send nuts to CBS (in reference to a comment actor Skeet Ulrich said during the final episode and the fact that the network was crazy to cancel the show) that fans found a rallying initiative to keep their beloved *Jericho* on the air. (John is employed by BlogTalk Radio.) Within a few days, over forty thousand pounds of nuts had been delivered to CBS network's president of entertainment, Nina Tassler, who eventually wrote a letter to fans stating the network would create seven more episodes of the series. She also urged fans to spread the word about the show—and to stop sending the studios nuts.

Daily's guests the night of *Jericho*'s season finale included executive producer Carol Barbee and co-creator Joel Steinberg (it was the next night that Daily urged fans to send in nuts). The fact that Daily's program allows people to call in to the show meant fans could interact directly with the show creators. Multiple text forums provided an outlet for fans to express their passion, but the two-way audio interaction of Daily's show allowed show producers to listen directly to feedback in real time. Hearing directly from fans obviously had an impact on executive producer Carol Barbee, as she reported to Amy

Amatangelo in the *Washington Post*. In response to getting the show back on the air, Barbee stated:

> We had nothing to do with it. The fans all did it themselves. . . .
> [In the future] I will want to interface with them and want to
> listen to them. It's been a huge eye-opening experience and,
> I think for all of us, the great equalizer.[1]

CBS featured videos on one of its Web sites of Daily interviewing stars of the show, along with forums and a fan-focused blog. Actors from the series even thanked fans by video, as Daily notes in a video documenting the *Jericho* campaign produced by CBS for their site.

CBS earned a massive amount of trust and respect from fans when they showed they listened to them and brought *Jericho* back on the air. By engaging in call-in shows like Daily's and producing videos to prove they were taking action in response to fan initiative, they demonstrated how using interactive and rich media speaks to consumers.

CBS also demonstrated the importance of embracing consumers and providing platforms for them to talk about a brand. Their forums and other online platforms let fans know they were being heard. As Paul R. LaMonica from CNNMoney.com stated in his article, "The Nuts Save Jericho," "The fact that CBS blinked and is bringing back the show only three weeks after dumping it is yet another stunning sign of how the Internet can be used to organize grassroots campaigns." Alan Levy, cofounder and CEO of BlogTalkRadio, stated in the same article that "the Internet is transforming how TV will be produced. I have never seen anything like this. This could be a transforming event since it shows the ability for networks and producers to engage their audience."

Engagement involves dialogue that centers around trust and respect. By using video and other rich media, you can provide your brand's fans with platforms to have the conversations they're having elsewhere.

Ultimately the revived series was unable to sustain even its original fan base, with viewership dropping in its second season, leading CBS to cancel the series permanently. But opening the process to fans and involving them gave it a chance, which ultimately strengthens the bond between TV viewers and the network. Presumably those lines of communication remain open for future engagement around other projects.

Help for the Hill: Politics Gets Personal?

Micah L. Sifry is senior editor for the Personal Democracy Forum, an annual conference focused on the impact of technology on politics, which is held every year in New York City. Over the past few years, Sifry has also been exploring how the transparency implications of Internet technology can change the nature of America. For instance, He sees no technical reason that every person in the United States can't watch a congressional hearing in real time: "From a technical point of view, there is no reason now why we can't have that level of access to the levers of government—being able to see how the sausage is made. It is surprising what Congress and what government still thinks it is their prerogative to hide from us even though we pay for it."

A number of sites and organizations are working to help U.S. government become more open. One helpful site to track is OpenCongress.org, which "makes it easy to track any bill, issue area or Member of Congress." Another is the Sunlight Foundation, with which Sifry has worked on various projects to get elected representatives to be more accountable for their actions by tapping into technology. Sunlight has established "Congresspedia" and the making of "transparency grants" among other initiatives.[2] The Sunlight Foundation is cajoling members of Congress to start posting their daily work calendars online; about ten members have taken the foundation up on the offer so far. These calendars allow voters to see whom members are meeting with, along with other vital information that helps keep these legislators accountable to their constituents. Eventually these meeting calendars will be viewable on a month-by-month basis mapped on a Google map. Senator Jon Tester (D, Montana) publishes his schedule, and as Sifry points out, it shows that he mostly holds meetings with people from his home state. "And that is exactly what he should be doing, right? Where it gets weird is when you see the meeting with the head of the New York Stock Exchange, or the head of some other powerful interest that has nothing to do with his state, but for the most part, I think Senator Tester will gain from being transparent with his constituents about what he does because they will be able to judge themselves if this is the kind of work their representative should be doing."

Another member of Congress takes the earmarks (specialized requests in legislation that don't go through any standard review process) he receives for his district and puts them up on Google Earth. As Sifry explains, "You can actually go and view his congressional district in Google Earth and literally see the location of the variety of places where money is being spent on a medical center or police station and so on."

Sifry and the Sunlight Foundation's focus on technology in government demonstrates the growing inevitability of the public desire for greater transparency. It's a desire that's equally targeted toward the business realm as well as toward politics, and studying how forward-thinking politicians use multimedia tools to engender trust with their constituents gives a good example to follow for any organization.

It is dizzying to imagine the uses to which tools like Google Earth and Google Maps can be put. For example, Google Earth now features red flame icons over Darfur, and mousing over each one produces information about the daily death and destruction there. Zoom in, and the flames spread out, showing even more destruction, and satellite images give a close-up bird's-eye view of the devastation. Produced in cooperation with the U.S. Holocaust Memorial Museum, the project is an eye-opening look at how something as simple as a map can become a power-ful communication tool in the interactive, online world, making remote parts of the world transparent to anybody with a computer and an Internet account.

The GE on Demand Audio and Video Series

Josh Karpf, one of the chief strategists behind GE's audio/video series called "GE on Demand," had been experimenting with podcasting since early 2005. In a desire to open the company to the outside world, his team brought cameras to GE's Global Research Center in upstate New York, where nine lab managers told viewers what they were working on. Speaking in lay terms, the world-renowned scientists' views, according to Karpf, "made really compelling stories."

For many of us, GE has a mystique as a company not unlike the Willy Wonka Chocolate Factory. We embrace its products but wonder what could actually be taking place inside the walls of their labs. By creating a series of videos featuring the scientists behind GE products, we're allowed a glimpse into the nature of invention and innovation that has shaped one of the world's leading firms. The company transforms from a monolithic giant into a group of passionate workers engaged in worthy pursuits. Even if we don't identify with all the ideas provided by a leading nanotechnologist, we certainly appreciate his desire to share his ideas with us in a transparent fashion.

"We are a big company," says Karpf, "and podcasts, both audio and video, let us share our stories with our stakeholders in a new way. It gives them the freedom to learn more about any topic within the GE universe and watch and listen to it on their own time."

Karpf is alluding here to the notion of just-in-time, which describes the process of delivering a message using media that consumers or employees can consume when it's best for them. For instance, an audio podcast can be listened to while walking the dog or driving, where reading would be impossible (or, at the very least, unsafe). And many would rather watch a short video than read an entire white paper. It's up to companies to provide messaging in multiple formats to suit the preferences of the people they're trying to reach.

How Nike Plus Builds Community and Changes the Role of Advertising

In a combination of savvy use of technology and community integration, Nike has created a unique product and experience around its Nike Plus initiative. Working in conjunction with Apple (and its iPod Nano), runners can place a sensor in their sneakers (Nike Plus footwear has a special pocket designed for this) that tracks data about a run and reports the information in real time to a runner's iPod Nano. Pace, time, distance, and calories burned are reported and saved so runners can upload their progress for themselves or share it with others around the world. They connect with an international community focused on a passion for running and get motivated by peer support.

From a multimedia perspective, letting a runner hear her progress while listening to music means Nike reaches consumers exactly where they are, as opposed to assuming they'll engage in typical forms of advertising. Connecting with consumers on this level is a trend Nike plans to continue, according to Stefan Olander, global director for brand connections at Nike, who reported to *New York Times* writer Louise Story that "we want to find a way to enhance the experience and services, rather than looking for a way to interrupt people from getting to where they want to go. How can we provide a service that the consumer goes, 'Wow, you really made this easier for me'?"[3]

The success of the Nike Plus program is demonstrated by the fact that consumers who use the product typically come back to the site three times a week. The ramifications of this form of pull advertising are significant, considering that Nike has dropped its television budget 55 percent from ten years ago.[4] Money is being focused on new media applications and initiatives focused on "advertising as experience" like the Nike Running Club on the third floor of its New York City store, where five coaches and seventeen pacers are available to lead runs three times a week in Central Park. Although people are not hit with multiple marketing messages, many visitors are still seen with the Nike swoosh on their shirts and sneakers during runs.

People want to be associated with good ideas, especially ones that suit their lifestyles, educate them on their passions, and introduce them to others who share their interests. Integrating audio and video with an online community and creating an experience for users is a growing trend that will likely supplant in-your-face marketing before the end of the decade.

How Companies Use Multimedia for Internal Applications

Podcasting and IBM's Media Library

George Faulkner has led IBM's podcasting initiative since 2005 and works on the corporate new media team at Big Blue. In a blog post from November 5, 2007, he eloquently describes how podcasting was a natural extension of the company's blogging initiative and the benefits of using audio to complement text: "The power of the human voice can be an extremely effective communications tool and, for the first time, we would be able to have a platform for sharing our joy, our pain, our triumphs, our experiences."

The media library provides tools to help IBMers create content, and Faulkner reports that the most common forms of media produced are audio interviews, speeches, and recordings from conference calls. (Video is catching up in the form of audio-enhanced slide shows.) In a recent speech, Faulkner noted that one of the company's most popular podcasts featured a battle of the bands comprising IBMer rockers. "That was the moment I realized this wasn't about knowledge sharing; it was about community building."

For a company as large, diverse, and spread out as IBM, audio and video are playing a decisive role in building community. And reading about a battle of the bands pales in comparison to hearing songs played or seeing bands in action. As the focus on creating media grows with the adoption of updated technology, the trend for companies to create libraries like IBM's will continue to grow. And when organizations provide such a forum, they show employees that they're interested in hearing their voices, not just those of management.

Podcasting and Microsoft's Academy Mobile Program

Microsoft's Academy Mobile program, like IBM's media library, provides employees with the tools and platform to create and share media with colleagues. As noted on the Microsoft Sharepoint Product Group Blog, Academy Mobile provides a "social computing experience with podcasts, RSS feeds and community driven dialogue." To help encourage participation in the program, Microsoft distributed six thousand micro-SD memory cards (these are a small flash memory card) to sales team members with preloaded information on how to create media. It also created a rewards program for top contributors. In short, it is working to facilitate the easiest introduction and adoption of new media tools as possible.

Academy Mobile boldly does what so many companies are concerned about doing: put communications in the hands of employees. The audio and video podcasts produced are not corporate controlled and are not subject to any kind of review and approval process. The program facilitates the transfer of knowledge from employee to employee using an engaging tool employees will want to use, both to share their own knowledge and consume that of their colleagues.

In a video describing Academy Mobile produced for a meeting of field employees and then uploaded to YouTube, employees describe how users can rate and comment on other people's podcasts and build community around content. The video is also largely aimed at Microsoft's large sales force and describes the program's aim to provide a one-stop shop for short, role-based content that can educate people in the field. Director of the academy and events Phil Morel comments on the focus behind the program: "I believe that 99 percent of what the field needs to know is already out there in the field. I believe our responsibility is to connect you in the field to other people in the field and to share that experience and to share that knowledge."

If you've ever worked in sales, you know how vital it is to talk to colleagues and share best practices. No matter how good internal documentation or training may be, hearing from colleagues in the field on techniques they've employed to close sales is of the utmost importance. Selling takes place outside your environment, so encapsulating customer reaction to products, services, and pricing is critical to gaining an accurate picture of how you're perceived in the marketplace.

The just-in-time aspect is another compelling reason to provide a sales force with tools, as Microsoft has done. Many sales representatives drive for hours to visit clients. To best make use of that "windshield time," consider creating training modules that consist of colleagues discussing best practices from the past week. Think how better equipped sales representatives will be if they walk into a meeting after a long drive, having just finished listening to advice from ten top-selling colleagues on the issues most important to customers. In this way, providing transparent tools for your organization boosts profit margins as well as community and trust among your employees.

Conclusion

The uses to which multimedia can be put for any organization are endless: town hall meetings using podcasts, video diaries in forums for consumers, or audio white papers downloaded onto iPods for employee training. And the media should be coming from your audience as well as management to encourage dialogue and best practice ideas vetted by the community at large. Trust begins when people who aren't normally listened to are provided a platform to speak. Find ways to foster conversation and take a step back to see how people honestly engage with your brand.

Transparency accrues from multimedia in a variety of ways, not the least of which is the ability to see and hear real people, making it far easier to judge their credibility than with more traditional text. And as an added benefit, the barriers to the production of multimedia have crumbled. What once required a professional crew, expensive equipment, and costly distribution channels now can be produced for little, or even no, money and distributed over the Net at little or no cost.

If you truly want to show your face to the world, multimedia is one of the best channels for doing so.

13

PROFILE AND PRIVACY

Transparency in Social Networks

Elli Font is one of the animal stars of GE's Ecomagination commercial and owner of a MySpace page replete with her picture, blog entries, and personal information. She's a fictional pachyderm, mind you: the profile was created for General Electric by advertising agency BBDO Worldwide in an effort to "explore media beyond conventional commercials and print." Reporter Stuart Elliott quotes Judy L. Hu, global executive director for advertising and branding at General Electric, as to the motivation behind the campaign: "It's a challenge whenever you try to do something new, but it's energizing. Clearly, we're taking a risk, but that's what you need to do to break through."[1]

The overall campaign was a large success, inasmuch as viewers who watched the spots clicked through to GE's site and spent an average of two-and-a-half minutes there. But the creation of the MySpace profile also demonstrated that GE recognized the importance of reaching audiences where they were: both where they spent their time online and in a fashion that resonated with the culture, standards, and norms of that community.

Elli's profile demonstrates the kind of payoff a company can earn if it is willing to take the time to analyze the profiles of MySpace residents. It's written in a playful but not mocking tone and shows that someone spent time creating a page that reflects the personality of an imaginary pachyderm versus thinly veiled marketing rhetoric. GE/BBDO recognized that posting anything akin to an advertisement would instantly turn off the MySpace community and harm the brand more than help.

The New Watercoolers

Where do you think the real work gets done for an organization? It has long been posited that it's the discussions in the hallways during a conference or deals made over drinks that demonstrate the real corridors of power for business. In other words, social environments provide an atmosphere of openness and authenticity not found in the typical office setting. The corporate paradigm shifts from formal to frank, and business is expedited largely due to transparency. It's harder to hide or lie in a social environment.

Online social networks like Facebook and MySpace provide virtual venues to build an authentic rapport with colleagues, employees, or customers. Depending on the network, implied or stated standards of conduct allow varying degrees of intimacy in regard to information you can share about yourself or your organization. Knowing how to navigate the various environments can provide you with multiple venues to engage in transparent conversation with people who can help you improve your products, services, and brand perception.

Participating in social networks for your organization also presents important legal and privacy issues that must be addressed when people are creating posting profiles willy-nilly across the Web. When digital footprints exist online in perpetuity, campaigns need to be structured in order to comply with the guidelines established by your organization before profiles or media are created and posted. Companies need to determine the makeup of various networks and reflect their brands according to the voice and tone of each community. The online identity for you and your business has much to do with the perception of where that identity exists. The context of where your message lives provides as much information as the message itself. Positioning yourself according to the environment you're entering is of utmost importance for the modern brand.

Social Networking

For a number of years, forums were the main tool used by people wanting to communicate with others online. Via AOL or other entry points, people would chat in text form, typically congregating around common subject matters or interests. Although the forums could be called social, they were disparate in nature, meaning you would typically encounter the same individual in separate forums either because you connected and agreed to meet elsewhere, or by sheer luck or similar interests found one another frequenting the same boards.

Social networks like MySpace, Bebo, and Facebook provided a key step in the evolution of online interaction since members of a community can connect, share photos, and leave messages for one another, all within the same environment. In Facebook, for example, you can e-mail a friend without having to use Outlook or another client: simply send a message or write on the person's wall without ever venturing to a new URL. For many, having this closed community provides an intimacy and comfort level not found with other tools online. Social networks also take on their own feel and inherent community etiquette, so comments or photos on MySpace may take on a different quality from those on Facebook. This phenomenon is akin to leaving one nightclub and going to another where the atmosphere and population vary from one location to the next.

Although there are multiple ways to network socially online, sites like Bebo provide a context for Internet interaction that is new for many users and is providing a unique paradigm to forge friendships and business connections in a context unlike any seen before.

A Cultural Context

A good way to think about venturing into the social networking space is to ask how you might approach visiting a club or group to which a friend has invited you. Would you burst through the door spouting your company's URL or passing out glossy photos of steak knives? Of course not. Even if the group focused on business networking, you'd take the time to socialize and network before passing out a business card or talking up your firm. The same mentality applies online. You'll be ignored if you don't establish your own voice for your profile. Being passionate about your business isn't an issue, but hawking your wares without providing real value or education means you won't get visited more than once.

A good rule of thumb before posting in any community is to visit pages and profiles for at least a couple of weeks before even commenting on others' pages, whether it's a "wall" (the communal watering hole on Facebook) or the comment section of somebody's blog. What's important to the overall community? What groups do you naturally gravitate toward for yourself or your business, and why? What's the tone of most posts? Like any other social relationship, the first step toward understanding online networks is listening to the people who already populate the network.

A topic for a book in its own right, social networks are now rivaling traditional news organizations with their ability to rapidly disseminate information to niche communities and galvanize them to action. A recent example is the Virginia Tech shootings in 2007 and the use of Facebook and other social networking sites like LiveLeak that students used to report moment-by-moment updates of events. An article in the blog "Mashable" by Pete Cashmore highlights how widespread and culturally relevant social networks have become for the users who frequent them, stating, "These groups are becoming the main way for students to express their condolences."

Another example of the impact of social networks on the culture at large is the use of Twitter to help aid workers during recent California wildfires. Twitter allows users to send short form text-based messages to a large number of users in groups organized around a particular subject matter. For the fires, "tweets" (the nickname for Twitter messages) conveyed up-to-date information on the fires and allowed people to talk about their situations in real time faster than if they had used traditional media.

Beyond the integration of citizen reporters into the journalism mix, the use of social networking tools during the forest fires demonstrates that a growing population is available only or primarily through those networks. Targeting people to learn about your business means recognizing where they spend their time and how they communicate. If they live online (Internet or mobile phone), your company needs to understand this and reach out to them there. More important, being transparent and authentic means you need to work to identify with a community you want to approach and speak with authenticity as a participant in that community.

A Multicultural Context and SAP's Global Survey

Shel Israel, prominent blogger and coauthor of *Naked Conversations*, one of the first books to look at the impact of blogs on business, has worked in conjunction with SAP to create a global survey to discover the impact of social media on culture and business.[2] As of February 2008, Israel had interviewed people in more than thirty-two countries. He worked in conjunction with Mike Prosceno, vice president of communications at SAP, who recounts the origins of study as a means to understand how the world at large uses social media tools:

If we [SAP] were going to move down this path with any kind of a meaning to what we were doing, we really had to understand how the world uses social media; whether they call it social media, the tools they use, local language is important, how this culture applied to engagement with the market at all. This was an incredibly eye-opening experience for me personally but also the learnings that we're getting from the survey are being utilized inside the organization in as many different capacities as one could imagine.

The survey has helped SAP work with its developers, customers and partners, and "every aspect of the ecosystem or community that surrounds SAP," according to Prosceno. Because SAP is a global brand, understanding the nature of how people communicate online around the world plays a vital role in the organization's success. For instance, working in the BRICK countries (Brazil, Russia, India, China, and Korea) requires companies to be proficient in the languages of those countries from both a literal and cultural standpoint. The Global Survey has helped SAP understand that in a country like Russia, where a fairly controlled media environment exists, large citizen-journalism sites are springing up all the time, "And they don't have ten contributors," Prosceno points out. "We're talking on the order of magnitude of hundreds or close to *thousands* of contributors. So if we're going to put all of our eggs in a basket for speaking to the people of Russia, it benefits us to have a dual strategy of going to traditional media outlets as well as these new citizen journalism sites."

Israel points out another dimension of social media: "In every one of the thirty-two countries where we spoke to well over fifty people, it was clear that social media were driven by people under the age of thirty. This survey gives me a data point that makes it pretty clear that young people are emerging to be the market of the future." Israel concludes that when these young people from all over the world come into the workplace, they're going to look for social media tools on the job. Their primary modes of communication rely on social networking tools, and if those tools aren't part of an organization, people won't want to work there. "So to me," Israel continues, "the message to businesses of all sizes, or to organizations of all sizes, is that if you're going to try to see what your business is going to look like three, five, and ten years down the line, you've got to turn to social media for a way of doing business."

The survey provides a great example of the pragmatic nature of tactical transparency along with the massive benefits enjoyed from working to communicate effectively with other cultures around the world. Social media and social networks break down language and cultural barriers to allow people to communicate about the business or other issues they're most passionate about. Not knowing how young people or other countries use modern communication tools to speak to the world means you won't be speaking their language or doing business with them anytime soon.[3]

Getting Down to Business

It's easy to discount social networking sites as having little or no value for business, but the lines between outlets that are strictly for business or strictly personal have blurred. A network you frequent for entertainment purposes may lead to business, for instance. The speed at which you can build relationships over the Internet also provides an accelerated way to network never available before today. Avoiding the opportunity to create relationships in these environments would be like skipping *all* conferences because some may be considered a waste of your time.

Most important, any environment that allows authentic business relationships to form or mature is certainly of interest to any business. Reaching employees or colleagues is as crucial to a business as reaching a customer.

Anatomy of a Profile. Profiles are the pages or areas individuals create within a community to present specifics about themselves they want to share about themselves. Although sites vary, profiles typically have this information:

- *Personal information.* Name, location (usually general rather than a specific address), age, and gender.

- *An avatar.* This can be in the form of a picture, a cartoon, or a second-life avatar image. (A second-life avatar is a virtual representation of one's identity within a second life. People create their bodies and clothing and can take human or other forms.)

- *Contact information.* Typically this encompasses where a person works (if it's a personal blog) or other URLs, e-mail, Skype handle, and so on.[4] Most new media creators are not shy about letting you know where to contact them. Social networks like LinkedIn and Facebook also allow participants to share previous employment, academic history, and other résumé-like information.

- *Who's in their community.* Often you'll see a square box somewhere on the page with the pictures of other people's avatars who are part of the network. For services like Twitter, you can follow or be followed by users interested in your posts. These messages can aggregate and appear online, or be "pushed" to your phone by short messaging service or instant messaging so you're always up to date with your friends' activities.

- *Links to favorites.* Sometimes called a *blogroll*, this is where a person lists favorite sites, blogs, podcasts, or other sites. What's implied is that if someone reads their work, they'll also like the people on their blogroll.

- *Media subscription.* If a person has created media in the form of a podcast, videocast, or blog, others are typically encouraged to subscribe to a person's RSS feed so they can have it delivered whenever fresh material is created. Measuring how many people have subscribed to a show or blog not only allows a creator to gauge an audience but to potentially go to advertisers with those numbers if they choose to monetize through ads.

- *Other elements*. Depending on the nature of the tool used— a blog, a microblogging utility, a profile on a social network like LinkedIn or MySpace—a profile can contain any num-ber of other elements, including a geographical location, a list of groups to which the individual belongs, and a place for visitors to make contact.

Depending on the community, profiles can vary in tone from professional to candid. But they quickly allow a user to identify areas they want to highlight to the virtual world around them.

Self-Branding. One intriguing aspect of social networking is the notion of self-branding. A relatively new phenomenon, this is the practice of creating multiple profiles in various commu-nities to create an aggregate overall picture of who you are online and off. How and what a person chooses to portray about essentially equates to a new media bio, demonstrating how active he or she is in various communities. For instance, you may list your LinkedIn profile, Twitter information, Skype handle, Flickr photos, Second Life Avatar name, and MySpace page location. Six simple links let visitors to your site or page know a wealth of information about how you live online. But beyond your interests, you're providing multiple portals to see what you choose to share with the world.

Jonathan Vanasco, founder and CEO of FindMeOn, an online identity syndicator and management system, considers how we tend to separate our various personas online:

> My LinkedIn and my Facebook account are more professional and collegiate in tone than my MySpace page, which is a lot more laid back. In real life I try to keep these things separate. But online I know that when I post on MySpace or LinkedIn or Facebook that I am the person who is the combination of all these different sites.

Vanasco's words echo the importance of understanding the individuals within any social networking community you're trying to reach. They provide insight into the multiple dimensions of the individuals who have different motivations for participating in the various online arenas where they engage. "People sometimes forget that the way they'd like to talk and present themselves on one network or blog," he continues, "might not actually be in line with the prevailing social norms of that group."

Self-branding in this fashion is relevant to business because your brand is being discussed in different ways and examined from different angles on each of these diverse networks, Web sites, and online forums. And when seeking to engage in those conversations, you need to be aware of the community you enter to obtain real value for your efforts.

The Trust Filter. Social networks provide a speed of information. However, they also serve as a trust filter through which you have access to various perspectives on and reactions to news delivered through your network. By the time you've heard five different people chime in on the same subject, you not only have a sense of a story but can deem it credible or not based on what you have learned about the sources doing the reporting.

Rachel Happe, who leads IDC's research on the digital business economy, describes this filtering process by noting that with social networking tools, "conversations are persistent, transparent to wider audiences and more inclusive." The nature of conversations within this paradigm produces a greater trust and perceived authenticity that alters the landscape of business communication.

Most of us couldn't imagine not having the Internet as a news resource. We also can't remember life without e-mail, which, with a single click, allows us to reach out to dozens of friends to ask their opinion on subjects of import or interest. Social networking expands the size of the population you are able to interact with on a regular basis, and it doesn't matter where they live. You may use Twitter most often with friends in Australia or poke friends on

Facebook who live in Tokyo. But when major news breaks, any or all of them may immediately contact you over the network, giving you a unique perspective that you couldn't have gotten in the past.

Happe's point about the conversational nature of social networking is important to note as well. Reading a press release is nothing like hearing information on a subject sent by a friend. And although emotion in messaging may imply subjectivity, it doesn't signify a lack of sincerity or integrity.

The filtering process will grow increasingly important as online networking matures, for both individuals and for organizations. Now, most organizations getting involved in social networking are trying to decide which sites to invest in and how many people to "friend" or connect with on a regular basis. Sometimes it's hard to distinguish substance from noise. But the filtering question is largely technical; individuals will soon choose to whom they want to listen, through which channels, and when. But the power of those rapid, informal, and trusted communications is one of the most compelling facets of social networking.

LinkedIn: Your Virtual Rolodex

People tend to forget that LinkedIn is a social network, perhaps because it has been around longer than other networks or isn't as interactive as some sites. However, the nature of the site is clearly articulated, in a large font, on LinkedIn's "About" page where it states that "relationships matter."

LinkedIn has become almost universally accepted as a primary means of networking for business online. When researching a competitor, identifying someone you'd like to target for business, or checking a friend's latest résumé, it's an invaluable tool to learn not only what a person has posted about himself or herself, but who has recommended this person and who he or she knows. We tend to judge people by the company they keep, and LinkedIn provides a marvelous context for understanding someone's overall community much more than a simple résumé alone ever could.

The site has also created new features to improve the quality of social networking for business. One tool allows you to see events in your industry and know who will be attending them— an invaluable application to help you best maximize your time at events or avoid them if nobody you need to meet is attending. This provides an excellent example of how transparency can provide business value. By knowing the details of colleagues' schedules, you can better plan your own time. It's a marvelous application of using social networking tools to streamline your calendar and maximize your networking.

Hire Learning: Ernst & Young's Paid Facebook Page

Creating profiles on social networking sites has become commonplace for major brands, and it's companies like GE with Elli that are reaping the benefits of interacting in an authentic way with an online community. Companies whose profiles read essentially like ads, however, are seeing either no response or a negative one because they aren't grasping the essential nature of these sites. The sites are social, so posting sales pitches is only going to turn people off and prove you don't know what you're doing. The networking part of the sites also means that when you enter a community, you're expected to bring value along with your participation. Simply asking for favors without giving back will get you ostracized sooner than later.

Ernst & Young is one organization that has been having great success with its sponsored Facebook page. (Companies pay for sponsored pages, a form of advertising, as opposed to the free and purely social profiles individuals create.) Geared toward recruiting entry-level workers and interns from the ranks of college graduates, the page contains discussion boards and other information designed to smooth students' transition into the

E&Y workforce. As of January 2007, about fifty-one hundred Facebook users linked to the E&Y page, and the feedback on the initiative has been largely positive, as Steven Rothberg notes in CollegeRecruiter.com: "College students and other members of Gen Y reward employers who embrace transparency. Recruiters who tell highly qualified candidates that they must apply through traditional channels will lose those candidates if those candidates want to connect through newer channels such as Facebook."

It's of huge importance to note that not using social networking tools well means a company runs the risk of appearing irrelevant to younger or future employees. Not grasping the essential nature of communicating in an authentic manner with the technology effectively tells digital natives you're not willing to speak to them in their own language. More than seeming out of touch, you may appear downright clueless to them.

Facebook Fridays: Serena Software Redefines Productivity

Jeremy Burton is CEO of Serena Software, an eight-hundred-employee firm based in San Mateo, California. He recently instituted the practice of "Facebook Fridays," where he encourages employees to spend one hour of personal time at the office "on their Facebook profiles and connect with co-workers, customers, family and friends." In an article Burton wrote for ZDNet Asia, he makes the case for encouraging employee interaction on social networks instead of blocking them: "For most people, the human drive to connect and share is stronger than the duty to spend every possible moment "being productive." If your employees are going to socialize at work anyway, why not encourage them to channel their social media impulses in smart, safe ways that can potentially help your business?

Burton provides concrete examples of how employees can help the business through their social networking activities and suggests that even though some problems are likely to arise, they're minor compared to the benefits to the company.

I Am What IM: Twitter

Twitter allows a person to post up to 140 characters of text that can be read online or over the phone (through an instant message client or short message service). By creating a tweets group with friends or colleagues, you can also send "tweets" that will be read only by the specific individuals you choose to direct your messages to. You can also post a widget (that is, a small icon) on your blog that displays your latest tweets online.

Initially people were encouraged to tell others what they were doing over their tweets. And many still do. But as evidenced by the forest fire example, rapidly deployed short-form communication can be put to multiple uses, and Twitter has become a sort of Web 2.0 telegraph system (one that uses Internet services on devices in addition to a computer—typically the phone via text messaging).

Beyond the speed and trust filter elements of messages received via the Twitter network, "microblogging" (as many have started to call Twitter, along with its brethren like Jaiku and Pownce) also provides an enormous level of intimacy not found in any other online medium. Many people announce where they're going throughout the day over their tweets, whom they're meeting with, and so on. Reading a person's Twitter Stream is akin to scanning his or her diary. Chris Brogan, a new-media authority and cofounder of the unconventional gathering called Podcamp (known as an "unconference"), is a well-known Twitter fanatic (at the time of writing he had posted well over ten thousand tweets; many call him the "Mayor of Twitterville"). In regard to the personal nature of Twitter, he says, "Twitter is the social medium that is bringing a sense of humanity to our living web right now and it is helping gather unstructured, unformatted information that otherwise wouldn't have a home in a blog post or something like that."

Brogan raises an interesting point about information that wouldn't normally have a home and is now being transmitted via Twitter. Formulating a blog post or podcast or other form of media typically means you're preparing and editing versus communicating off the cuff. Because they tend to be more spontaneous, Twitter messages typically have a level of authenticity and transparency because of their raw nature. More often than not, people text their message, and they're done. There's only so much editing you can do with 140 characters.

Along these lines, people have also come to realize that Twitter can be a powerful marketing tool. It's a newer medium and can rise above the clutter of e-mail messages and phone calls. It's like getting a virtual nudge from a friend who can speak volumes with just a few texted words.

The nature of Twitter as a new paradigm for communication makes it extremely interesting for the enterprise environment, and many are exploring its applications within the workplace. One simple use is to set up Twitter groups for your company when you go to a conference so you instantly contact everyone at once ("meet us in the café for lunch in ten"). Many more applications are on the horizon, although issues of privacy and how to manage tweets for your brand are still being explored.

Employees Twittering about work—say, with other members of the Twitter community who have the same types of jobs—fall into the same category as employees blogging about work. It provides customers and members of other publics with an unfiltered, authentic, and honest view into the company.

Keeping It Safe While Keeping It Real

Although there can't be a heavy-handed policy to stifle authentic communication, guidelines for conduct at the workplace (and the communications sent while there) provide employees with a sense of how they can be brand champions while still expressing their unique ideas. Guidelines should also provide employees insights into how their conduct away from the workplace (online and off) could also reflect on their organization. The line between our personal and business lives has blurred with quick access to our personal information online, so companies need to set standards for behavior that allow for authenticity within set boundaries.

One of the most thorough examples of guidelines for social networking online is IBM's *Virtual World Guidelines*, established for employees engaged in worlds like Second Life. Beyond the standard caveats found in most blogging guidelines, IBM's messaging delves into the nature of avatar ownership and how an employee should handle his or her avatar when not at work, when being identified as an IBM employee could have repercussions.

Of interest here is that if general business culture begins to actively participate in virtual worlds, issues of identity will become of paramount importance. For instance, if you're in Second Life and someone's avatar approaches you and says he or she works for IBM, how can you prove that? How can the other person? And if you decide to conduct business together, will you do so within Second Life or decide to call each other on the phone in the real world? Whatever transpires, IBM's guidelines provide a model to emulate for creating guidelines of your own.

Proving Your Online Identity: BeenVerified.Com

It's easy to sound as if you know what you're talking about when posting a comment on a blog, but how do people really know who you are? You could say you're a doctor, but would you seriously consider medical advice left as a comment on a blog unless you could verify that the author did indeed go to medical school, earn a degree, and obtain a license to practice medicine?

BeenVerified.com is a service that provides online tools that allow people to prove that they are who they claim to be. "There's a difference in the quality of the content [you read online] because of the source," says BeenVerified CEO Josh Levy. "Our service allows enough transparency so that if you see a Wikipedia posting about cancer, you can know if it was a doctor who made the post or some guy who runs a repair shop."

The service provides a number of pragmatic steps that can be emulated by any organization seeking to adhere to social networking guidelines. For instance, BeenVerified allows people to show just their credentials and accomplishments without identifying their name (when a user posts information on their site). In this way people can achieve a level of credibility while retaining anonymity.

Levy says that although many companies were providing ways for people to work and meet online, "what they were missing was that one extra step that let the people within the community trust each other." Many social networking sites are susceptible to scams of one form or another, where having online identity tools in place could help thwart such practices. In fact, to prove the point, Levy started a profile on LinkedIn for a nonexistent woman who supposedly went to Harvard University and began linking her identity with other people who were at Harvard the same year. "She now has 12 LinkedIn friends that have all gone to Harvard," says Levy. "I created this profile of a person who doesn't exist—it's crazy what you can really do on the Internet if you really want to."

Participating in services like BeenVerified and others like it will become commonplace for individuals and organizations in the near future. And their call for online accountability is certainly welcome in an atmosphere where conversations take place out of context with regard to identity. Knowing who you're really talking to is a vital step toward authentic communication.

Conclusion

Social networking offers an opportunity for companies to engage in authentic conversation with their employees and customers. It's immediate and personal and allows modes of communication that can't be found in traditional e-mail or phone conversations. But a social networking strategy also needs to be implemented for an organization, largely based on Jonathan Vanasco's notion about thinking:

> The Internet reflects this very classical American tendency of instant gratification and instant interaction. You don't really think before you post online. You don't think about the context or tone of what you're saying or how does it fit into a larger dialogue. I think for the most part what people need to do more is think.

Remember that overall, the online community values transparency and authenticity above any flashy marketing campaign. Entering into any social network means understanding how that world operates and respecting cultural standards. And you're allowed to explore and investigate; you don't need to launch a major initiative your first time creating a profile.

What to Do Next

- Visit a number of social networking sites and see how they work. You don't have to join until you feel comfortable doing so. Think of yourself as a digital tourist, and soak in the various online cultures to get a sense of the people in their communities.

- Revisit sites that capture your attention. Becoming an active member in any community, online or off, takes time. Getting to know the nuances of a particular social network means that once you join, you'll know how to operate within the context of that environment.

- Join a network (or more than one) where you feel a kinship with a community. Some networks are so large (like Facebook or MySpace) that you can join and connect with a limited group of friends to explore how the tools within that community function as a user. Experiment with community tools to discover which ones you like and which ones don't work for you.

- Blend your online personas by listing the networks you belong to at your central online portal (your main Web site page or blog, for instance). Posting this information will allow people to connect with you because you've organized and presented this information where it's clearly visible.

- Adapt the lessons you learn for your personal interactions with social networks for your business. Once you've developed a shorthand within various communities, you'll know where you can talk about your work and not be perceived as a salesperson. Being passionate about what you do is not pitching, especially if you're engaged in dialogue versus digital soap boxing.

14

THE CASE FOR FACE-TO-FACE

Transparency in Person

There's just no substitute for meeting in
meatspace. As Facebook, Twitter, and other
social tools become more prevalent on the Web,
it's easy to stay connected to the people we meet
online and off, but there's something indelible
about coming together to make something
great happen.

—Eric Skiff, community evangelist,
Clipmarks.com

Transparency is hard to fake in person. Someone who confronts
you at work or a party will see your expression and your body
language as a response to his or her accusation. In the same way,
when you see a friend, you can hug your friend and look into his
or her eyes without relying on a webcam.

Knowing it's impossible to meet face-to-face as often as we
might like, business relationships can be greatly enhanced (or
diminished) by the ways we interact when we *are* able to connect in person. Fortunately, a lot of business events are shifting
to embrace transparency in the way they're organized in an
effort to stimulate interaction among attendees. And digital
natives of all ages hunger for in-person interactions where they
can eschew their computers and phones, at least until later,
when they will Twitter about the event or upload audio or video
about the people they have met.

The "Unconference" Movement

Traditionally most business conferences are not designed to be interactive. There are parties to attend, to be sure, but the content at events is delivered by keynotes and panelists. Attendees listen passively unless there's time for a few moderated questions at the end of a session.

"Unconferences" do away with much of the formality that exists around the traditional conference model, largely because everyone who comes is an active participant rather than a passive attendee. Wikis are typically used for registration—for people who want to come and those who want to speak. The logic here is that everyone has something to say, so why shouldn't they say it? For some unconferences, there's even a model under which you're expected to speak; being a wallflower isn't even an option.

Many unconferences are called "camps" in reference to the origin of one of the earliest (if not the earliest) unconferences, Barcamp, the first of which took place in Palo Alto, California, in August 2005. Hosted by Ross Mayfield, founder of wiki provider Socialtext, the first barcamp took place as a spin-off of O'Reilly Media's annual invitation-only Foo Camp. Inspired by the participatory nature of Foo Camp and pushing the democratic nature of the event to allow anyone to attend or speak, barcamps struck a chord and have now taken place in over thirty-one countries.

Multiple camps have arisen from the original barcamp, each with its own unique spin. Podcamp initially focused on podcasting but has since come to embrace all forms of new media. Startup Camp focuses on the start-up community. Whatever the name, unconference sessions often feel like fifty minutes worth of the hallway discussions you have at typical conferences. Monologues are replaced with dialogues, and the conversation becomes the focus rather than an accidental by-product.

Unconferences offer a unique form of organization and self-policing that lend tools to the transparent nature of events:

- *Organization as facilitation*. Unconference organizers are usually unpaid volunteers whose chief role is to help events run smoothly versus designing content for the event. Wikis are used for participants to register to attend and to speak.

- *No pitching*. Unconferences mirror traditional conferences in the sense that speakers are strongly urged not to use their sessions as thinly veiled advertisements. Speakers who ignore this rule at unconferences are likely to receive a fierce backlash of online vitriol due to the democratic and open nature of the event.

- *Rule of two feet*. As a further safeguard against potential pitches and as a way to ensure an event can be exactly what participants would like to make it, people enter and leave unconference sessions throughout a talk. The philosophy here is that no one should have to endure a topic he or she is not interested in just to subscribe to common conference etiquette. Speakers are reminded of this practice so they don't take offense, but it's also a challenge to make their talk as captivating as possible and work to provide an interactive atmosphere where everyone is engaged.

- *Show me the money*. As part of the wiki for an event, organizers are urged to either disclose direct contributions from sponsors (as most unconferences are free) or reveal other funding sources. Full disclosure is a given for unconferences as a safeguard against any unwanted sponsor influence over content or misallocation of funds.

- *Sticky spontaneity*. Many camps don't require or even ask for people to sign up for sessions before the day of the event; rather, they provide an empty wall and multiple colored sticky notes for people to simply post what they'd like to talk about and when. Organizers provide rooms and times, and speakers talk on a first-post, first-speak basis.

Transparency takes place in context. If you're attending a conference that's focused on listening versus participating, it may be easier to avoid interacting with other attendees and keep to yourself. And it should be noted that the surge in popularity of the unconference model does not diminish the value of the traditional conference model; we all have times when we want to focus more on listening than on speaking or interacting.

But being face-to-face with peers in a setting like an unconference means you'll be challenged not just to socialize but to participate. Transparency is typically most apparent in action: how you respond during discussions and deal with immediate input gives others an intimate glimpse into who you really are. Talking in real time means you can't hang back and craft a blog post as part of an ongoing discussion. Events like unconferences are challenging in the sense that you're expected to bring your voice to the overall conversation taking place. If it's your honest voice, you'll be embraced. If you're pitching or saying what you think you should, you'll be challenged. Face-to-face or in your face: the choice is up to you.

Eric Skiff, quoted at the start of the chapter, sums up a central value of unconferences and the need for transparency found only in face-to-face interaction: "It seems that we've all got an innate need to share what we know, and a platform to do that is as welcome to those who get to listen as it is to those who speak. We've got just as much to learn from our peers as we do from selected speakers, and we need a way to get together and share that knowledge."

Here's an assignment: go to www.flickr.com and type in *unconference, barcamp, or podcamp*. You'll get a sense of the excitement people have in an environment that embraces multiple opinions, where barriers to entry are stripped away and conversation is king.

The popularity of the unconference model is beginning to make inroads in the business world. Mark Ragan, CEO of Lawrence Ragan Communications, hosted two unconferences before paid conferences and grew enamored of the concept:

> I have found the Ragan unconference to be one of the worthiest endeavors ever undertaken by my company. Indeed, I have fallen in love with them as a way to bond with the customer. As a reporter and publisher, there is no better way to learn what's on the mind of my readers. As a marketer, the unconference tells me more about what's hot in the marketplace than any other tool I have. Finally, I have never learned more about the business from any other tool.

Ragan is planning to host stand-alone unconferences in a number of cities. Any organization that hosts meetings or conferences, for employees or other publics would be wise to consider adopting a similar approach.

Jeff Pulver and Friends:
The No-Barrier Breakfast

Jeff Pulver, social media luminary, cofounder of Vonage, and creator of the popular VON (Voice on the Net) conferences, recently wrote on his blog that "back in 1996 I first wrote that 'the more virtual we become, the more we need to have face-to-face meetings' and I feel even stronger about this in 2008." To implement his vision, Pulver has created a breakfast networking initiative: "Breakfast with Jeff Pulver and Friends." In his own words, here's why he felt there was a need for this type of event:

> Rather than host "just another business networking breakfast," where it has been my own personal experience to be a place for people to gather, look for "that person or persons" to speak with, then pretend to listen to the special guest speaker and eventually

leave while asking, "Why did I go there?" I have been applying concepts from the online world of social media and introducing them into the world of face-to-face meetings.

Pulver organizes his events on Facebook, which allows attendees to connect with each other after a breakfast so they don't need to worry about exchanging business cards. It also allows people to get to know each other on Facebook before attending and find common interests to chat about when they meet.

Pulver has come up with a unique and fun way to implement the tools of online media in person: his "Personal Social Networking Toolkit," a variety of items given to attendees at the door for a breakfast, usually in a zippered plastic bag. The following list of items is taken from Pulver's description of the toolkit:

- A *pen*.
- A *name badge*. Beyond writing your name on the badge, you're urged to pen your personal tagline to help inspire discussion and interactivity. Two of Pulver's recent taglines were, "I take fun seriously" and "I travel for breakfast."
- A *series of small labels*. These are used for real-time social tagging: you write something about a person and stick it on his or her name tag.
- A *personal tag cloud label*. A tag cloud is a series of keywords clustered in a paragraph format, typically at the bottom of a blog or web page. It serves as a table of contents of sorts for subject matter indexed by keywords. A personal tag cloud label mirrors these tag clouds. At one of Jeff's breakfasts, this means you will have a number of small stickers attached to your name tag with labels people have tagged you with.
- A *stack of sticky notes:* These go on your "wall" and mirror the personal walls people have in social networking sites like MySpace and Facebook.

The event has taken off with dozens of breakfasts across America and has expanded to Israel, Amsterdam, and London. It has also been featured in the press, most recently when *Fortune* senior editor David Kirkpatrick wrote an article after attending one of Pulver's breakfasts. Here's how he describes the process of assigning a personal name tag for yourself:

> Pulver explained to each arrival that they must put not only their name on the tag, but also a descriptive phrase. His said, "I take having fun seriously." Another guy (an old-media refugee) had tried one line, crossed it out, and then penned in big letters, "I'm terrible at this."[1]

Kirkpatrick goes on to describe how someone at the breakfast later posted a note to his personal tag cloud that said, "reporter." One might think people would be intimidated by the prospect of interacting in such a way with the senior editor of *Fortune*, but the setting reflects the open-source mentality that has become so prevalent online and off in the past few years. Events like Pulver's reinforce the idea that all voices are equal and everyone should expect to have their ideas challenged or discussed despite their status, titles, or where they work. As Pulver puts it, the event "breaks down walls around you—people are there to network and socialize . . . you are the speaker, and you have the chance to speak to anyone you like."

There's another vital aspect to the event that's mirrored in one of Pulver's taglines: it's serious fun—serious in the sense that you're interacting with peers and networking in an effort to build your business or your contacts, fun in the sense that it's hard to keep up a veneer of any kind when people are posting sticky notes on your chest while chomping on a piece of bacon.

The techniques Pulver uses are more than just entertaining icebreakers. By mirroring how we interact online, they require people to consider what their labels will mean when applied (literally and figuratively) to someone in person. It's easy to post a comment on a blog when you can't see someone's reaction to gauge how it has affected this person. In addition, you can post and come back later, a far more controlled activity than dealing with someone's reaction right away. Pulver's breakfasts demonstrate another example of transparency in context, where being there means you can't hide your true self. Moreover, being shy won't serve as an excuse for not expressing your opinion.

Pulver asserts that these techniques could be used in other settings. Why not put some sticky notes to use in your office and try a tagline on for size? You'll likely be surprised by how much fun you have while fostering better communication at work.

An Interview with Scott Ginsberg, "That Guy with the Name Tag"

Scott Ginsberg (www.hellomynameisscott.com) wears a name tag all the time (he has even been known to tattoo a temporary name tag to his chest for certain occasions). The *Wall Street Journal* calls him the "authority on approachability."[2] He's written multiple books and has launched an online TV network, www.nametagtv.com, that offers multiple tips on how to network, market, and sell effectively while embracing transparent principles focused on engaging people in a genuine manner. Here are his answers to the questions that John posed to him:

• • •

What's the importance of face-to-face networking today? Isn't it easier just to connect online via social networks like Facebook? Easier doesn't mean better. "Connected anonymity" is the term for it, which means we can easily connect, but not on a deeper level. Be careful not to spread yourself thin.

Why should companies put time into having face-to-face meeting opportunities? To gauge emotion and reaction and reinforce approachability.

How can individuals and companies make their meetings more transparent? Share your follies. Lead with a story of how you did it wrong and lessons learned.

What tips do you have for helping a shy person learn to network effectively? Small victories first. Talk to people who won't reject you, like bartenders and hosts, and build up your confidence.

How can people avoid being pitchy or salesy in networking situations? Detach from outcomes, and solve, don't sell. Deliver value first. Have fun.

Do you agree with the "lottery" idea that the more people you meet, the more likely you are to "hit" on the person that can change your life? Yes. You just never know.

What question did I not ask that I should? You should ask, "What's the secret to making a name for yourself?" Answer: working your butt off.

• • •

Wearing a name tag 24/7 may not work for everyone, but it has made Ginsberg's career. However, his advice and wisdom demonstrate that his name tag habit is more substance than stunt. He has created a way to introduce himself that typically induces a smile (since they're not used to seeing someone wear a name tag at a diner, for instance) and opens the door for genuine conversation. People appreciate that wearing a name tag in front of strangers involves risk and that vulnerability is a form of transparency.

You'll note that Ginsberg has a focus on hard work from his last question. Meeting face-to-face is not always easy, and some people are more gregarious than others. But here's a simple truth: the fewer people you meet, the fewer chances you have for business success. Period. Everyone is connected to someone else, and if you aren't working to increase your network, you'll stay limited by the people you already know versus the ones you could.

Paltalk President and COO Joel Smernoff: Face-to-Face Online

Paltalk is the largest real-time video-based community in the world, with 4 million active users. The service allows people to participate in multiperson video chatrooms in real time. It has also incorporated a social network into its platform allowing people to bring prerecorded videos or other media into their profiles, a process Paltalk's president and chief operating officer calls "social casting." While users may not literally be face-to-face, they can certainly see the expressions of friends and strangers in chat. As Joel Smernoff states:

> Something like 85 percent of human communication tends to be nonverbal, and a lot of it has to do with seeing someone's face. When someone smiles on video, you can see if they are being genuine. You can see if their eyes crinkle and note the subtleties that you can't pick up via text or voice chat. How they carry themselves says a lot and informs you a lot about who the other person is that you are talking to.

A number of couples have met on the service and gotten married, and participants in some chatrooms have also started having annual meet-ups around the world to network in person. A fundamental aspect of Paltalk's business model is the actual source of its income: a subscription fee (from fifteen dollars a month to sixty dollars a year) lets users see other people's webcams (there is no fee to set up an account that comes with a chatroom in the ability to participate by text in other chatrooms). As Smernoff notes, "The fact that we do have hundreds of thousands of paying subscribers really tells you the power of that transparency—that people are willing to pay to see other people because they get value in that."

The service has been around for about ten years and has a set of protocols for moderating chatrooms, which provides a good example of tactical transparency. Called Pal Helpers, these individuals serve as a sort of "neighborhood watch" and are available if a situation arises that causes concern to a user. They can enter a conversation or conflict and work to help resolve any disputes that may arise. They aren't censors; they simply work to reinforce the site's overall guidelines for use and individual chat members have established for their rooms. If a visitor to the chatroom violates these guidelines, the owner of the room can call on a Pal Helper to moderate. A visitor who won't comply can be banned from a room. "These are the kind of infrastructural steps that you need to take to make sure your environment is pleasant to hang out in," says Smernoff. "It takes time to develop these, and it really has become a core competency and something that we are very proud of."

Safeguards like the Pal Helpers program mirror the idea that transparency doesn't mean full disclosure or a chaotic environment where anything goes. Using social networking tools to build community and allow interactivity still requires setting up guidelines and respecting whatever environment you're in, online or off. Video reinforces this notion. As Smernoff notes, "Being able to see who is talking to you is actually quite powerful, and there is a safety factor to that transparency as well."

Seeing people, even if they don't share their names, provides a layer of protection for a user since nobody can hide their actual physical identity from a webcam (or in person) unless they wear a disguise. Knowing someone's identity provides another layer of transparency in the form of accountability.

Online Anonymity

The opposite of face-to-face transparency is anonymity. Although there are certainly cases where being anonymous is acceptable, such as bloggers or reporters in repressive cultures who conceal their names for fear of imprisonment or harsher ramifications, most online anonymity hinders genuine communication. There are a number of tools, some described in this book, that can help prove someone's identity as part of a social network, even if their identity is limited to verification of their work history, versus their name or address.

But the point remains that some use anonymity as a means to act in ways they wouldn't in person. Trolls like these have various motivations behind their actions. Jonathan Vanasco, founder and CEO of www.findmeon.com, a company that deals with online identities, has identified three kinds of trolls in his research: marketing trolls, evangelical trolls, and contrarian trolls. Marketing trolls lurk on sites and pipe up in moments when they feel pitching their wares will result in a sale. Evangelical trolls have a strong voice and wait for subjects to arise they're passionate about to state their opinions in bombastic tones. Contrarians are the ones who like to pick fights and start flame wars; sadly this behavior can go to extremes. Two cases of this involve the death threats leveled against blogger Kathy Sierra and the case of Megan Meier, a teen who hanged herself after a horrific cyberbullying attack launched by two adults who created the fake identity of a teenage boy supposedly attracted to her. Forbes even featured a cover story, "Anonymity and the Net" where author Victoria Murphy Barret wrote:

> Question this right of Net anonymity and you risk an unmitigated thrashing (anonymously, of course). So maybe we are asking for trouble when we dare to say that Internet anonymity is out of control. Today the Net still protects the abused and the disenfranchised, people who go online for help because they can do so in secret. But it also shields creeps, criminals and pedophiles. It emboldens the mean-spirited and offers them a huge audience for spewing hatred and libel.[3]

The good news is that the tide has begun to turn online, and many noted new-media luminaries are calling for accountability no matter what the forum. One of these is noted technologist and conference maven Tim O'Reilly who posted a Blogger's Code of

Conduct (largely in response to the Kathy Sierra incident) as well as a wiki on the subject, where he encourages people to create their own code by combining any modules that encourage responsibility for one's words, the need to connect privately before publishing online, and to "think twice—post once."

A blogger code of ethics has little chance of adoption. Codes of ethics are usually introduced by associations that can enforce them among their membership. There is no compelling reason for bloggers, particularly those inclined to violate the guidelines, to embrace such a code. However, the modules provide an excellent basis for any blogging or social networking behaviors and also serve as a call for transparency. Connecting privately is a good example; it's a lot easier to send a snarky comment using Twitter than it is to pick up a phone and work through a problem. But guidelines like O'Reilly's acknowledge the fact that effective conversation involves accountability.

Anil Dash, vice president at Six Apart (the company behind blogging platforms like www.typepad.com), echoes the need for accountability online:

> The failing of those of us in technology for many years is that we have been very willing to let people behave completely without accountability in terms of identity. But guess what, if you go to any city in the U.S. they'll still say that you can have a public gathering about any topic you want but people can't have their faces covered. . . . This shows that people are willing to do a lot more destructive things when they are not accountable, when they are anonymous.

This accountability also needs to be reflected in the voices that guide organizations. Hiding behind a title to deliver unpleasant news or invoking marketing rhetoric erodes trust among employees and customers alike. While you may not be anonymous delivering such messages, you certainly aren't being transparent.

Conclusion

While social networking provides numerous ways to help you keep in touch with friends and colleagues and build your business, it's essential to network in person to have the kinds of interactions possible only in the live environment. If you're a shy person, challenge yourself to go to some unconference-style events where you can share your views in a small group, or lead a session and let people know you've never spoken before. Your transparency will elicit sympathy from your listeners, and you can encourage them to join in the conversation, particularly when your organization serves as the host of such events.

As Jeff Pulver pointed out, the growth of online and social networking calls for a balance of face-to-face events where we can distance ourselves from a keyboard and see people's expressions in real time. Meetings encourage accountability, vulnerability, and a reflection of a basic human need: to convene in person to learn, network, and get away from the office.

Part Three

MAKING IT REAL

15

THE TOOTHPASTE IS OUT
OF THE YOUTUBE

Addressing Loss of Control
with Transparent Tactics

On April 16, 2007, Apple's stock plummeted based on the publication on the world's most popular blog, Engadget, of an internal e-mail that reported a delay in the release of two highly anticipated products: the iPhone and the Leopard operating system. It turned out there was confusion associated with the initial e-mail (as Engadget pointed out in a clarification of the post), but the fact remains that the stock still dipped, people lost money, and both Engadget and Apple each suffered a major loss of credibility.

This all happened within minutes. Welcome to the digital age.

Loss of control of your company's message is nothing new. Negative public relations of all stripes has tarnished or ruined the reputations of countless companies for as long as businesses have been hanging shingles. Social media and the improvement of digital technology have simply increased the speed at which messages about your company and your brand can be transmitted by people over whom you have no control. Still, most organizations behave as though they do have control, issuing formal statements and heavily edited press releases. Yet if even Steve Jobs and company can suffer at the hands of a few misplaced e-mails, how can other companies deny that they cannot control messages about their organizations?

The answer is that they can't. People blog. They record podcasts. They write reviews. They submit negative stories to sites like Digg, where others vote to promote those stories, making them more visible. They share information in social networks and on message boards. Countering these uncontrolled messages requires you to infuse your organization with a mind-set geared toward transparency so you can deal with negative situations rapidly and with consistent integrity that will build trust.

But you can't run away. You can't pretend your organization is immune to the proliferation of consumers knowledgeable in how to use social media tools to voice their concerns. Consider the case of Vincent Ferrari, who recorded his attempt to cancel his America Online (AOL) account, then posted the recording to his blog. During the conversation, an AOL employee tasked with retaining customers repeatedly refused to honor Ferrari's request, going so far as to ask the adult to put his parents on the line. Mainstream media coverage of the event included a roster of highly regarded outlets like *The Today Show* and the *New York Times*, which noted that such encounters rarely became the stuff of widespread conversation in the days before the Web.

On the Monday after the public debut of Ferrari's recording of his call to AOL, Scott Falconer, an AOL executive vice president, sent an e-mail message to company employees alerting them to Ferrari's blog post and warned, 'On any interaction, you should assume that it could be posted on the Web.'"

AOL also fired the account representative who handled Vincent's call, subjecting the company to even more ridicule. After all, he worked for the company's "Retention Queue," not the cancellations department. In other words, he was doing exactly what AOL paid and trained him to do. The problem wasn't the individual representative; it was AOL's approach to any customer calling to cancel an account.

At the end of his *Today Show* report, host Matt Lauer asked Ferrari if he felt guilty that the representative was fired. The implication was that it was Ferrari's fault that AOL terminated his employment, not that AOL provided horrific customer service or was hypocritical in its firing if an employee whose tenacity as a "retention consultant" would have been viewed by the company as laudable in the light of AOL's customer policies.

Control What You Can

Before moving on to some case studies, let's review the lessons learned from the Engadget and AOL examples:

• • •

Be vigilant in your corporate communication policies, especially e-mail, so information that should remain confidential is not leaked. (Engadget)

Be vigilant in your fact checking. Bloggers are not immune from the risks in both leaking a story before it is set to break or in printing erroneous information. (Engadget)

Report retractions or corrections of previous stories, as the editors of Engadget did with its Apple information.

Provide multiple ways for customers to opt out of your service, online and off. It's better to send "we want you back" e-mails or letters in the future with discount offers than badgering someone who wants to cancel right away. It's not up to you to decide what's best for your customer. (AOL)

Always remember that your customer service representatives not only represent your company; they *are* your company to the customers they interact with. A-list blogger Jeff Jarvis's accounts of his difficulties getting Dell to fix his computer include an abusive comment from a summer intern working at CGI Digital Media, which Dell had hired to address online public relations issues. When Jarvis called CGI on the comment, company executive Paul Walker wrote, "It is important that you understand the intern's comment in no way reflects the points of view of Dell or CGI. Dell's aims with [its blog] are positive and they have every intention of making it a forum for open conversations with Dell customers." Jarvis didn't buy it: "The person who answers the phone, or now responds to a blog post, *is* acting on behalf of Dell and to the customer *is* Dell, since that person is our connection to Dell." Companies cannot scapegoat the representatives acting on their behalf. Instead, they must take responsibility for employees' actions and always place customer service above saving face. (AOL)

Apologies ring hollow if companies don't demonstrate they are working to remedy the problem at the root of the customer complaint. Compensating the complaining customer without addressing the core issue isn't enough. JetBlue Airways' Customer Bill of Rights provides an excellent example of how a major organization put an initiative into place after a negative situation (storms that kept its fleet on the tarmac for long stretches of time). Beyond offering refunds, the Bill of Rights provides specific ways in the future that JetBlue Airways will compensate customers in any number of situations they might experience. Being accountable in this way builds trust with customers; it's something they can point to in the future and hold a company to their word. (AOL)

The Greatest Fear

All companies share similar fears about the loss of control that social media could bring to their organizations. For this chapter, we focus on the top concern facing businesses today: "Web logs are the prized platform of an online lynch mob spouting liberty but spewing lies, libel and invective. Their potent allies in this pursuit include Google and Yahoo."[1]

Is it any wonder companies fear the power of digital media? Social media tools have made it easy and affordable for anyone to create content over a blog, podcast, video, or live audio/video stream. And they post their thoughts online where millions of people have access to them within seconds.

It's fair to be scared. But you can't stay uninformed. Andy Sernovitz, author of *Word of Mouth Marketing: How Smart Companies Get People Talking*, states:

> You'll never be able to control the blogosphere conversation. Don't even try. You'll never be able to manage your blog coverage like you manage the press. Don't even try. But what you can do is participate, earn respect, and tell your story.[2]

Before panicking about this loss of control, ask yourself this question: "How do I earn respect in real life? If I'm perceived as having integrity, why is that the case?" The answer lies in how you conduct yourself through all aspects of your professional life. You earn genuine trust with colleagues and clients because you treat them with respect, do what you say you'll do, and deliver value.

The online world allows you to do the same thing, just faster and with the whole world watching. Corporations tend to forget the power of the personal online. When you blog about your experiences at work, for instance, the average reader is allowed a glimpse into a world she may otherwise never get to. You don't need to reveal proprietary information. You can discuss the same things you would in a standard press release, but using your own words. And you can tell readers why you're passionate about your announcement beyond the fact that it will make you money. Now you've communicated in a way that sounds as if you're chatting with a friend versus presenting to your board. In fact, you've just done the three things Andy Sernovitz said you need to do: you've participated, earned people's respect, and told your story.

However—and here's where things might get a little scary again—earning respect online actually goes one step further. You need to engage in conversation about your work and the media you create, so your blog post needs to let people add their comments. While the prospect of negative comments appearing on a Web site owned by the company strikes many executives as counterintuitive, remember that you should practice comment moderation, stifling any egregious comments that would violate your published policy if they ever appeared.

But it's essential to remember that a genuine conversation, in real life or online, allows differences of opinion. You will instantly lose credibility online if you don't post comments of people who may not like your product or service but have a valid or constructive opinion. Although it's unpleasant to think of someone's negative words remaining in full view, remember that you can comment after they comment or write a whole new post in response and demonstrate that you're interested in their viewpoint. When you receive comments positive or critical, post them right after you've approved them. As long as they don't violate a publicly posted code of conduct, letting others read them demonstrates that your focus is on creating authentic conversation, not on shoving more marketing rhetoric down people's throats.

In Chapter Four, we pointed out that customers need to be listened to. The only thing worse than not listening is actively censoring their contributions. If they've posted a comment to a blog and you don't post it, they'll know. They may even write about it on their own blogs, as McDonald's found out when the company posted an item to its corporate social responsibility blog explaining, in response to criticism, its rationale for including a toy Hummer in Happy Meals. The article appeared on a Friday afternoon, after which company employees went home for the weekend. Comments flooded in, but nobody was there to approve them. Not knowing that nobody would be available to read the comments until Monday morning, several of those whose comments had not appeared took to their own blogs to accuse the company of censorship.

So what do you do when people post negative comments? How will that affect your brand?

Case Study: Bigelow Tea—Get Them Talking on Your Turf

As a leader of a company, events occur outside your realm of influence that can transform your business. Sometimes these are positive things like a rise in stock price or an unexpected news piece that sends a number of new customers in your direction. But sometimes the event isn't positive.

On April 4, 2007, radio talk show host Don Imus made now-infamous and derogatory comments about the Rutgers women's basketball team that sparked a media frenzy; eventually CBS, his employer, fired him and canceled his show. Cindi Bigelow, president of Bigelow Tea, was caught in the firestorm of public uproar because her company was a sponsor of Imus's show. Instantly the Bigelow blog became a central online conduit for discussion of the incident; a post about the controversy received 139 comments within a few days. As company president, Bigelow had to decide whether to keep sponsoring Imus's program while managing the public relations fallout sure to accompany any decision she made. She chose to continue supporting the show, citing Imus's work with children's charities and her belief in his apology made to the Rutgers team.

Bigelow made the decision she felt was the right thing to do for her company and explained the decision-making process, a fundamental example of transparency, on her blog:

> The blog is a wonderful tool that I think CEOs, etc., would be remiss if they weren't using. There are people out there who are saying [they] want to know more about my brand and the things that [they are] buying on a daily basis. The need for CEOs and presidents to establish a direct form of communication with their consumers and constituents is very important. It provides a beautiful opportunity to let the consumer know who you are, what's important to you and what motivates you. It gives you an opportunity to establish a real relationship.

Fortunately, the company had already established its "Tea Talk" blog with the help of Valorie Luther, founder and CEO of Creative Concepts, a public relations, marketing, and social media consultancy. When the Imus situation erupted, Luther understood the nature of the blogosphere concerning moderating and posting comments:

> The very big thing that happened with the blog is that none of the comments were ignored. We did look through them to make sure there wasn't any inappropriate language, but every single legitimate comment was posted regardless of their opinions about Bigelow Tea, Imus or any of the other players in the situation. Since we didn't censor any comments, the blog ended up being a landing place for people who had an opinion about the situation. They knew they were both being heard and not being screened. It was really pretty monumental for a corporate blog to play host to such an outspoken community . . . a community that had a lot to say not only about Imus but about Bigelow Tea as well.

It's instructive to visit the Bigelow Tea blog from April 10 and read the string of comments.[3] Cindi starts off the post with candid words about her thoughts on Imus, conceding that his actions "put our future sponsorship in jeopardy." (At this point she had not decided that Bigelow would continue sponsoring Imus's show.) What's interesting about the uncensored comment stream is that Bigelow (Cindi and the company) quickly took a back seat to more general questions of race and gender. The Imus situation clearly set off a powerful emotional reaction nationwide, and the Bigelow Tea blog gave people a place to be heard. Whether they agreed with Bigelow's decision or even drink her tea, they recognized that their opinions mattered enough to Bigelow to post them in a public forum.

According to Bigelow, her company accrued value from the candid and open exchange with her customers:

I'm not going to say that it wasn't a very challenging period. I remember getting one letter from a woman who was going to hang me from the highest tree because she thought I was going to drop Imus. I wrote her a letter saying I respect your opinion, but we actually want to give Imus the opportunity to work with the young women from Rutgers and see what good can come from this. Then she wrote me a beautiful letter as a follow-up and said how much she appreciated my taking the time to write to her directly. So I think the consumer today appreciates that opportunity just as much as I want to be heard as the company president that they want to be heard as our consumer. And that's what the blog offers.

She goes on to point out the tactical transparency a blog can offer:

My feelings are that [even] if you don't provide a blog, or something like it for your company, people are going to talk about you and your products, so why not provide them an environment where people can talk in front of you and not behind you. I'd rather you yelled at me directly than behind my back; this way I can at least explain where I'm coming from.

Creating an open channel of communication for your brand tells customers you're willing to listen to them. If you demonstrate that you'll listen to what customers have to say, positive or negative, you'll earn their trust. Think of the famous scene in *Miracle on 34th Street* where a woman approaches a Macy's employee and says she can't believe that the store Santa Claus told them to shop at Gimbels for a product that wasn't available at Macy's. Initially shocked that Santa wouldn't recommend Macy's, the employee is delighted when the customer says, "I can't believe you'd be so honest. Now I'm going to shop here all the time."

Stephanie Rogers, director of interactive strategy for PARTNERS + Simons, shared this advice she gives to clients who are thinking of entering the blogosphere and need to address their concerns over loss of control:

Education: The first thing I do to help clients get acclimated with the online space is to have them get out there via Technorati (www.technorati.com) and Google (www. google.com) and read what is being said about the brand. I remind them that the online world is an evolving market-place, so education is an ongoing process.

Commenting: The second step to help clients get comfortable is to have them comment on other blogs and become part of the conversation before they start their own blog. I remind clients that they need to be aware of the context of a con-versation before just jumping in with random thoughts.

Etiquette: By this point, clients start to get excited about starting their own blog, but typically want to remove negative com-ments automatically. In this regard I have to educate them about the etiquette of the blogosphere—moderating com-ments is standard (to delete spam, racist commentary, etc.) but it's de rigueur to post all comments, positive or negative.

The gut check. In regards to posting negative comments, you have to do a gut check and make an intelligent decision as to whether the comment adds good insight and is a legiti-mate concern or whether it's totally off topic, irrelevant, and they're abusing the commenting function. But you should follow up with everyone who posts so you can let them know they've been heard. The worst thing you can do is ignore the ranters—they'll find other places online to rant if you do.

Other Fears to Consider

What's the ROI?

One of the most often-heard objections to engaging in social media is the financial risk. There are costs associated with participation (consider the fact that Southwest Airlines had to hire additional staff to handle the moderation of comments on its blog), and there are potential losses from missteps, ranging from lost sales to fines for regulatory violations that might be levied when somebody misspeaks.

Companies, however, routinely balance these costs with the expected benefit of an activity. The calculation is known as a cost-benefit, or risk-benefit, analysis. In the social media space, the analysis is simple to conduct. Add the cost and the realistic potential risk, then subtract that sum from the expected benefit. If your calculation produces a positive number, the benefits outweigh the costs.

We've moved beyond the point in social media where we can pass it off as a gimmick or fad. It's also impossible to deny there's money to be made online. A forecast from ZenithOptimedia "expects Internet ad sales to hit $44.6 billion in 2008, and increase its total share of the market to 9.4% (up from 8.1% this year). Zenith predicts that that Internet will overtake radio in percentage of total ad spend next year [2009], and overtake magazines in 2010."

To suggest there's no benefit to participation in social media is reminiscent of the belief common in the early 1990s that the Internet was a fad. Rather than wait until your competitors have created a video series, blog, or podcast that's engaging your customers, why not get to know how social media tools work? More important, don't wait to discover negative conversations about your brand in portals where you don't have a voice.

Given the number of corporations producing blogs, podcasts, Facebook pages, MySpace accounts, and a broad range of other social media, it is clearly a channel that has entered the mainstream.

We're Going to Look Stupid

It's natural to worry about "the online lynch mob" poking fun at your first attempts to go viral with your brand. However,

remember that the introduction of transparent media demonstrates respect for the blogosphere. Picture yourself at a party: if
you don't know anyone there, do you walk in yelling about how
wonderful you are, or do you begin a monologue at someone you
don't know for fifteen minutes without letting the person get a
word in edgewise? If you do, you'll likely spend a lot of lonely
hours at the punchbowl.

Here are some basic rules to help you get over the fear of
losing face online:

- *Test with friends*. There's no rule that says your first effort
  needs to be highly visible and of broad interest. Experiment
  with a blog, podcast, or social networking site like Facebook
  on your own or with a few trusted friends.

- *Get specific*. The majority of blogs, podcasts, and videos fail
  on the business and consumer front because they're not
  focused. Who is your audience? What is your expertise, and
  how can you bring them value? Nobody wants to hear you
  turn on a recording device of any kind and ramble while trying to be interesting. That's the kiss of death. Just because
  user-generated-content tools allow you to create media
  instantly doesn't mean you shouldn't prepare.

- *Get feedback*. It's the rare person who can speak and write
  extemporaneously and be perfect the first time. It's critical
  to get honest, candid, and specific feedback from friends
  and colleagues about the content you're creating. An easy
  way to have people provide you feedback is to whip up a
  quick survey using a service like www.SurveyMonkey.com.
  Remember to keep it short, and try to avoid essay questions.
  For a blog, ask questions like these: Was it too long? Could
  you hear my voice in the writing? Did I prove my point? For
  audio/video media, ask questions like these: Was it too long?
  (shorter is better when starting out); How was my diction?
  Did the video play okay in your browser?

Remember that by and large, the blogosphere and social media community is very supportive when anyone tries to create work that comes from a place of passion versus profits. It's okay to want to make money, mind you, but don't lead with a multilevel-marketing mind-set. Show people you respect them and their time enough to create interesting, entertaining, and value-added material that will improve their lives and make them want to join your conversation.

From Loss to Leverage

Transparency is hard. Being open with strangers assumes a level of vulnerability that's not common for most organizations. The temptation is to hide behind press releases that have gone through a gauntlet of lawyers and public relations folks before being released to the public, and it's no fun to have people criticizing your business. It's difficult to demonstrate your viewpoint with humility and candor in an ongoing conversation, but it's really no different from getting a phone call from an angry customer. Will it help that person to read to him or her from a script, or is it better to genuinely listen to the complaint and work to remedy it?

Creating transparent portals for your brand actually protects you from more online negativity than by staying silent. Silence implies you don't care and aren't listening. And when clients think you're not listening, they lose trust and buy from your competitors. That's the real loss you should be focused on.

Remember that perception of control is just that: perception. The fact is, the organization has already lost control. You are being talked about on blogs and podcasts, in groups on social networks, on message boards, even on street corners and in coffee shops. The conversation is happening with or without you. Customers are rejecting the typical corporatese that characterizes these stiff, formal communications and (as the Edelman Trust Barometer reinforces) opting to do business with organizations whose employees interact with them as real people engaged in real conversations.

You may be familiar with Bazooka bubble gum. This gum comes with a comic strip wrapped around the gum featuring Bazooka Joe. Years ago, one of those comics featured Joe walking along the street at night when he encountered a man on his hands and knees, bathed in the light of a streetlight. Joe asks what the man is looking for.

"A quarter," the man says.

"Where did you lose it?" Joe asks.

"Across the street," the man answers.

"Why are you looking for it here?" a baffled Joe asks.

The man responds, "The light's better."

This comic stands as an object lesson for companies that insist on continuing solely to communicate through old channels because leadership is more comfortable with them. You may be communicating where the light's better, but your publics are across the street, in the dark where it's uncomfortable and risky, engaged in conversations that influence perceptions and purchase decisions.

It's time to get involved in the conversation. It's time to become transparent. It's messier, but the payoff is far greater than maintaining opacity.

16

YEAH, BUT . . .

Overcoming Objections

Every organization will face resistance to transparency from forces that see only the downside. Organizations that have thrived on opacity will be the hardest to change, but even those inclined to embrace the principles outlined in this book will run into roadblocks from lawyers, regulatory affairs staff, IT departments, some occupants of the executive suite, and external critics.

The objections fall into these major categories:

- *Legal and regulatory.* Transparency will make it too easy to violate laws and regulations.
- *Competitive.* Opening our organization will make it too easy for the competition to see what we're doing.
- *Technical.* We don't have the resources to manage transparency.
- *Investment.* Time and money are both raised as issues standing in the way of implementing the tools to support transparency.

In this chapter, we review each of these issues in turn. Before undertaking this review, however, it's important to get the big picture. If, as we have maintained throughout this book, transparency is the right thing to do, then it is the role of the company's leaders to find ways to overcome the objections and reap the benefits while minimizing the risks.

Michael Hyatt, CEO of Thomas Nelson publishing, puts it this way:

> Leadership, whatever else it takes, it takes courage. You've got to be willing, as a leader, to set the pace, to be the example, to model what you're asking others to do and to be courageous in the face of people who might be fearful or are only looking at the downside. You have to focus also on what's the upside, and with very, very modest investments, the returns [on transparency] are huge.

The benefits are indeed huge. In these pages, we have talked about increased trust among employees, customers, and other stakeholders. We have seen that transparency makes it easier to recruit, identify product and service opportunities, avoid onerous regulations and legislation, and forge alliances and partnerships with people and companies that can help your company achieve results that weren't possible before. We have seen transparency create loyalty among customers, confidence among investors, and fairness from the media.

We believe without equivocation that these benefits far outweigh any risks, a point Hyatt, the CEO of a multimillion-dollar company, also makes: "Sure, if you're transparent, some people will use that to their advantage, but the benefits offset that. Much [of the risk] is in our minds; it's usually exaggerated. We have never been sued, we have never been threatened, [our transparency] has never been an issue."

Much of the fear that keeps companies from embracing transparency is analogous to the child who starts crying when he sees the needle but before he has been given the injection, which winds up hurting a lot less than he thought it would.

Let's begin our examination of the major categories of resistance.

Legal and Regulatory

In the early 1990s, Buckman Laboratories CEO Bob Buckman acquired a private CompuServe forum for his employees. (Predating the Web, CompuServe allowed Buckman's employees to participate in forums using a global network of telephone dial-up numbers.) Convinced that the answers to customer problems resided in the heads of his global employee team, he instructed employees to begin using the system's message boards to alert others about issues and to answer questions and solve problems as they arose. The system produced huge payoffs for the company, not only solving customer problems but leading to sidebar conversations that resulted in new product development.

Then the U.S. federal government and several U.S. states filed antitrust charges against Microsoft. As part of the legal discovery process, Microsoft subpoenaed the transcripts of message boards from Netscape, the distributor of the first commercial Web browser that Microsoft was trying to unseat by integrating its own Internet Explorer into the Windows operating system. (The integration of Internet Explorer into Windows was part of the basis of the antitrust charges.)

Realizing that any company's internal message board transcripts could be made public through legal action, Buckman's lawyers told him they needed to shut the system down. Buckman was nonplussed. He calculated the value of the system: the customers who were at risk of canceling contracts but who were retained because the network led to a solution to their problems, the customers who increased their orders due to their satisfaction with the company based on how quickly their issues were resolved, the referrals to new customers, the development of new products and the improvement of existing ones. With a rough estimate of the dollar value the network had produced, Buckman asked his lawyers if the threat of discovery might cost the Buckman Laboratories more than that.

No, the lawyers said; they didn't see how any legal action could produce a judgment worth *that* much. In that case, Buckman said, "Get out of my office."

Thomas Nelson's Michael Hyatt had much the same reaction when his outside counsel resisted the employee blogging program he wanted to launch. "It's one of the advantages of being CEO," he says. "I thanked them for their counsel, which

I respect, but said I had a different view and that I was going to proceed anyway." It's a decision he does not regret.

Lawyers should not be blamed for their reticence. It is their role in the world to minimize their clients' legal and regulatory risks. To be sure, there are risks. But two principles can help a company proceed in the face of those risks:

- *Conduct a risk-benefit analysis.* Companies conduct such analyses every day. When the benefit adequately outweighs the risk, most companies proceed. (Note: we're not talking about consciously breaking the law or violating regulations. The risks are usually associated with the likelihood of lawsuits or other discretionary legal actions.) It is even possible to conduct a thorough return on investment (ROI) analysis using a tool produced by Forrester Research's Charlene Li. Li's ROI formula assigns dollar values to a variety of potential costs and risks associated with corporate blogging, as well as the various benefits, such as improved employee retention and reduced cost of customer service. The actual formula is simple: add the risk and costs together, and then subtract them from the benefit. If you have a reasonable positive number, you should undertake the blog.

- *Offset the risk.* Take steps to make sure your transparency efforts do not violate laws or regulations.

This last point is one that bears some scrutiny. One of the reasons so many people are agog over Paul Levy's blog, "Running a Hospital," is based on the number of regulations that govern the health care business. Levy, though, is untroubled. "HIPAA is my biggest concern," says Levy, CEO of Beth Israel Deaconness Hospital in Boston. HIPAA, the Health Insurance Portability and Accountability Act, became U.S. law in 1996 and is designed primarily to protect health insurance coverage for workers and their families when a worker loses or changes the job that provides the coverage. Title II of the act, however, focuses on privacy.

HIPAA was the reason Thomas Nelson changed its policy about issuing prayer requests for employees in the hospital. As human resource vice president Jim Thomason put it in his blog, "Within weeks [of HIPAA's passage] every HR department, hospital, doctor's office, or any facility that handled private medical information had to put in safeguards to make sure personal information did not become publicly known." The result was no more prayer requests for employees since Thomas Nelson didn't want to run afoul of the law.

The same approach works for Levy: "I do my best to make sure I comply with [HIPAA]," he says. When he blogs about a patient, he conceals the patient's identity, changing name, gender, and even the condition for which the patient is being treated. "I use a little bit of poetic license so nobody can ever tell who it is. I also ask the permission of the patient, or of the family members if the patient is no longer alive."

In other words, the solution for the legal and regulatory issue is pretty simple: *Don't violate any laws or regulations*.

It is this simple rule that led Dell to launch the first investor relations-focused blog, written by the company's vice president of investor relations, Lynn Tyson. In an interview, Tyson said:

> The ability for an investor relations department to execute this and do it well quite frankly is predicated on how well they do their jobs every day. And if there's confidence in their ability to exercise sound situational judgment over the phone or over e-mails or in one-on-one meetings with investors or group meetings with investors or drafting press releases, then there should be that same level of confidence by the company in their ability to have a dialogue over the Internet.

Tyson also sees the benefit of the conversation, noting, "People [here at Dell] have learned that there is little downside to having conversations."

The pharmaceutical industry is one of the most reticent when it comes to transparency for fear of violating any of a number of regulations imposed not only by the same institutions regulating all companies, but also the Food and Drug Administration (FDA). FDA closely monitors drug companies for any promotion of off-label indications. (Drug makers are restricted from recommending a drug for anything other than the conditions for which the FDA has given its approval.) Off-label indications top the list of pharmaceutical company fears that a blog may induce.

But if those sales and marketing representatives know enough to avoid making statements about unapproved indications at trade shows, why would anybody think they would forget that rule while writing a blog post?

The concerns of the pharmaceutical industry do seem to be eroding, ever so slowly. In an op-ed piece for the trade publication *PRWeek*, Ketchum Communications' director of global health care and brand advocacy wrote, "Now is the time for an active dose of leadership to forge change, before change is enforced upon us. Unless companies boldly confront online communications issues, the industry could suffer further reputation damage and lose the opportunity to shape its own communication future."[1] Again, the balance of risk versus benefit seems to weigh in favor of the advantages.

Lawyers may have some confidence that executives will negotiate the legal and regulatory mine fields. It was GM's Bob Lutz who noted that as vice chairman of the company, he has the experience and knowledge to know what he should and shouldn't say, not unlike Dell's Tyson. But what about average employees? In companies where employees are encouraged to blog about their jobs, isn't the risk greater?

IBM's Mike Wing, vice president of strategic communications, answers this question with a tone of genuine confusion: "Why would we have hired these people if we don't trust them?"

Of course, as President Ronald Reagan suggested when negotiating nuclear disarmament with the Soviet Union, trust is enhanced through verification. At IBM, as with so many other companies, that verification is proactive, taking the form of employee blogging policies to which employees agree to abide. Interestingly, IBM developed its policies by opening a wiki and inviting employees to submit their ideas for what the policy should include.[2]

There is one other concern some have about employee blogging: employees will make forward-looking material statements that can cause problems with agencies like the Securities and Exchange Commission, which requires companies to abide by the fair disclosure regulation, known as Reg FD.

The policies to which employees agree should be enough to calm those fears, but Forrester Research senior analyst Jeremiah Owyang finds the concern mostly baseless: "People have been hired because of their area of subject matter expertise." And that, he says, is what they'll blog about. So far, employee bloggers for companies that have embraced the concept have shown Jeremiah's view to be true. At Microsoft, recruiter Heather Hamilton blogs about recruiting. Thomas Nelson publishing's Jim Thomason, the vice president of human resources, blogs about human resources. Sun Microsystems' Robert Eckstein works on Java, and his video blog is (of course) about Java.

Sun Microsystems president and CEO Jonathan Schwartz used his blog to ensure employees understood that they couldn't be *too* transparent by leaking confidential information into the marketplace, something that had happened often enough to capture his attention:

I have no problem at all with Sun talking to the marketplace. I don't care if we're falling on our sword or evangelizing a solution, they both have value. We also have a responsibility to our customers not to leak what they've shared with us. We have legal obligations because we're subject to Reg FD, which says we have to share with everybody at the same time information that might be deemed material to our performance. For folks to

> violate those principles because it's convenient or expeditious isn't a good thing. Everybody can talk to everybody, I don't have any problem with that, but everybody should remember that we have signed confidentiality agreements with folks and we have to honor them. There are a lot of people who do business with us because they know we can keep a secret.

Telling employees so on his public blog was enough to remind employees of their obligations. Between such clearly communicated, strongly enforced policies and the fact that employees blog about their own work, not big-picture company issues, it's highly unlikely that the organization will encounter any serious problems as a result of its blogs or other initiatives employing social media to build transparency.

While companies can use these techniques to minimize risk, one last issue remains. You know that you can control what you write, but what about comments from the public left to your blog or other property?

The answer to this is the simplest of all: no company should allow comments to appear on its blogs or other social media sites without first moderating them. The moderation function is a simple on-off switch on most blogging platforms. Be sure to include a policy that covers what is unacceptable in a comment; then don't publish comments that violate the guidelines.

"I don't post things with bad language, and I don't post, for the most part, individual personnel issues or individual patient issues," explains Beth Israel Deaconness Hospital CEO Paul Levy, dismissing concerns about inappropriate comments. Instead, he responds directly to those who submitted the comment that the topics are private and he cannot allow them to appear:

> If someone complains, for example, about the way they've been treated as a patient, I can't reply without violating the law. I refer those to our HR department.

That being said, sometimes [a commenter submitting a comment he cannot publish] raises a general issue I *can* talk about. I turn down the comment, but in my own comments, I'll say something like, "Dear Mr. Smith: I got your post. I can't publish it for the following reasons, but I'll be happy to speak with you personally."

Competitive Issues

When you throw open your organization's windows and let everyone look inside, your competitors are among those with a clear view of your operations. That, according to many, is the definition of insanity.

We refer back to the opening chapter of this book and our discussion of the definition of transparency. It does not mean revealing absolutely everything. To begin with, there is information you simply are not allowed to share, such as employee medical information and undisclosed material financial information. Next, nobody expects a company to share plans for products or services still in development. Even Sun Microsystems, where Schwartz touts transparency as one of the company's most formidable competitive weapons, told employees in a public blog post, "The unauthorized sharing of Sun confidential information is illegal, and against company policy." Michael Hyatt concurs: "transparency about most things" serves the interests of his organization, but not transparency about everything.

One issue that stymies many organizational transparency efforts is a degree of concern over just what a competitor could use if it were exposed to the light of day. One very smart (and clever) person once said, "Nobody ever won a tennis match by keeping his eye on the scoreboard." The idea is that your ideas will already have been turned into profitable products and services by the time a competitor is able to do anything about it.

Furthermore, as author Dov Seidman notes in his book *How*, how you conduct business in today's transparent world is more important than what you do.[3] Seidman, an expert in business ethics and chairman and CEO of LRN, a company dedicated to inspiring principled business practices, says that competitors can copy any product or service within weeks of its introduction. Thus, it becomes equally important to focus on the things that build trust and loyalty, including your relationship with customers, your commitment to keeping your promises, your treatment of employees, and the degree to which you collaborate and crowdsource (the practice of reaching out to customers and other publics for ideas to implement). Procter & Gamble, for instance, has been forthright in noting that some 70 percent of its new products come from ideas submitted from outside the company. In other words, being transparent about how you do things is going to earn you more business than good products and services alone, since those can be duplicated in a heartbeat.

Technical Issues

Most technical objections, emanating from the information technology (IT) staff, come in one of two flavors:

- Employee visits to social networking sites increase the risk of infection from viruses and other bugs that exist on the Net.
- Introducing social media to the intranet (for the purpose of internal networking behind the firewall) requires considerable time and expense in order to test the applications to make sure they don't conflict with other, mission-critical tools.

Let's tackle these in order.

Risk of Infection

The business case for employees accessing social media sites using company computers should be clear by now. In case it's not, look at the results of recent research from research company

Gartner, which recommends that organizations not block access to social networking sites; rather, they should embrace them as a means to encourage creativity and collaboration on the job. The recommendation follows a survey of fifteen hundred chief information officers from around the world. Half of those CIOs noted that they plan to invest in Web 2.0 technologies (blogs, wikis, podcasts, RSS feeds, social networking capabilities, and more) during 2008.

In order to enable that open access, David Lavenda, vice president of marketing and product strategy for WorkLight, a Web 2.0 company, suggests, "The research alerts that in the near future businesses will require their IT security systems to provide secure access to Web 2.0 services like Facebook rather than block the facility." Lavenda adds that it is important that consumer tools support enterprise levels of security before they are introduced to the workforce. In other words, it's a task for IT to ensure employees can access these sites without incurring a risk.

At the same time, it's important to keep in mind that many of the fears of infection are unfounded. For example, an urban myth suggests that Facebook hosts malware, which can infect company computers. That is not so; what you'll find there is called scareware. According to the blog Mashable:

> These ads that show up on your Facebook pages in a similar manner to content-specific Google Ads have been found to be scamming folks left and right. Some of the discovered ads are posing as a dating service, redirecting you to a site that says "Your machine could be infected" and then onto a site for a product called Malware Alarm.

While this is still deplorable behavior, there is nothing dangerous about scareware; it cannot find its way onto company computers. The vast majority of these sites, including blogs, Twitter, and other tools, are perfectly safe.

Risk of Conflict with Existing Software

Some IT departments have told those interested in implementing Enterprise Web 2.0 tools that the test phase for vetting the applications can cost tens of thousands of dollars and take close to a year. To be sure, it is important to verify that any new software will work with existing applications. You don't want intranet blogging software to bring down the sales database, after all.

Still, there are options that can help you avoid this situation. The first involves the use of a particular software application, but it's one that many companies are already using: Microsoft SharePoint. The 2007 version of the enterprise software includes virtually all the social media functionality a company might look for, including blogs, wikis, RSS, and social networks. Since companies have already vetted SharePoint, no testing is required, although many companies will need to upgrade to the latest edition. It is SharePoint 2007's social media integration that has allowed companies like Wachovia (the fourth-largest bank in the United States) to move ahead with an ambitious internal social media initiative.

The other option is to have your social media tools hosted externally. A number of companies provide this service, including Awareness Networks, the option selected by Northwestern Mutual Financial Corporation for its internal blogs and RSS feeds. The notion of external hosting may produce immediate dismissal from IT. "Our content is too sensitive," they will tell you; "it *must* be kept behind the firewall." However, we have never seen a company that maintains its employees' retirement data on its own servers. This information is housed instead on the servers of the investment company that manages the plan, like Fidelity Investments. The truth is, companies already host data externally. Part of the due diligence a company performs on a company that hosts social media externally should focus on the security of the data. But it is a viable alternative and one that is becoming increasingly common.

Investment

Cost is another objection frequently raised by IT departments. It's a specious argument, though, given that most social media tools are either very inexpensive or free. While some companies have a blanket ban on the use of open-source software (which includes the top blogging platform, WordPress), it is time for organizations to rethink this approach. Even the Walt Disney Company has employed open source software, Drupal, to serve as the content management system for a significant part of its intranet.

If a company opts for more costly software, such as the enterprise-level social media tool available from Traction Software, it makes sense to subject the cost to a cost-benefit analysis. If the benefit of the tools—increased collaboration, faster time to market, greater knowledge sharing, and improved employee retention, to name a few—exceeds the cost, then the company should be able to invest to make it happen.

17

YOUR ROAD MAP TO TRANSPARENCY

Creating a Plan

Transparency often leads you to the right
path. What is the worst-case scenario with
transparency? You're being honest and are
saying things that are real—the right outcome is
eventually going to come out of that.
　　　　　—Dave Balter, founder and CEO of BzzAgent

By now you should be keenly aware that no organization can hide its head in the sand and avoid implementing the tools that will help it create better dialogue with customers, partners, and employees. This transformational process should take place in the steps set out in this chapter.

Many of these steps have been discussed in previous chapters. The template in this chapter is a self-contained guide you can use to walk through the planning process. It has been crafted to work from the inside out to expose your brand to the new-media marketplace at large.

Step One: Assess

You will detect a pattern in the structure of Step One: the first few choices for each question reflect traditional methodologies that organizations use to deal with feedback from employees and customers. By and large, these are all one-sided conversations where management tells people what they think and the implied message is, "If we want your opinion, we'll send you a survey." The latter answers to these questions reflect methodologies employed by more progressive organizations that use tactical transparency to better position their brand in the marketplace.

Ask yourself the following questions about your organization as specifically as possible:

- What communications tools does management have in place to communicate to employees?
  - ❑ Company wide e-mail blasts
  - ❑ Company newsletters
  - ❑ Leadership pages on the intranet
  - ❑ Town hall meetings
  - ❑ CEO or management blogs that allow for comments from others
  - ❑ CEO or management podcasts, videos, or interactive, real-time, rich media where employees can contribute their thoughts

- How can employees respond to those communications?
  - ❑ If they have concerns or questions, they e-mail their manager to resolve.
  - ❑ They can submit an article for the company newsletter.
  - ❑ They can submit a comment, question, or suggestion using an intranet form.
  - ❑ They can respond by commenting on CEO or management blogs.
  - ❑ They can add comments to existing intranet content.
  - ❑ They can interact directly with a CEO or manager using real-time, rich media.

These next two sets of questions reflect the mind-set of a traditional office that is not concerned with capturing feedback unless there's a direct need to respond. No dialogue is requested, and employees and customers typically don't have a feeling of ownership for their brand. Their loyalty goes as far as their paycheck or waiting until a competitor offers a lower-priced product or service.

- Do your employees genuinely feel that their opinions and concerns matter to management and that their interests are factored into management's decision-making process?
  ❑ Not sure why it matters.
  ❑ I don't know.
  ❑ No, but at least we're listening.
  ❑ Yes, and here's how I know [insert specifics here].

- What tools do you have in place to capture employee thoughts and ideas?
  ❑ Employees can submit thoughts and ideas to their managers for discussion.
  ❑ Employees can submit thoughts and ideas in departmental meetings where appropriate.
  ❑ Employees can submit thoughts and ideas by commenting on company blogs or other rich media presentations.
  ❑ Employees can submit thoughts and ideas using the media they create on blogs or other formats.
  ❑ Employees can use an online submission tool that allows other employees to comment and vote on ideas and issues that are raised.

The answers to these questions demonstrate that a company is providing tools for dialogue. This is the first step toward true transparency because it shows that the organization is listening to a variety of sources and publics. It also demonstrates preparedness to accept and address criticism, because the comments people make may not always be positive. If those comments stay public so they can be dealt with, trust is invariably given to management since they didn't silence a critical voice.

- Are your employees champions for your brand away from the workplace?
  - ❏ Not sure why it matters.
  - ❏ I don't know.
  - ❏ No, but we're working to empower them to feel ownership of our brand.
  - ❏ Yes, and here's how I know [insert specifics here].

- How do you communicate with your customers?
  - ❏ By posting updated news and press releases on our Web site
  - ❏ Through media outreach (placing articles in the mainstream and trade press)
  - ❏ Via our customer service representatives online or by phone
  - ❏ Via our various department blogs and other rich media where we have a direct dialogue with our customers
  - ❏ Via the blogs and social community we've created for our customers so they can create discussions around our brand by themselves

The final answers represent an ultimate goal for tactical transparency: providing your employees and customers tools to create media around your brand for themselves, outside of what management is doing. Enlightened leaders understand that conversations around their brand are taking place all the time, so why not create a community for users that you can host? Let them speak freely about your products and services in an environment where you can prove you're listening all the time.

Step Two: Adjust the Culture

By creating dialogue-rich environments, you also provide a platform to quickly communicate your thoughts when problems arise. Whatever the situation, you've earned the trust to have your voice heard in the context of a community you've helped create. And you can show people how you plan to deal with the negative situation that calls for transparency. Dave Neeleman, founder and former CEO of JetBlue Airways, speaks to this idea in the YouTube video he created apologizing for a series of negative events surrounding JetBlue Airways' stranding of passengers as flights were canceled during severe ice storms in New York City in 2007: "As with all challenges that come your way you can ignore it and pretend like it was an aberration, or you can do an examination and determine if there's something you can do internally to make sure that never happens again."

Transparency within your organization must involve every employee. The research you undertake to assess the degree to which transparency already exists must therefore be comprehensive. If you undertake a survey, be sure it captures a scientifically valid and representative sample of the employee population. Be sure employees can respond anonymously to ensure candid responses. Assess the following factors in any research effort.

Top-Down Transparency

Your CEO or high-level managers don't necessarily need to be the ones blogging or creating interactive media, but they do need to bless the process. Employees need to know (via set blogging or new-media guidelines) what tools are in place, how to use them, and why the company has implemented them to be most effective.

It Takes Time

You can implement tools to foster dialogue, but transparency takes time to filter throughout an entire organization. As Dave Balter, founder and CEO of BzzAgent, puts it:

> The thing that people don't ask really is, How do you get everybody in the company to align with this? How do you teach an executive who spent their days hiding from bringing anything public to do it this way? That is where it really becomes a job onto itself. I think the thing that people should know about this is that transparency is sort of a long-term cause. It is not "flip the switch tomorrow morning and everybody gets what the reality needs to be." It may look simple on the outside in a lot of ways, but it takes some work to get people to experience transparency and use it and understand that it can really help them.

Experiencing transparency is a multifaceted phenomenon and often involves critique. That is, if you ask for someone to talk about your brand, this person may say things you don't want to hear. But if he is being honest and gives you actionable insights, he may provide you with an opportunity to improve products or services you otherwise might never have discovered. So while initially the process may feel uncomfortable, the end result is improvement on your part while demonstrating your willingness to listen to the people who most care about your brand.

How Open Is Right for You?

J. D. Lasica, cofounder of Ourmedia.org and the Social Media Group, helps elucidate three levels of transparency that an organization needs to consider when assessing the status quo and goals moving forward toward achieving tactical transparency. "The first," Lasica states, "is *operational transparency* that involves the ethics codes, conflict-of-interest policies, or other guidelines your organization has established."

A number of exceptional blogging and new-media guidelines have been highlighted throughout this book. Here are a few as a refresher:

- "WOMMA's Practical Ethics Toolkit," http://www.womma. org/adoption/
- "HomeGood's Openhouse Blog Code of Conduct," http://openhouse.homegoods.com/index.php/ homegoods-blog-code-of-conduct/
- "IBM Social Computing Guidelines," http://www.ibm.com/blogs/zz/en/guidelines.html/
- "The New PR Wiki," a community-created resource that includes a list of internal blogging policies from a variety of organizations, including Thomas Nelson publishing; http://www.thenewpr.com/wiki/pmwiki.php?pagename= Resources.BloggingPolicy

J. D. Lasica describes his second kind of transparency as *transactional transparency,* "and that means out there in the field, how does transparency really work?" Guidelines like these provide boundaries for your employees to know how they can participate in the conversation you're creating at the office and out in the world. That is, can they have a personal blog away from work, and if so, can they discuss work at all? What shouldn't they talk about?

The disclosure rules that professional journalists follow provide a good model. Lynne d Johnson, director, social media, for FastCompany.com, explains that if she writes about a phone call she received from a company like Nokia, she is required to include language like this: "In full disclosure, I received this phone call from Nokia." Bloggers for your company will need to be trained for situations like these so they don't put your organization in an awkward position for the press or other partners.

Guidelines like the ones above for your customers provide a means for you not to post comments that break stated policies or address someone not respecting the community you've created. Fostering an environment to discuss your brand doesn't mean welcoming racism, bigotry, personal attacks, or foul language. Embracing dialogue doesn't mean posting thoughts that don't improve a conversation with helpful critique or thoughtful insights. Remember that your community will welcome your moderation if you are actively involved in forums, blogs, or other media you create and work to maintain a welcoming environment.

The final type of transparency Lasica posits is what he calls *lifestyle transparency*:

> There are these rivers of personalized news that are coming out of sites like Facebook and Twitter, these RSS streams where everything you do now becomes transparent. This is, I think, one of the major new things that is happening in the world of online media, and it all really comes down to how much you ought to disclose. All these sites are giving you options, but for the most part, the assumption is that you are going to be transparent about it; you have to really go the extra mile if you are trying to protect your privacy and not share that information with someone.

Lasica points out an essential aspect of tactical transparency: it's as important to decide where you aren't going to be open as where you are. Identifying the information about your organization that it makes good business sense to keep confidential will allow you to work to foster dialogue in other areas where you can speak freely. Typical examples of items most companies won't reveal or open to dialogue include these:

- *Financials*. Many "unconferences" like Podcamp (www. podcamp.org) require that a ledger for all expenses incurred and paid out for an event be publicly disclosed. Organizers employ this type of tactical transparency as a way of demonstrating public accountability. What to post and when about any financial aspects of your organization, however, needs to be approved by all departments of your organization. You also need to be aware of the ramifications of your disclosure. Although your philosophy or mind-set may promote full revelation of certain aspects of your financials, if other individuals' or organizations' information is involved, get explicit written permission from them before posting items that include them.

- *Proprietary information.* Full disclosure about products in development could provide your competitors with an edge to ruin your business. There's a vast difference between being open and revealing your secret sauce to the world. Playing some of your cards close to the vest doesn't automatically denote obfuscation.

- *Personal information about employees.* Being transparent involves sensitivity. Blogging or talking about individuals without their permission is gossip, be it digital or otherwise. And being shy doesn't mean a person isn't open, just not in the way that others are. Chris Anderson, senior editor for *Wired* magazine, puts it this way:

> Not all individuals are as comfortable with living in public as I am. My instinct is to do everything in public. I've got a thick skin, and I can take it. Other people may be shy, or they may not crave attention as much as I do. I think that transparency is something that people embrace rather than being forced to do. And what I will not do is tell people that they must be transparent or they must blog early and often. I leave that to them. I tell them they have permission to do so, and I'll lead by example where I can, but fundamentally each of them is going to have to find their own comfort zone for transparency.

Again, we see the need here for your transparency audit to encompass your entire organization and for you to think on multiple levels regarding how best to institute effective policies for dialogue. One vital aspect of this process is to determine who will serve as the voice for your organization on a blog or other social networking outlet. How can you prepare employees at the front line and supervisory levels to interact with customers authentically and appropriately and without coming off sounding like a company shill? Customers will react badly if they feel they are simply hearing carefully crafted PR messages or if their concerns are being ignored.

Step Three: Establish Your Voice

Your communications efforts need a defined voice or feel that reflects your company's culture and brand. For instance, an internal video created for MTV would likely differ from one made for PBS. The impact and effectiveness of your messaging rely on demonstrating that you know your audience, largely because you're having a real conversation with them.

Another dimension to your voice is the nature of objectivity in your communications. How can you demonstrate to your employees and customers that you're speaking truth and not just saying what people want to hear or what you want them to believe?

Traditional journalists provide insight into the level of objectivity in regard to how they consciously work to eschew their personal opinion for the sake of maintaining objective credibility for their story. Anthony Moor, deputy managing editor for the interactive department for the *Dallas Morning News*, points out:

> Nobody is purely objective. I think that traditional journalism is done in a framework that gives a lot of checks and balances to the reporting process that ensure we can provide a true picture of the world. It is just a question of the degree to which you want to see objectivity and how much credibility you place in things. People may place a lot of credibility in Robert Scoble

[the popular tech blogger] because of his background, right? But if we know that he is an opinionated person, we know that he is unlikely to be concerned about mixing opinion with reporting.

A traditional journalist doesn't want to mix opinion with his or her journalism. That is sort of a hallmark of the way in which traditional journalism operates. I do think going forward we are faced with the need to recognize that the world has changed and that because there are more and more voices available to people, we have to ask ourselves, How do we fit in? How does traditional journalism fit into this new world?

In an intriguing counterpoint to Moor's stance on objectivity, Andrew Baron, founder of the popular video series Rocketboom, talks about the trust created when you tell your audience you aren't objective:

I started to notice something really different about what we were doing, especially because people kept saying, "We really love Rocketboom instead of Fox News," for instance. I kept wondering why. People were saying they really trusted our information and they really believed in what we were doing and thought it was valuable. They kept [juxtaposing] it to other typical news stations, and eventually I figured out it had to do with these other news shows trying to attain the journalistic goal of being objective. What we are doing instead is saying, "No way; there is no such thing as objectivity, and we are being entirely subjective." It's just our personal take. If you don't like it, go away or tell us because we're apt to change and say we were wrong or whatever.

That kind of a sentiment behind our information actually seems to be more valuable for people because we're able to live up to the integrity behind what we say. In other words, you can't say that you are objective because that is futile really, and so you'll always be failing. When you say that you are only showing one side and you are subjective, then people can't really knock you down for that.

The nature of objectivity in journalism is a never-ending subject of debate, but it reflects the fact that your corporate voice needs to be aligned among all the practitioners communicating to employees or the outside world. And beyond the nature of the conversation in terms of factual accuracy (although that's extremely important), it's your attitude that will most clearly resonate with your audience. You may be an expert about your products and services, but you can't dictate how your customers will respond to your brand. Addressing them with a lack of respect or not hearing their objections comes off as arrogant, not informed. More and more, it's a good rule of thumb to pretend your online conversations are equivalent to having someone sitting across from you at your desk for a chat. If you're not honest about where you're coming from, they'll know it and likely never come back.

Step Four: Create an Action Plan

It's time to address some specific areas or situations where tactical transparency can transform your business:

- Crises
- Major change initiatives
- Financial matters
- Dealing with the media
- Employee interaction with the outside world
- Accessibility of management to strategic publics

Crises

We discussed the characteristics of being OPEN regarding tactical transparency in Chapter Two:

- Objectivity
- Purpose

- Esteem
- Navigation

These characteristics reflect the action points to take when you confront a crisis that involves the speed with which you address a situation, how you respond, your organizational voice, and action plans employed to deal with crisis in the future. Cindi Bigelow, president of Bigelow Tea, recounts how her team pulled together to deal with a difficult situation revolving around company sponsorship of radio shock jock Don Imus after his comments about the Rutgers University female basketball team:

> I pull together what I call our SWAT team to talk about crisis situations. We understand what everyone's role is and the chain of command in the situation. For the Imus situation, I pulled in all parties that this would touch. I explained how we needed to deploy our actions. Then everybody threw in their thoughts and what they thought the timing was. We formulated a plan on a whiteboard and assigned who was going to do what. We got together a minimum of at least twice a day to go over any new information. Then we just did whatever we had to do. We were constantly getting together and seeing if we needed to change course. Then we debriefed about how we could do better.

Have you got your own SWAT team for your business? If not, here's a place to start:

- Create an action plan for crisis before you're in a crisis.
- Determine the key players in your organization who are involved in different types of crises (for example, legal, media-related).
- Establish the methodology for how all key players will be communicated to and how: e-mails, phone calls, how to reach people away from the office or on vacation, and so forth.

- For the first meeting of all key players, have the person most knowledgeable about a situation format a brief depicting what the crisis is as specifically as possible, along with an agenda. This person should present three or more potential ways to deal with the crisis to expedite formulating a response.

- Establish a time frame for dealing with the crisis and all the departments and people any action will touch within your organization.

- Discuss the ideas on how to deal with the crisis, and evaluate all possible outcomes.

- Evaluate all scenarios in the light of authenticity: Are your solutions focused on saving face for the company or honestly communicating your position in a way that builds trust with your key stakeholders?

- However you decide to respond to a crisis, provide channels of feedback for key stakeholders about your decision.

Major Change Initiatives

Your company may be facing multiple layoffs or is in the process of being acquired. How do you incorporate tactical transparency to address these seismic changes?

- *Hold certain conversations face-to-face.* If your company is dealing with layoffs, for instance, you need to congregate a town hall or other meeting format to provide the specifics of what's happening to the company. If you attempt to address issues this sensitive in an e-mail or press release, you'll be creating an environment rife with fear, distrust, and resentment.

- *Share the news quickly after your management team has determined it needs to be announced.* Remind employees or other stakeholders that the information is private and confidential, but that you've created an open format to allow people to ask questions and vent.

- *Keep it constructive.* Create an agenda for a town hall or other meeting format that goes beyond sharing news about your change. Action counters fear, so provide steps that listeners can implement to help them work to implement change or take steps for other actions where needed.

- *Provide multiple forums for feedback.* Change is an ongoing process; you'll therefore need to demonstrate you're listening on an ongoing basis. You can't do this with a traditional suggestion box. Think about posting an internal blog about your change process where comments are encouraged, and make sure to blog when suggestions are put into practice.

- *Follow up.* Once you've worked through a major change, put together a report documenting the process. Include multimedia if possible, with audio testimonials from employees or video training modules. Get as specific as possible about what the crisis was, how it was dealt with, and perceived or actual results. Reports like this will allow you to emulate or modify your change process in the future.

Financial Matters

There are two distinct audiences to address with your numbers: employees (inside) and everyone else (outside). Of course, the numbers are the same, but the uses to which people put them are vastly different. An open-book approach to your financials with your employees is the first step to employee accountability for the numbers of which they have control through the performance of their work duties. Externally, the more you reveal and explain, the more likely you are to be trusted by publics that count within the financial community: individual and institutional investors, analysts, and the financial media.

This does not mean you must expose every last spreadsheet to public scrutiny. Thomas Nelson's Michael Hyatt keeps the privately held company's profits secret to avoid giving away too much information to competitors, but shares information on sales, even though there is no requirement for him to do so. Thus, your key planning steps for financials are simple:

- *Decide what to reveal.* Inventory your financial information, and decide which you can share and which you should continue holding close to the vest.
- *Set the context.* For financials you decide to make public (beyond those you are required to disclose by law), identify the context that will help your audiences make the most out of them.
- *Choose the channel.* For each category of financial information you are going to share, identify the best channel for getting it into the hands of your chosen publics.

Dealing with the Media

The line between traditional and new-media outlets is blurring at a rapid pace. Dealing with media could mean talking to a prominent blogger as much as providing a quote for the *Wall Street Journal*. And saying "no comment" isn't a viable choice in an overall atmosphere that will assume that any reticence to speak indicates culpability. So consider the following steps for interacting with any media outlets:

- *Set parameters for your interview.* Gone are the days when you talked to reporters and hoped for the best in regard to how they wrote their article. Follow the lead of Michael Hyatt, and tell reporters you are amenable to an interview only if you can post their questions and your answers to a blog or other public outlet before (or at least at the same time) the article is released. Bring your own tape recorder to the interview, and transcribe your thoughts word for word; if a reporter misinterprets your thoughts, you can point to an audio or text transcription to provide the context for your thoughts.

- *Understand your audience.* Who is asking you questions about your organization, and who do they write or report for? It's a compliment for someone to interview you (unless you're in a crisis situation), and your due diligence involves reading or viewing some past posts to get a sense of the outlet's voice and general take on things. Beyond the etiquette involved in knowing their work, you'll be better armed to understand how they deliver news and the audience they're targeting. This doesn't mean you should work to say what you think a reporter wants to hear; it's a question of how best to communicate your message. Acting in a Shakespeare play is different from doing children's theater, but both audiences are just as precious and will let you know if you're not reaching them.

- *Ego surf.* Whether you use Google News alerts or another method to cull the Internet for mentions of your organization, getting these instant alerts to news about your company means you can react quickly to any media-oriented situation. If one of your products is mentioned negatively on a blog, for instance, yours should be one of the first comments addressing how you're working to correct or improve said product. The more you can speak in an honest voice and provide specifics of how you're working to remedy a situation, the better. And when someone has been kind about your company, take the time to thank the person. Be specific about what he or she has written or produced so the person knows you're listening.

- *Be creative.* The social media news release is one way you can interact with the press that moves beyond standard press releases or sound bytes. But you can also create audio or video press releases, articles written by your entire company created on a wiki, or any other project that shows you're reaching out to the public as a unified, transparent whole.

Employee Interaction with the Outside World

The outside world invades the workplace more than ever before. Work colleagues may e-mail you via Facebook, and within seconds you're writing on the wall of a friend you're meeting after work. Employees may also blog at home and write about your company while not realizing they could be discussing sensitive subjects that could damage your brand. Establishing policies along these lines provides parameters your employees will appreciate since they'll know how to act in various situations:

- *Show them the plan.* Employees won't know how to act in certain situations according to your organization until you tell them. A number of specifics will have been addressed in the hiring process, but until they're working and immersed in your corporate culture, guidelines exist as an idea versus a reality. Whatever policies you have in place have to be readily available to employees, and it's incumbent on you to ensure they read and understand them.

- *Get specific.* Employees take pictures and post them to Flickr, Facebook, and MySpace. Do you want them to have a separate personal account for profiles with their personal pictures? Or should they create a new profile for networks they use for work? They may not want to create these other profiles, but it's one way to delineate between their personal and work identities. What can't they discuss away from work? Have they signed nondisclosure agreements to that effect? It's your organization's place to determine what behavior away from work will reflect on your brand and how to deal with it. Just be aware if the guidelines are too restrictive or unrealistic, you'll have a harder time hiring people.

- *Get feedback.* Issues like these are always evolving. At the time this book was being written, Cisco updated its employee blogging policy in reaction to an employee blogging anonymously about various policy and legal matters within Cisco. The amended policy states, "You must clearly identify yourself as a Cisco employee in your postings or blog site(s) and include a disclaimer that the views are your own and not those of Cisco." You will invariably face situations that require your policy on employee behavior inside or outside the workplace to be updated. Make sure you have a vehicle to communicate these updates quickly and specifically to avoid repeating similar situations.

Accessibility of Management to Strategic Communities

Accessibility of a company's leadership is a key characteristic of transparent companies. Whether it is through a regularly updated blog or a quarterly response to questions that drops jaws with its candor, management's willingness to reply to inquiries and address issues that arise will influence audience perceptions of just how open and trustworthy a company is:

- *Identify the go-to leaders*. Agree at the senior-most levels of the organization which (if not all) leaders will be available to address questions from various publics.
- *Choose the channel*. How will these leaders interact with key stakeholders? Through a blog? A podcast? Webcasts? A question-and-answer submission form? Phone calls?
- *Set a process*. Accessibility does not mean a customer can pick up the phone and call the CEO expecting the CEO to answer the phone. Media calls still go through media relations, for example. But remember that at ExxonMobil, anyone can e-mail a member of the board and will get a direct answer. Establish the processes through which various publics will be able to reach out to the diverse members of your leadership team.

18

WHAT'S NEXT?

The Future of Transparency

So where do we go from here?

The future of transparency is not a matter of asking how much more transparent your organization should be in the future. As we've noted repeatedly, there are really only two approaches to transparency:

- That which is required by law
- The division you make between what you will keep hidden, for competitive or other legitimate reasons, and what you will subject to public scrutiny

From this perspective, the notion of the future of transparency seems a bit shallow. But there are a few factors to consider.

More Regulation

If the events that led Senators Paul Sarbanes and Michael Oxley to introduce legislation that forced transparency on organizations aren't enough to make it clear, we'll reiterate this critical point: opacity will lead to more regulation.

Sarbanes-Oxley, implemented to address egregious wrongdoing, has produced unintended consequences. Legal staffs have implemented policies restricting the free flow of information in organizations because that information must be reported. In most cases, it's not the fear that those communications contain evidence of illegal or unethical behavior that led to the policy.

Instead, it is the time and expense required to collect and sub-mit it. The work involved in satisfying the requirements is a huge distraction that siphons resources away from the company's core activities: serving customers. It's often easier to simply not allow the communication so the company doesn't have to worry about reporting it. As a result, valuable processes are tossed in the trash, and the company, not to mention its customers, is the worse for their absence.

Consider the voluntary transparency on which this book has focused as proactive actions to quell any demand for further reg-ulation. If business is forthcoming about its inner workings, decision-making processes, the quality of its staff, the deals it does (and decides not to do), and the other issues raised in this book, then nobody should sense a need to force companies to disclose information through regulation. After all, what more is there to reveal? It is in a business's enlightened self-interest to behave ethically and put that behavior on display for everyone to see.

Of course, we must reiterate that tactical transparency does not mean revealing all your cards. Transparency extends as far as the best interests of your company and its owners allow, provided you aren't using opacity to conceal the kind of behavior that will, when exposed (and it will be exposed), lead to calls for more daunting, expensive, complex, and restrictive regulation.

The Moving Target

Once you have set your transparency strategy, don't rest on your laurels. Things change. Specifically, there are two moving targets to keep in mind: changes in business and changes in communication.

Changes in Business

Boeing's introduction of its 787 aircraft has been lauded as a symbol of one kind of change taking place in the business world.

Airplanes, like so many other products, traditionally have been manufactured in one place and by one company. In developing the 787, Boeing recognized that in twenty-first-century manufacturing, the old approach would be unacceptably expensive and cumbersome. Instead, Boeing partnered with a number of other companies around the world, leveraging their capabilities and expertise. Huge parts of a 787 are manufactured and assembled by partners. These parts are shipped to a central location where they are put together into a finished aircraft.

This dramatic change to a business model opens a Pandora's box of issues. In their book about the business elements of transparency, Dan Tapscott and David Ticoll explore Boeing's need to be transparent with its new partners; keeping secrets could only hinder the manufacturing process.[1] These same issues have led Boeing to consider information it makes available to the public, from investors to the media to readers of "Randy's Journal," produced by Randy Tinseth, vice president of marketing for Boeing Commercial Aircraft. In the United States, *outsourcing* has become a four-letter word to a lot of people. To be sure, there are times when companies outsource work simply because it will save them a few bucks; they don't care about the human cost. In many instances, though, outsourcing is a recognition of the global nature of business. Companies have done a terrible job explaining why outsourcing certain types of jobs increases the economic benefit to the company, its owners, its customers, and the public at large, introducing new jobs that pay better and helping the economy move forward.

Boeing, however, has gone to great lengths to explain the process, its risks, and its benefits. Given public sentiment about outsourcing, it surely must have been tempting to downplay the global manufacturing process introduced with the 787. But the company took the right course and worked hard to be transparent. The result has been praise for the process and few complaints about jobs done outside the United Sates.

Boeing's global, multicompany manufacturing scheme is just one example of how business is undergoing change. Technology and other factors will drive more and bigger changes we can't even imagine to business models we take for granted. We will need to be ready to apply transparency strategies to these new dimensions of business as soon as they emerge—or risk being accused of returning to our old, opaque ways.

Changes in Communication

The communication channels employed by business, media, and the public change at a pace that's hard to keep up with. New tools are introduced, it seems, every day (and sometimes several times a day). In the beginning of the social computing era, there were blogs. Today there are podcasts, wikis, microblogging tools like Twitter, democratized content networks like Digg, file-sharing utilities, social networks, niche social networks, and virtual social networks. We have every confidence that something new will have been introduced between the time this book goes to press and the time it becomes available. We will lament the fact that this new tool isn't covered in the book, because its use will increase the ability of publics to peer inside the organization and report what they find, which will have consequences for business.

Staying on top of these tools will enable you to figure out how to:

- Assess their potential impact
- Incorporate them into your monitoring efforts
- Use them as part of your own transparency strategy

Conclusion

Transparency is not a choice. It is a legal, moral, and competitive requirement. Choice factors into the equation in terms of what you will make transparent and keep secret, and in terms of the strategies and tools you will use to behave in a transparent manner.

Whether your organization recognizes this and adopts the practices we've outlined (or others that serve the same goal) or remains opaque and risks the unintended exposure of practices and behaviors you wouldn't want your mother to read about in the newspaper is immaterial.

Either way, we'll be seeing you.

Literally.

Notes

Foreword

1. J. Hendler, "Agents and the Semantic Web." *IEEE Intelligent Systems*, March/April 2001.

Chapter One

1. D. Tapscott and D. Ticoll, *The Naked Corporation* (New York: Free Press, 2003).
2. *Simpson's Contemporary Quotations*, http://www.bartleby.cm/63/42/8242.html.

Chapter Two

1. J. Robertson and M. Wong, "Apple's Jobs Sorry for iPhone Price Cut," *USA Today*, Sept. 6, 2007.
2. From J. Fields Awake at The Wheel blog (http://jona thanfields.com/blog), *Is JetBlue Using Twitter to Spy on Its Customers . . . or Blow Their Minds?* May 5, 2008: http://jona thanfields.com/blog/jetblue-twitter-customer-service-or-to-spy/:
3. M. Barbaro, "Target Tells a Blogger to Go Away," *New York Times*, Jan. 28, 2008.

Chapter Three

1. M. Straus, "Food Giants Mull How Much to Push Organic," *PRWeek*, Mar. 19, 2008.
2. Edelman Trust Barometer, 2008, http://www.edelman.com/trust/2008/TrustBarometer08_FINAL.pdf.

Chapter Four

1. M. Port, *Book Yourself Solid* (Hoboken, N.J.: Wiley, 2006) and *The Contrarian Effect: Why It Pays to Take Typical Sales Advice and Do the Opposite* (Hoboken, N.J.: forthcoming).

2. D. Mamet, *Glengarry Glen Ross* (New York: Grove Press, 1984).

3. You can read Solis's original blog post at http://www. briansolis.com/2007/06/future-of-communications-manifesto-for.html.

Chapter Five

1. Edelman Trust Barometer, 2008, http://www.edelman.com/ trust/2008/TrustBarometer08_FINAL.pdf.

Chapter Six

1. The reference to former CBS News anchorman Dan Rather is about another blogstorm: the revelation by bloggers that a document purporting to prove U.S. President George W. Bush shirked his Air National Guard duty was a forgery. Rather's traditional response—"We stand by our story"— ultimately led to the end of his career with CBS.

Chapter Seven

1. Fleishman Hillard, "Rethinking Corporate Social Responsibility: A U.S. Perspective" (St. Louis, Mo.: Fleishman Hillard, 2006).

2. S. Strom, "Corporate Conscience Survey Says Workers Should Come First," *New York Times*, May 31, 2006.

3. A. Kleiner, "Jack Stack's Story Is an Open Book," *strategy + business*, Third Quarter 2001, www.strategy-business.com/ press/16635507/20088.

4. J. Stack, "America's Twenty-Five Most Fascinating Entre-preneurs," *Inc.*, April 2004.

5. Cartoonist Scott Adams lambasted ghost-written executive blogs in a wonderful installment of his *Dilbert* comic strip. The pointy-haired boss approaches the tech writer, Tina, and says, "I'm starting my own blog." Tina responds, "Oh, dear God, no." The boss continues, "Every day, I will record my personal thoughts about our business. I need you to write the first one by noon. I can't wait to see what I'm thinking."

Chapter Eight

1. T. Defren, "Social Media Engagement Turns Lemons into Lemonade," *Fortune Small Business*, Mar. 2008, p. 68.
2. R. Scoble and S. Israel, *Naked Conversations* (Hoboken, N.J.: Wiley, 2006).

Chapter Nine

1. Boeing also maintained a blog during the period the Boeing 777 overwater aircraft was undergoing flight tests. The blog was written by the test pilots themselves, offering a fascinating behind-the-scenes look at what a test pilot does and how an aircraft is tested.

Chapter Eleven

1. Edelman Trust Barometer, 2008, http://www.edelman.com/trust/2008/TrustBarometer08_FINAL.pdf.
2. Edelman and Intelliseek, *Talking from the Inside Out: The Rise of Employee Bloggers* (New York and Chicago: Edelman and Intelliseek, 2005).

Chapter Twelve

1. A. Amatangelo, "Battle-Scarred 'Jericho' Marches On," *Washington Post*, Feb. 10, 2008.

2. Congresspedia is defined as "the citizen's encyclopedia on Congress that you can edit" at http://www.sourcewatch.org/index.php?title=Federal_Funding_Accountability_and_Transparency_Act. The Sunlight Foundation says that its transparency grants are designed for "organizations that are using new 'Web 2.0' technology to further the organization's mission of making information about . . . the federal government more accessible" to Americans. http://www.sunlightfoundation.com/grants.

3. L. Story, "The New Advertising Outlet: Your Life," *New York Times*, Oct. 14, 2007.

4. Story, "The New Advertising Outlet."

Chapter Thirteen

1. S. Elliott, "Got a Second? G.E. Has a Quick Message," *New York Times*, May 5, 2006.

2. R. Scoble and S. Israel, *Naked Conversations* (Hoboken, N.J.: Wiley, 2006).

3. Israel's entries on the report can be found on his blog here: http://redcouch.typepad.com/weblog/sap_research_report/index.html, and you can read updates on the Survey at Mike's blog here: www.accidentallyonpurposeblog.com.

4. Skype is a voice over Internet protocol product that allows users to make phone calls online for extremely inexpensive rates and also allows them to instant message people they have connected with using the service.

Chapter Fourteen

1. D. Kirkpatrick, "Geography, Social Media and Breakfast," *Fortune*, Feb. 29, 2008.

2. J. Zoslow, "First Impressions Get Faster," *Wall Street Journal*, Feb. 18, 2006.

3. V. M. Barret, "Anonymity and the Net," *Forbes*, Oct. 25, 2007.

Chapter Fifteen

1. D. Lyons, "Attack of the Blogs," *Forbes*, Nov. 14, 2005.
2. A. Sernovitz, *Word of Mouth Marketing: How Smart Companies Get People Talking* (New York: Kaplan, 2006).
3. http://www.bigelowteablog.com/2007/04/10/bigelow-tea-responds-to-imus/.

Chapter Sixteen

1. A. Moravick, "Pharaceuticals Need Online Medicine," *PRWeek*, Mar. 17, 2008.
2. You don't have to invent your own blogging policies from scratch. You can find a large sampling of policies from a number of companies at "The New PR Wiki," http://www.thenewpr.com/wiki/pmwiki.php?pagename=Resources.BloggingPolicy.
3. D. Seidman, *How* (Hoboken, N.J.: Wiley, 2007).

Chapter Eighteen

1. D. Tapscott and D. Ticoll, *The Naked Corporation* (New York: Free Press, 2003).

Acknowledgments

Two names appear on the cover of this book, but far more people have been involved who deserve more praise and credit than we can ever hope to provide.

Yvonne DiVita and Tom Collins from Windsor Media Enterprises, our agent and legal representatives, provided invaluable assistance to us in guiding this book through the proposal stages and laying the groundwork for a great relationship with the publisher.

Kathe Sweeney, senior editor for the business/management group at Jossey-Bass Publishers, was cheerfully responsive to our never-ending stream of questions, requests, and issues.

Natasha Nicholson, vice president of communications at the International Association of Business Communicators (IABC), believed in this effort from the start and brought it to the attention of Jossey-Bass, with which IABC has a publishing partnership.

This book is far more than our own observations. The interviews we conducted, specifically for the book as well as for our respective blogs and podcasts, provided case studies that bring theory to life, insights that fleshed out concepts, and observations that ground the book in the real world of business. We can't thank the following people enough for their time and experience:

Jonathan Schwartz, CEO and president, Sun Microsystems; Robert Duffy, Open Port Group, Intel; George Faulkner, Corporate Communications at IBM; Jimmy Wales, founder of Wikipedia; Dominic Jones, principal of IR Web Report and founder of Clarity! Communications; Jeff Pulver, founder of

Vonage and Pulver.com; Lynne d Johnson, director, social media, for FastCompany.com; Michael Hyatt, CEO, Thomas Nelson publishing; Alan Levy and Bob Charish, CEO and COO, respectively, cofounders of BlogTalkRadio; Christopher Carfi, cofounder of Cerado; Bill Sobel, principal of Sobel Media and founder of the New York Media Information Exchange Group; Jeremiah Owyang, senior analyst with Forrester Research; Ludovic Fourrage, group program manager for the Academy Mobile Program at Microsoft; Sean O'Driscoll, general manager, customer service and support, for Microsoft; Chris Anderson, editor in chief, *Wired* magazine; Todd Defren, partner at SHIFT Communications; Andy Sernovitz, author of *Word of Mouth Marketing* and founding CEO of WOMMA.org; Gabe Dalporto, chief strategy office for Zecco.com; Tom Foremski, author of the Silicon Valley Watcher blog; Bob Langert, vice president for corporate social responsibility at McDonald's; Mike Prosceno, head of new media relations at SAP; Mike Wing, vice president of communication strategy for IBM; Lynn Tyson, director of investor relations at Dell; Shel Israel, coauthor of *Naked Conversations*; John Czwartacki, executive director of external communications for Verizon; Chris Heuer, principal, the Conversation Group; Chris Brogan, new media consultant and cofounder, Podcamp. org; Brian Solis, principal of Future Works PR; Andrew Horowitz, president and founder of Horowitz & Company and author of *The Disciplined Investor*; Timothy Sykes, CEO, Bullship Press; and author of *An American Hedge Fund*; Tia-Carr Williams, CEO at EveryMedia and chief network officer at www. NovumInstitute.org; Michael Port, nationally acclaimed speaker and author of *Booked Solid*; Dave Balter, founder and CEO of BzzAgent; Joel Smernoff, president and chief operating officer of PalTalk; Josh Levy, CEO of BeenVerified; Paul Levy, president and CEO of Beth Israel Deaconess Medical Center, Boston; Jonathan Vanasco, founder and CEO of FindMeOn; Andrew Baron, founder of Rocketboom; Gerald Baron, founder of AudienceCentral and author of *Now Is Too Late*; Anthony

Moor, deputy managing editor/interactive for the *Dallas Morning News*; Micah L. Sifry, senior editor, Personal Democracy Forum; J. D. Lasica, founder of Ourmedia.org; Stephanie Rogers, director of interactive strategy for PARTNERS + Simons; Anil Dash, vice president, Six Apart; Robert Scoble, managing director, FastCompany TV and coauthor of *Naked Conversations*; Eric Skiff, community evangelist at Clipmarks.com; Paull Young, senior account executive at Converseon; Scott Ginsberg, The Nametag Guy; Jason McClain, founder of the Institute for the Development of Evolutionary Awareness; Andrew Kaplan, CEO at MediaMensch Networks; Cindi Bigelow, president, Bigelow Tea; Valorie Luther, founder and CEO, Creative Concepts; Sean Bohan, an advertising and marketing executive; and Lauren Wood, senior program manager, Sun Microsystems; Matthew Knell, general manager, JetBlue Airways; Morgan Johnston, corporate communications, JetBlue Airways; Brian Lusk, manager of customer communication and corporate editor, Southwest Airlines; Bill Owen, lead planner in the Schedule Planning Department, Southwest Airlines; and Paolo Tosolini, new media business manager, Microsoft.

Alan Levy and Bob Charish, CEO and COO, respectively, of BlogTalkRadio, encouraged John to conduct his interviews and use the transparent tools they had created for their social broadcasting network.

Arlene Magargal of Magargal Office Support provided transcriptions of many of the BlogTalk Radio interviews we conducted.

Susie and Scott Adamson provided John with some peace and quiet by opening their home to him for writing while his wife dealt with the far noisier environment in which the Havens' young children romped.

Which leads us to our families, whom we can't thank enough for their patience and understanding as we took time away from them to prepare and write this book—on top of the time we put into our day jobs.

The Authors

Shel Holtz is principal of Holtz Communication + Technology. With more than thirty years of experience, he consults, writes, and speaks about the convergence of the online world and organizational communication. Before forming his consultancy in 1996, Holtz managed communication for two Fortune 500 companies and worked as a communications practice leader for a global human resource consulting firm. He has written several books and manuals and dozens of magazine and journal articles on communication. In 2005, he was named an IABC Fellow, the highest honor of the International Association of Business Communicators, which has also designated him an Accredited Business Communicator.

• • •

John C. Havens is vice president of business development at BlogTalkRadio. He is also lead organizer of PodCampNYC, a social media "unconference" that attracted over 1,500 participants and 150 speakers in the two years it took place in the greater New York area. He is a founding member and serves on the advisory board of the Association for Downloadable Media, a member of the Online News Association, and the inaugural Guide to Podcasting at About.com. A former professional actor, Havens appeared in principal roles on and off Broadway, television, and film for over fifteen years. He is a frequent speaker on new-media topics.

• • •

To hear ongoing interviews, read updated posts, or learn more about Shel and John's latest work on transparency, please visit www.tacticaltransparency.com.

Index